P9-CJE-643

DISCARD

GARBAGE AND WASTE

Other Books in the Current Controversies Series:

GARBAGE AND WASTE

David Bender, *Publisher*
Bruno Leone, *Executive Editor*

Scott Barbour, *Managing Editor*
Brenda Stalcup, *Senior Editor*

Charles P. Cozic, *Book Editor*

CURRENT CONTROVERSIES

363.728
G213

No part of this book may be reproduced or used in any form or by any means, electrical, mechanical, or otherwise, including, but not limited to, photocopy, recording, or any information storage and retrieval system, without prior written permission from the publisher.

Cover Photo: © Paul Conklin/Uniphoto

Library of Congress Cataloging-in-Publication Data

Garbage and waste / Charles P. Cozic, book editor.
    p. cm. — (Current controversies)
    Includes bibliographical references (p.   ) and index.
    ISBN 1-56510-566-4 (lib. : alk. paper).—ISBN 1-56510-565-6
(pbk. : alk. paper)
    1. Refuse and refuse disposal—United States. 2. Hazardous
wastes—Health aspects—United States. 3. Recycling (Waste, etc.)
—United States. 4. Environmental law—United States. I. Cozic,
Charles P., 1957–   . II. Series.
TD793.25.G37   1997
363.72'8—dc21   97-23
                                                                          CIP

© 1997 by Greenhaven Press, Inc., PO Box 289009, San Diego, CA 92198-9009
Printed in the U.S.A.

Every effort has been made to trace the owners of copyrighted material.

Contents

of landfill space, and lightweight plastics are more ideal than other materials for packaging and for disposal in landfills.

Chapter 2: Is Toxic Waste a Health Hazard?

Yes: Toxic Waste Is a Health Hazard

Chapter 3: Is Recycling Effective?

many cases, curbside recycling is more cost-effective than trash dumping. Local and state governments can adopt a number of approaches—such as optimizing the collection of recyclables and providing incentives to households—to make curbside recycling more effective.

Some families have made a strong commitment to recycling. They have adopted consumer habits that produce only a minimal amount of garbage that cannot be recycled. These families provide examples of how waste can be minimized through recycling, composting, and conscientious lifestyle choices.

New technologies are facilitating the recovery and recycling of plastic materials such as soda bottles. Innovative companies are using these technologies to convert plastic flakes and shrink wrap into products including sheeting, parking lot blocks, and mailbox posts.

No: Recycling Is Not Effective

Advocates exaggerate the extent to which recycling can succeed. Promoters of recycling do not adequately consider the costs of collecting, storing, and transporting recyclable material. Moreover, recycling can eliminate only a small portion of the waste stream, and prices for recycled products exceed those for products made from virgin material by as much as 15 percent.

Ample and inexpensive landfill space and the high expense of collecting recyclables have combined to make curbside recycling of household discards uneconomical. Curbside collection costs households hundreds of millions of dollars annually, and states spend millions of dollars each year to subsidize recycling businesses and programs.

Frequently, more energy and resources are used than saved by recycling. Two examples of such waste are the recycling of disposable juice containers and of polystyrene, which cost less to manufacture and less to dispose of than recyclable glass bottles and paper products.

Chapter 4: Are Government Regulations Necessary for a Cleaner Environment?

Yes: Government Regulations Are Necessary

Conservative members of Congress have waged an assault on landmark environmental and public health protection laws. Led by

No: Government Regulations Are Not Necessary

Foreword

By definition, controversies are "discussions of questions in which opposing opinions clash" (Webster's Twentieth Century Dictionary Unabridged). Few would deny that controversies are a pervasive part of the human condition and exist on virtually every level of human enterprise. Controversies transpire between individuals and among groups, within nations and between nations. Controversies supply the grist necessary for progress by providing challenges and challengers to the status quo. They also create atmospheres where strife and warfare can flourish. A world without controversies would be a peaceful world; but it also would be, by and large, static and prosaic.

The Series' Purpose

The purpose of the Current Controversies series is to explore many of the social, political, and economic controversies dominating the national and international scenes today. Titles selected for inclusion in the series are highly focused and specific. For example, from the larger category of criminal justice, Current Controversies deals with specific topics such as police brutality, gun control, white collar crime, and others. The debates in Current Controversies also are presented in a useful, timeless fashion. Articles and book excerpts included in each title are selected if they contribute valuable, long-range ideas to the overall debate. And wherever possible, current information is enhanced with historical documents and other relevant materials. Thus, while individual titles are current in focus, every effort is made to ensure that they will not become quickly outdated. Books in the Current Controversies series will remain important resources for librarians, teachers, and students for many years.

In addition to keeping the titles focused and specific, great care is taken in the editorial format of each book in the series. Book introductions and chapter prefaces are offered to provide background material for readers. Chapters are organized around several key questions that are answered with diverse opinions representing all points on the political spectrum. Materials in each chapter include opinions in which authors clearly disagree as well as alternative opinions in which authors may agree on a broader issue but disagree on the possible solutions. In this way, the content of each volume in Current Controversies mirrors the mosaic of opinions encountered in society. Readers will quickly realize that there are many viable answers to these complex issues. By questioning each author's conclusions, students and casual readers can begin to develop the critical thinking skills so important to evaluating opinionated material.

Current Controversies is also ideal for controlled research. Each anthology in the series is composed of primary sources taken from a wide gamut of informational categories including periodicals, newspapers, books, United States and foreign government documents, and the publications of private and public organizations. Readers will find factual support for reports, debates, and research papers covering all areas of important issues. In addition, an annotated table of contents, an index, a book and periodical bibliography, and a list of organizations to contact are included in each book to expedite further research.

Perhaps more than ever before in history, people are confronted with diverse and contradictory information. During the Persian Gulf War, for example, the public was not only treated to minute-to-minute coverage of the war, it was also inundated with critiques of the coverage and countless analyses of the factors motivating U.S. involvement. Being able to sort through the plethora of opinions accompanying today's major issues, and to draw one's own conclusions, can be a complicated and frustrating struggle. It is the editors' hope that Current Controversies will help readers with this struggle.

"Science is decades away from being able to pinpoint the hazards of the thousands of chemicals that permeate our environment."

Introduction

In 1994, researchers discovered unusually high rates of lupus and multiple myeloma (a bone marrow cancer) among Arizona residents in Tucson and Nogales. These researchers theorized that the high rates could be attributed to exposure to toxic chemicals. In Tucson, fifty thousand people had consumed water contaminated with trichloroethylene, a degreasing solvent. On the U.S.-Mexico border in Nogales, pollution from approximately one hundred Mexican *maquiladoras* (factories) and smoldering waste dumps had long filled the area's air and bodies of water with toxic waste. According to *Los Angeles Times* environmental writer Marla Cone, Nogales "is plagued with so many sources of pollution that no one has a clue which chemical— or more likely which combination—might be playing a role in the lupus and myeloma."

Americans are currently exposed to more than seventy thousand chemicals and their toxic waste by-products, including benzene, chlorine, dioxin, lead, mercury, PCBs (polychlorinated biphenyls), and pesticides. Such waste—generated by trash incineration, crop spraying, paper bleaching, water chlorination, and other industrial activities—can accumulate in the human body and are suspected of causing birth defects, cancer, learning and reproductive disorders, respiratory illnesses, and other ailments. Because of this potential health threat, government regulations restrict the use of many toxic chemicals in order to prevent their waste by-products from entering the air, land, and water.

Exposure to Dioxin

But environmentalists and industry representatives continue to debate whether toxic waste actually does cause long-lasting illnesses, particularly cancer. Consider the case of dioxin, a by-product of industrial processes such as plastics incineration, herbicide manufacturing, and paper bleaching. Experts have called dioxin, which does not readily degrade in soil or water, the world's most toxic substance. The Environmental Protection Agency's (EPA) Dioxin Reassessment estimates exposure to dioxin to carry a cancer risk of one in one thousand to one in ten thousand. However, critics contend that not one case of cancer has ever been conclusively linked to dioxin. Environmental educator and writer Mike Weilbacher writes that research on dioxin, "the most studied chemical in history, produces no consensus on . . .

its health effects." A lack of consensus applies to other chemicals as well. According to *Business Week* writer John Carey, "Science is decades away from being able to pinpoint the hazards of the thousands of chemicals that permeate our environment."

The chemical industry and others defend the use of many toxic chemicals. According to the Chemical Manufacturers Association (CMA), a trade group that represents nearly two hundred chemical companies, many "chemicals make a valuable contribution to our economy and standard of living. They are important in curing diseases." Chlorinated compounds, for example, "are an essential component in the manufacture of 85% of pharmaceuticals," notes the Chlorine Chemistry Council. Rhodes University professors Ben Bolch and Harold Lyons contend that "chlorine, in its use for water treatment, has probably saved as many lives as any other chemical." Furthermore, many chemists worry that Americans are becoming needlessly fearful of all chemicals. Nobel Peace Prize winner Norman Borlaug warns that society is in the "grip of a virulent strain of chemical-phobia" induced by the "pseudo-scientific promoters of toxic terror."

Both the EPA and CMA maintain that chemical companies have substantially reduced emissions of chemicals listed on the Toxics Release Inventory (TRI), a list of six hundred chemicals monitored by the federal government. According to the EPA, some thirteen hundred companies that participated in an effort known as the 33/50 Program, which operated from 1991 to 1997, collectively achieved the program's goal of reducing waste from seventeen toxic chemicals by half. The CMA contends that under its Responsible Care program, which all members must adhere to, companies achieved a 44 percent reduction in TRI waste from 1988 to 1993. CMA president Fred Webber writes, "We're seeing the payoff from a lot of hard work and money invested by the chemical industry in preventing pollution."

Not So "Green"?

However, environmental organizations and activists argue that chemical corporations are not as "green" as they claim. They note that the CMA has sued the EPA to remove some chemicals from the TRI. According to the U.S. Public Interest Research Group, "The CMA vigorously opposes 'Community Right to Know More' legislation designed to provide community members with more complete information about toxic chemicals. It also opposes federal legislation designed to promote voluntary reductions in toxic chemical use."

Environmentalists assert that such a weak commitment to protecting the environment necessitates governmental restrictions or bans on certain chemicals, more rigorous testing of chemicals, and expansion and stronger enforcement of the TRI. In the words of the Natural Resources Defense

Council, approximately 90 percent of industrial chemicals "have never been subjected to adequate testing to determine their impact on our health." Environmental Research Foundation director Peter Montague maintains that "new chemicals should be assumed harmful until they have been thoroughly tested for all the kinds of harm we presently know about." Some environmental organizations have even waged campaigns to ban certain toxic chemicals. Since the 1980s, for example, Greenpeace has advocated a phaseout of all uses of chlorine.

Nevertheless, environmentalists and industries have reached some agreement on the issue of chlorine. According to the American Forest and Paper Association, a growing number of paper mills now employ a technique known as elemental chlorine-free, which makes dioxin levels "undetectable" and "not of concern to EPA."

But the two sides remain adversaries on the use of chemicals as a whole. Environmental activists contend that if there is sufficient reason to suspect that a chemical threatens health, then it should not be used. Conversely, chemical companies and other manufacturers assert that until studies prove that a chemical is a health hazard, then regulation is unnecessary. *Garbage and Waste: Current Controversies* examines the effects of toxic chemicals and waste in the following chapters: How Severe Is the Garbage and Waste Problem? Is Toxic Waste a Health Hazard? Is Recycling Effective? Are Government Regulations Necessary for a Cleaner Environment? The contributors to this anthology address these questions as they examine the issue of garbage and waste in America.

Chapter 1

How Severe Is the Garbage and Waste Problem?

Chapter Preface

Since 1992, freight trains from distant cities such as New York have been making daily deliveries of two hundred tons of specially treated sewage sludge to the small town of Sierra Blanca, Texas, near the U.S.-Mexico border. On the outskirts of town, sludge from processed toilet and sewer waste is spread along more than one hundred thousand acres of farmland.

In virtually every U.S. state, specially treated sewage sludge is being applied to agricultural land. However, observers, including the residents of Sierra Blanca, are divided concerning the agricultural use of sewage sludge. Opponents of this technique argue that such sludge is laden with toxic ingredients including asbestos, dioxins, pathogens, petroleum, and heavy metals such as lead. According to writer Weston Kosova in *Audubon* magazine, "The blunt reality is there are dozens of potential toxins in sludge that can pass through the EPA's seemingly rigorous testing process undetected." Stanford Tackett, a chemist and an expert on lead contamination, warns, "In truth, only 1 to 3 percent of the sludge is useful to plants." The remaining waste, Tackett argues, contains heavy concentrations of toxic lead and should not be spread close to where people live. Taking these arguments into account, some food producers such as Del Monte and H.J. Heinz now ban the use of "sludged" produce.

However, proponents argue, although treated sewage sludge can contain potentially harmful substances, it can also be safely applied to cropland by following federal regulations. In the words of Sarah Clark, a former Environmental Defense Fund senior scientist, sludge farming "is the best means of returning to the soil nutrients and organic matter that were originally removed. If the right safeguards are taken, it can be environmentally protective and even beneficial." Indeed, according to a 1996 National Academy of Sciences report, the application of sewage sludge to cropland, "when practiced in accordance with existing federal guidelines and regulations, presents negligible risk to the consumer, to crop production, and to the environment."

Whether treated sewage sludge and other types of waste are health hazards for humans and other species is the focus of the viewpoints in this chapter.

Industries Produce Massive Amounts of Toxic Waste

by Bruce Selcraig

About the author: *Bruce Selcraig is a writer in Austin, Texas.*

When the wind blows eastward across Utah's Great Salt Lake, which is to say most of the time, a long yellowish plume of chlorine often drifts from the stacks of a giant magnesium factory on the desolate west side, across the saline waters, fouling the view and sinuses of anyone in its path. Upon first sniff, downwinders wonder who spilled the Clorox.

About 30 miles to the south, in the pleasant small town of Grantsville, a bus comes through several times a day to ferry workers to and from that massive plant. It's not an easy bus to miss. You can smell it coming.

For Tooele County, Utah, the jobs pay well—$12 to $17 an hour. But the constant bath of chlorine that envelops workers can discolor their cars' paint jobs, leave workers with brittle "swimmer's" hair and cause headaches and respiratory problems. The workers who make it past their first few days learn to cope, often by making light of working conditions, such as the times when the caustic chemicals get so thick their skin begins stinging. That's when they say the "bees" are out.

America's Largest Air Polluter

Such is life under the influence of the Magnesium Corp. of America's 120-acre processing plant in Rowley, Utah, which, for the second consecutive year, earned the distinction of being not only the country's largest releaser of chlorine, but also the largest industrial air polluter in America. MagCorp released nearly 56 million pounds of toxics to the air in 1994—the latest year for which figures were available—and MagCorp plant manager Ron Thayer said he expected his plant to be the nation's leading air polluter in 1995 and 1996 as well.

"We don't dispute that," Thayer says. "Those are our numbers."

The "numbers" Thayer refers to are contained in the 1996 edition of the Envi-

From "The Filthy West" by Bruce Selcraig, *High Country News*, September 16, 1996. Reprinted by permission of the author.

ronmental Protection Agency's Toxic Releases Inventory, an inch-thick annual portrait of industrial pollution in America that reads like a trashy beach novel for toxic waste wonks.

The TRI figures—they're always two years behind, so these are for 1994—tell Westerners plenty about who is fouling the land, air and water in the West.

In TRI we learn that six of the top 20 companies with the largest toxic releases to the land—usually in the form of enormous slag piles—are smelter operations in the West: ASARCO in East Helena, Montana; ASARCO in Hayden, Arizona; Kennecott Utah Copper in Magna, Utah; Phelps Dodge Hidalgo in Playas, New Mexico; Cyprus Miami Mining in Claypool, Arizona; and the Phelps Dodge Chino Mines in Hurley, New Mexico.

> *"The TRI requires some 23,000 facilities in 20 manufacturing industries to report their release of 341 chemicals, in 22 chemical categories, to the air, land and water."*

We also learn that while the Rocky Mountain West is not often associated with big polluting chemical refineries, the Coastal Chem site in Cheyenne, Wyoming, is ranked as the nation's fourth largest disposer of toxic waste by underground injection. Coastal Chem pumped over 20 million gallons of chemicals beneath the ground—less than half the amount of big DuPont plants in Tennessee and Mississippi, but still enough to rank it eighth in total toxic releases nationwide.

Want more arcane data?

What facility is the largest "federal" polluter in the West?

That would be the Naval Petroleum Reserves facility in Tupman, California, one of 15 sites in the West among the Top 50 government polluters. Another fed in those ranks is, of all things, the Federal Correctional Complex (that's a prison) in Florence, Colorado, which released 90,000 pounds of toxics in the process of, we are told, making furniture.

Within this weighty volume of charts and number, or more likely, on its computerized version, anyone can find, say, a favorite polluting pulp mill, smelter or refinery, or the nation's most polluted ZIP code—won't that make some Chamber of Commerce proud!—or the company emitting the most neurotoxins and ozone depleters in all 50 states.

No wonder Al Gore likes it so much—the veep released the new TRI [Toxics Release Inventory] numbers in June 1996 at a White House ceremony—and some of Congress' least enlightened members want it disemboweled. Such has been the life history of this controversial but uniquely democratic law.

The Toxics Release Inventory

The Toxics Release Inventory was created in 1986 in the wake of the 1984 Union Carbide accident in Bhopal, India, which killed more than 3,500 people and acutely injured tens of thousands more.

The TRI requires some 23,000 facilities in 20 manufacturing industries to report their release of 341 chemicals, in 22 chemical categories, to the air, land and water, and by underground injection.

This somewhat obscure but powerful piece of the Emergency Planning and Community Right-to-Know Act, which only passed the House by one vote, has become not only the best barometer of industrial pollution in America, but also a useful tool for prying information out of stonewalling corporations. It also can focus public attention on a polluting company and arm activists.

> *"TRI's largest oversight by far is that it hasn't included every industry or facility that pollutes."*

The TRI has become indispensable to hundreds of groups, from environmental-justice activists to doctors, lawyers, school principals and insurance companies. Many chemical company officials credit TRI with speeding up the search for lower-pollution technologies, while labor activists have used TRI to broaden management's understanding of safety issues.

"Knowledge is power," says Robert Wiygul of Denver, managing attorney for the Sierra Club Legal Defense Fund, who has used TRI to challenge the siting of hazardous waste sites. "TRI is one of the most important statutes on the books."

"It's been incredibly helpful to us," says Lorraine Granado, director of the Cross Community Coalition in Denver, Colorado, which successfully used TRI figures to show that their north Denver community had been burdened with polluting industries. The coalition not only defeated a proposal to locate a medical waste incinerator in its community, which is 72 percent Latino, it also pushed Denver to adopt an industrial zoning code that takes into consideration how much pollution a neighborhood already suffers from.

Thousands Harmed

In Richmond, California, where in July 1993 General Chemical inadvertently released a mist of sulfuric acid over an eight-mile area and sent 24,000 people to hospitals, several community and labor groups used TRI numbers to sue the firm. The company now allows safety audits performed by the community's own expert, a concept unheard of in 1991.

"I would say that in at least two dozen major campaigns over the last several years, TRI has been essential to achieving victories for the community," says Richmond activist Denny Larson. "We've linked TRI numbers with race and poverty in Richmond. And we've shown how IBM was the number one ozone-destroyer in California and the nation. We use it on a daily basis."

Benefits of the TRI

But what do all the numbers really tell us?

Is living downwind from MagCorp worse than, say, living downstream from a gold mine or worse than breathing Mexico City's air for one hour? Can we compare factories across the nation, or even across town, and make any sound judgments about the danger they pose to communities? This is the conundrum that TRI poses.

"TRI gives you information as a starting point," says Paul Orum, editor of *Working Notes on Community Right-to-Know*, a Washington, D.C., newsletter. "But there's nothing in TRI that says this much exposure to a certain chemical will have this health effect. We're still sorely lacking in a public-health infrastructure that can tell people the impact of toxics to which they are exposed."

Where TRI is often the most helpful to communities is in identifying potential problems. If, for example, a community health study has identified clusters of cancer or birth defects, TRI may be able to isolate the facilities that were releasing carcinogenic and mutagenic chemicals. Even then, TRI is best used as a guide or model, not a smoking gun.

An Important Regulatory Tool

Despite its loopholes and limitations, TRI is often credited by community activists and industry alike with doing more to reduce industrial pollution in America than any other piece of federal legislation.

Since 1988, the first year of TRI reporting, overall reported toxic releases have declined some 44 percent, according to the Environmental Protection Agency.

"The chemical industry figures showed it released several billion tons of toxic waste."

Yet TRI doesn't give a full picture of a factory's total chemical use or production, or of those chemicals' effects on worker health. There are more than 70,000 chemicals used in commerce today, and the 1996 TRI reported on only 328 of them.

"A definitive TRI," says Paul Orum, "would also include air toxics from our carpets and walls, and from consumer products like cellular phones, and from the disposal of products, like the mercury in batteries."

But TRI's largest oversight by far is that it hasn't included every industry or facility that pollutes. If a company has fewer than 10 employees or processes less than 25,000 pounds of a certain chemical, they're usually off the hook. So are automobiles, trains and planes. And only since 1993 have federal facilities, such as military bases, been included.

Still missing are coal-burning power plants, electric utilities, commercial hazardous-waste treatment centers, petroleum storage terminals, chemical wholesalers, and, in a Grand Canyon-size loophole courtesy of the Reagan administration, the metal-mining and coal-mining industries.

That will change soon. Al Gore announced that the EPA will expand TRI to include all those industries, adding 6,400 more facilities and 300 more chemicals. (Industry is lobbying heavily against the expanded TRI.)

TRI Opponents

Although TRI flourishes today, it barely escaped with its life back in 1985. The Reagan White House, allied with the chemical industry and some EPA officials, were united in opposing so-called Right-to-Know laws that would require industry to more fully inform communities about chemical hazards. But after the devastating Union Carbide accidents in Bhopal and in Institute, West Virginia, prompted some states to draft their own laws, Congress passed a version for the nation.

"The opponents said (our) bill would be more effective than Communism in shutting the country down," recalled former Minnesota Rep. Gerry Sikorski, now a Washington lawyer.

> *"The TRI numbers often reflect what have become known as 'phantom reductions.'"*

TRI was never voted on by itself. It was contained within the Emergency Planning and Community Right-to-Know Act, which was defeated easily in a House subcommittee chaired by TRI opponent John Dingell, D-Mich. But a parliamentary procedure allowed the bill to be voted on by the entire House.

"The debate was intense and the lobbying furious," recalls the Environmental Defense Fund's Bill Roberts, who at that time was an aide to former New Jersey Rep. Jim Florio.

"We were down 211 to 212," Roberts remembers. "Everything stopped for a moment, and then someone switched their vote, and thank goodness George Brown from California, a supporter, was holding the gavel. He closed the vote immediately. Down came the gavel. We had won 212 to 211. It was one of the most dramatic experiences I had in my career there."

TRI's debut was memorable. Years before the first report came out in 1989, Rep. Henry Waxman, D-Calif., enjoyed throwing around estimates that chemical companies were annually releasing as much as 85 million pounds of toxic chemicals to the air. The chemical industry, in turn, blasted Waxman and whined about scare tactics and innuendo.

Then, in a modest press conference at the EPA, the first TRI figures were unveiled to the public.

Unwelcome Publicity

The chemical industry figures showed it released several *billion* tons of toxic waste. Shocked, and groping for an explanation, the chemical companies quickly changed strategies. They no longer denied the pollution, but said it wasn't that harmful; and they promised major reductions.

One company, Monsanto, knew that its first TRI numbers were going to be so unflattering that it issued a pre-emptive press release before the 1989 TRI report, promising to cut toxic emissions by 90 percent. Many companies followed suit.

It is now clear that TRI's power has never been in the threat of big fines or jail time, only in the threat that every CEO seems to viscerally comprehend—really, really, bad publicity.

With uncharacteristic foresight, Congress required the TRI data to be made available to citizens by computer—the first U.S. law so designed. This means that when the report is released by the EPA in Washington, it also is available on-line to thousands of activists, company officials and reporters

But public access alone isn't what made TRI so powerful. What made the TRI a news media hero was that the EPA, with some prodding by reporters, broke down the mountain of numbers into simple-to-read charts and graphs. This makes it possible for hundreds of newspapers—even timid TV stations—to boldly announce which company is their state's or county's worst polluter. And that stigma

> *"When companies arrive at new ways to figure their pollution, the numbers never seem to go up—always down."*

doesn't fade very easily, despite the increasing efforts of corporate squads of image-fixers. The damning numbers, of course, come straight from the companies themselves.

"TRI put many corporate CEOs in a very awkward position," says Bill Roberts, legislative director for the Environmental Defense Fund and one of TRI's intellectual fathers. "It had a fascinating effect, something I've never seen another piece of legislation do."

USA Today environmental reporter Ray Tyson, whose TRI stories are probably the most widely read in the country, says that when companies know they're going to post big pollution numbers, his phone starts ringing.

"The lobbying (by industry) is not particularly subtle," Tyson says, "especially if companies know they will be the top polluter or in the top 10. We've had a number come by to offer their help in 'interpreting' the data. Some even went over my head to my bosses to question our need to publish it." (To their credit, his editors haven't waffled.)

When Gore released the 1994 figures, he seemed pleased that industrial pollution—at least on paper—continues to decline, but a closer look at the 8.6 percent reduction from 1993 to 1994 shows that almost all of the improvement comes from just two fertilizer plants in Louisiana.

Phantom Reductions

This isn't to minimize the significant reductions made by companies that have invested hundreds of millions of dollars in new technologies and pollution safeguards, but the TRI numbers often reflect what have become known as "phantom reductions."

Sometimes the huge reductions trumpeted by industry reflect pollution that has simply been redefined, recycled or recalculated—never actually removed from the environment. A Citizens' Fund survey reported that only 13 of the top 50 facilities reporting reductions between 1988 and 1989 could point to specific programs to control pollution.

For example, every year many companies vigorously lobby Congress and the EPA to remove or "de-list" certain chemicals from the list they have to report under TRI. It's not hard to see why. If chlorine were ever de-listed, the Mag-Corp plant in Utah would look about as ominous as "Wally World." Not long ago the chemical acetone accounted for huge portions of some companies' TRI releases; then it got de-listed—despite protests that in combination with other chemicals it may increase one's cancer risk. De-listing allowed companies to retroactively remove their acetone numbers and make their previous TRI reports look cleaner.

Some reductions are achieved by using new math. Contrary to our logical assumptions, the TRI numbers are not a direct measure of pollution, that is, they aren't like odometer readings on a car. They're only estimates—complicated projections based on pollution formulas involving variables such as temperature, time and chemical reaction. They can and have been off by millions of pounds. But when companies arrive at new ways to figure their pollution, the numbers never seem to go up—always down.

Legitimate Gripes

On the other hand, some companies may have legitimate gripes when they say the TRI numbers don't treat everyone equally.

Say you're DuPont, and you have four chemical refineries on the Top 10 list for total toxic releases. You learn to accept this because you have huge plants, but what if, hypothetically, you've reduced pollution dramatically over the years by spending millions on state-of-the-art equipment and on a per-worker basis your pollution numbers are the best in the business? And what if the Acme Sludge Co., which is one-tenth your size, is located right next door and hasn't installed a pollution device since the Korean War? Who still ends up looking bad in the TRI reports?

That's partly the media's fault, says a big TRI fan, Ralph Nader: "Newspapers don't break down the numbers like they should to make it more understandable."

TRI rankings also don't discriminate about the relative danger of chemicals. The company that discharges a million pounds of ammonia to the ocean looks a lot worse than one that dumps a thousand pounds of lead or mercury into a river, though the latter has committed a far more grievous environmental sin.

Similarly, some plants may not pose as great a threat to public health as others, simply because of location.

The massive chlorine releases of the MagCorp plant in Rowley, Utah, merit scrutiny, but unlike dozens of chemical refineries in the South whose plant gates are sometimes within a hundred yards of clotheslines and back porches,

MagCorp is surrounded by a 30-mile buffer of desert and a near-lifeless salt lake between it and the closest town.

"If, as a society, you decide that you want to have a plant that produces magnesium," says Dwight Bird, an environmental engineer for the state of Utah who is reviewing MagCorp's pollution permit, "there aren't a whole lot of better places to have it."

Those sentiments, however, don't go down well with MagCorp-watchers like Chip Ward.

"That attitude is not a whole lot different from the idea we had not long ago, that oceans were a great place to dump things," says Ward, a local librarian and environmental activist. "Every polluter on earth thinks the West Desert is a haven for doing things that wouldn't be tolerated closer to people. And I think MagCorp helped set that precedent."

Assault on the TRI

In the polluter-friendly 104th Congress, TRI looked as though it would get battered like a country mailbox. Bob Dole and Sen. Bennett Johnston, (D), whose home state of Louisiana has the country's worst per-worker pollution totals, sponsored a "reform" bill that would have reduced by 90 percent the number of chemicals industry must monitor on its TRI reports. Other bills would have crippled or simply de-funded the whole program.

The business crowd is going after it, says Nader. "They see that TRI is effective."

Fueling the assault has been corporate PAC [political action committee] money. Citizen Action analyzed the contributions of 100 business PACs that represented companies affected by TRI and its Right-to-Know legislation. Those 100 PACs gave $3.7 million to members of Congress, according to Citizen Action, and 86 percent of it went to lawmakers who voted in July 1995 to weaken the Right-to-Know law.

And while the Chemical Manufacturers Association continued an advertising campaign on television about its Responsible CARE program, which casts industry as a caring and credible steward of the environment, it was lobbying hard for every amendment that would cripple TRI. The trade group also sued the EPA in 1996 in federal court to prevent the agency from expanding the TRI list of chemicals. The Chemical Manufacturers lost the case.

> *"The Chemical Manufacturers Association . . . was lobbying hard for every amendment that would cripple TRI."*

For now, TRI survives and looks surprisingly strong. Clinton and Gore have both mentioned it in speeches, and in a poll for the National Wildlife Federation, 78 percent of voters agreed that requiring companies to report on every toxic emission to the air and water is worth doing—even if the costs of doing so are passed on to the consumer.

Even natural enemies such as Idaho Sen. Larry Craig, (R), who is usually partial to the mining industry, have apparently found other targets. According to a staffer, Craig has no immediate plans of derailing TRI.

That could change, however, any time an anti-regulatory Congress decides the public already knows too much about Big Business and decides to restore the cozy secrecy the nation's biggest polluters once demanded—and got.

The Cleanup of Nuclear Weapons Waste Is a Growing Problem

by Linda Rothstein

About the author: *Linda Rothstein is the managing editor of the* Bulletin of the Atomic Scientists, *a bimonthly magazine focusing on nuclear arms and energy.*

Over the past 50 years, the United States has spent hundreds of billions of dollars—at 1995 rates—to design and manufacture nuclear weapons. Now that the East-West arms race has finally ended, the nation may have to spend hundreds of billions more just to stabilize the poisonous mess left in the weapons complex.

Although her predecessors were all cut from the same secretive military cloth, Energy Secretary Hazel O'Leary has flung open the windows and doors, presenting the weapons complex's problems for public inspection. Two of the department's reports issued in 1995—*Closing the Circle on the Splitting of the Atom*, a generously illustrated survey designed for the general public, and *Estimating the Cold War Mortgage*, a massive study prepared for Congress—underline how difficult the mess will be to clean up.

"Cleanup" Is Misleading

In fact, both reports make it plain that "cleanup" is the wrong term. Most of the weapons complex is not going to be cleaned up in the foreseeable future. Merely stabilizing the wastes is an enormously sophisticated technical enterprise.

The Energy Department estimates that a comprehensive cleanup could cost in the range of $500 billion over 75 years. The more conservative $230 billion figure presented in *Cold War Mortgage* is a baseline cost (in 1995 dollars) that would be spread out over the next 75 years. That money would buy "stabilization" of the worst sites, not cleanup.

From "Nothing Clean About 'Cleanup'" by Linda Rothstein, *Bulletin of the Atomic Scientists*, May/June 1995. Reprinted by permission of the *Bulletin of the Atomic Scientists*; copyright 1995 by the Educational Foundation for Nuclear Science, 6042 S. Kimbark Ave., Chicago, IL 60637, USA. A one-year subscription is $36.

Many parts of the weapons complex have long been poised precariously on the brink of environmental disaster. There is much to do: sites must be "characterized" (the contents of three-fourths of the units at weapons production sites that may leak contaminants into the environment remain to be assessed); nuclear materials that are now stored in aging facilities must be stabilized; and a variety of toxic wastes must be stored safely until they can be moved to permanent repositories. . . .

Environmental remediation will need forceful advocates over the 70 years the baseline study estimates it will take to accomplish the task.

As its authors warn, *Cold War Mortgage* presents only a gross estimate of costs, in part because the Energy Department's environmental task is without technical precedent. The department faces some problems for which no solutions are yet available. For example, there is no known remedy or technique for decontaminating groundwater.

Painful Certainties

Although the costs are uncertain, there are some painful certainties: *Cold War Mortgage* estimates that remediation will include disposing—somehow—of 403,000 cubic meters (106 million gallons) of high-level radioactive wastes; 2,600 metric tons of spent fuel; 107,000 cubic meters of transuranic wastes; 1,800,000 cubic meters of low-level radioactive waste; and 780,000 cubic meters of "mixed" (chemical and radioactive) waste. And there are the as-yet-unanswered questions about what can be done in the many cases where plant operations have contaminated the soil and groundwater.

Where waste water was dumped on the ground and stored wastes leaked into the earth, volatile organic compounds, heavy metals, and radionuclides have spread to surface streams and groundwater. There is no way to restore the groundwater. The baseline report simply recommends two approaches that might be called "holding actions": trying to eliminate further contamination, which includes repairing still-leaking storage sites; and, in some cases, blocking the migration of contaminated groundwater before it reaches major sources of drinking water.

> *"The contents of three-fourths of the units at weapons production sites that may leak contaminants into the environment remain to be assessed."*

The cost of remediation in the case of some river systems—the Columbia River (Hanford Site), Clinch River (Oak Ridge), and Savannah River (Savannah River Site)—was omitted from the baseline plan because no effective remediation technique is available. In some cases, remediation efforts themselves could cause unacceptable ecological damage. Some water is being treated at the Savannah River Site, but the treatment is expensive and of unknown efficacy.

27

Because it is impossible to destroy radionuclides and other contaminants like heavy metals, the Energy Department's baseline study rejects the "greenfields" concept—the idea that all nuclear weapons production sites can or should be returned to their original condition. Instead, the department's cost estimate is based on "in-place containment" whenever possible. Containment also offers the advantage of producing little or no secondary waste. Nearly every removal technology will produce additional waste during the transportation, storage, treatment, and final disposal stages.

> *"In some cases, remediation efforts themselves could cause unacceptable ecological damage."*

The following is a summary—based on *Closing the Circle* and *Estimating the Cold War Mortgage*—of the waste products that must be managed and the steps in the weapons production process that created them.

The creation of each gram of plutonium, reactor fuel element, and container of enriched uranium produced radioactive waste—virtually all of which remains with us today. The graphite bricks Enrico Fermi used for the first "atomic pile" at the University of Chicago were buried in a Cook County forest preserve. The acid used to extract plutonium for the first atomic test in the New Mexico desert is still stored at the Hanford Site in the State of Washington.

Not only do all the wastes remain, they pose a variety of hazards. Many are so toxic that they must be isolated for hundreds of centuries, and they need special treatment before they can be permanently disposed of.

During all of the nuclear weapons production period—and especially between 1943 and 1970—the nuclear weapons industry handled many wastes with little thought to the future. Billions of gallons of waste water were poured on the ground. Other liquid wastes were dumped into evaporation ponds, from which radioactive materials leaked, contaminating the soil and groundwater.

Weapons-complex wastes range from intensely radioactive acids used to separate plutonium to slightly radioactive items of clothing or chemical solvents used in purity tests. They differ in physical characteristics, chemical form, and radioactivity, and they need to be handled and stored in different ways. Among the great challenges to cleanup are the many deteriorating, unlabeled or unidentified waste containers whose precise contents are not known.

Waste has been the most abundant product of every step in the weapons production process: uranium mining and milling, uranium enrichment, handling spent fuel, spent fuel reprocessing, and plutonium production and plutonium parts manufacture.

Mining and Milling

The United States mined about 60 million tons of ore to produce 994 metric tons of highly enriched uranium and about 100 metric tons of plutonium. It

28

takes about 1,000 tons of uranium ore to produce one kilogram of plutonium.

The ore was first processed to produce concentrated natural uranium or "yellowcake," leaving behind vast quantities of slag or "tailings." These mill tailings (which contain toxic heavy metals, radium, and thorium) account for only a small fraction of total radioactivity in weapon production waste, but they constitute 96 percent of the total volume of waste. Tailings were typically abandoned, with some material blown away by the wind or washed away by rain. In 1978 Congress passed a law to insure that these mill tailings, whose major threat to safety is the radon they emit as a byproduct of radioactive decay, would be stabilized.

Enrichment

At the enrichment plants, uranium 235 was separated from the more abundant isotope, 238. But most of the material fed into the plants came out as "depleted uranium," also known as enrichment tails. About 600,000 metric tons of somewhat radioactive depleted uranium are stored in Ohio, Tennessee, and Kentucky. Enrichment plants contaminated the environment with solvents, polychlorinated biphenyls (PCBs), heavy metals, and other toxic substances.

At the uranium foundry in Fernald, Ohio, hundreds of tons of enriched uranium (in gaseous form) were converted to crystals, then blended with magnesium granules. When the mixture was cooked in a furnace, it ignited, converting the crystals to metal. Fernald's environmental legacy includes the release of uranium dust and landfills that have leaked chemical wastes.

Spent Fuel

The United States operated 14 nuclear reactors that produced plutonium and tritium for nuclear warheads. The last of these reactors was shut down in 1988. Most of the fuel rods and targets that were irradiated in the reactors were reprocessed to extract plutonium and leftover enriched uranium.

When large numbers of weapons were being produced, the spent fuel was stored only long enough for some radioactive decay to occur before reprocessing. But as warhead production declined, reprocessing tailed off. In April 1992, when the Energy Department announced that it was ending reprocessing, approximately 4,630 metric tons of spent fuel was stored in nearly 30 storage pools. (The Energy Department prefers to use a 2,600-metric ton figure, which represents the mass before the material was used as fuel.)

Nearly all of this fuel remains at the Hanford Site in Washington State, the Savannah River Site in South Carolina, the Idaho National Engineering Laboratory, and West Valley, New York, most of it in indoor pools of water that must be cooled and filtered. Some older spent fuel is in dry storage.

Although Energy has less spent fuel to contend with than does the commercial nuclear power industry, the two cannot be compared. Unlike commercial fuel, spent fuel from production reactors was not designed to be stored for any length of time. Its outer layer or "cladding" corrodes if it is stored in water. (But proper control of water chemistry can prevent or reduce corrosion.)

Eventually, the spent fuel will be placed in a deep geologic repository—when such a burial site becomes available. In the meantime, it must be stored above ground, and many of the existing storage facilities—some nearly 50 years old—do not meet safety standards. Some storage pools are unlined, with inadequate means for controlling water chemistry. Under some circumstances, both the rusted cladding and uranium will burn when exposed to air. A worst case scenario includes conditions that could lead to an inadvertent nuclear chain reaction or "criticality" event.

Secure Storage

Today, the spent fuel considered to be at highest risk is being moved from old storage sites, repackaged, stabilized, and placed in more secure locations. At the Idaho Laboratory, a storage pool that is earthquake resistant and can be chemically controlled is being used to consolidate spent fuel from other parts of the laboratory.

In contrast, Hanford's radioactive sludge and spent fuel are stored in aging tanks a few hundred yards from the Columbia River. One basin has leaked millions of gallons of contaminated water into the ground. Workers at Hanford are now beginning to move spent fuel and sludge away from the river, and an environmental study is looking into alternate storage. In the meantime, Hanford's pools must be repaired to minimize leaks and make them less susceptible to earthquake damage.

Because it is safer and more reliable over the long-term, dry-cask storage will probably be used for spent fuel that has cooled long enough. The spent fuel from the N Reactor at Hanford is a candidate for this treatment.

When a deep underground repository is available, the spent fuel will have to be encapsulated in metal containers that meet the requirements for long-term (10,000-year) performance. Damaged fuel will probably have to be processed before it is stored. The department may need to process spent fuel that contains uranium enriched to the weapon-grade level to avoid both potential security and criticality problems. But new technologies, such as "minimal dissolution and non-extractant solidification" might make it possible to stabilize spent fuel without reprocessing.

> *"Waste has been the most abundant product of every step in the weapons production process."*

Reprocessing

Reprocessing of spent fuel produces the most chemical and radioactive wastes and is the most environmentally costly of all weapons-related work. Reprocessing wastes contain 99 percent of all the radioactivity produced in the weapons production process.

After spent fuel was irradiated in a production reactor, the plutonium and uranium had to be recovered—separated from the remaining material, which includes a variety of intensely radioactive fission products. The spent fuel was dissolved in acid and chemically separated, with the acids and chemicals used in the reprocessing retaining most of the radioactivity. The intense radioactivity is caused by the relatively rapid decay of fission products. This waste will generate only one-tenth as much heat and radiation after 100 years, and it will have decayed to one-thousandth of its original level in 300 years. Rapid decay may make its ultimate disposition easier, but high-level waste must still be isolated from the environment for a long time—essentially for as long as spent fuel.

> *"Many of the existing [spent nuclear fuel] storage facilities—some nearly 50 years old—do not meet safety standards."*

Hanford had five reprocessing facilities, Savannah River two, and Idaho one. These reprocessing buildings, and the underground tanks where their wastes are stored, are among the most radioactive places in the United States. Four of Hanford's plants and one at Savannah River extracted plutonium. Two others—the second at Savannah River and the one in Idaho—extracted highly enriched uranium from spent fuel. At the fifth Hanford facility, uranium was recovered from high-level waste. The government also built and operated a demonstration plant in West Valley, New York, for reprocessing commercial fuel.

Tank Storage

These operations produced about 100 million gallons of high-level waste (the equivalent of 10,000 tanker trucks full). Most of it is stored in underground tanks in Washington, South Carolina, Idaho, and New York. The tanks contain a variety of radioactive liquids, solids, and sludges. Some of the liquid has been converted to a dry, concentrated form.

When the emphasis was on weapons production, the tanks were often filled with little regard to what sort of a brew was being created. The waste was not generally sampled and records were not kept. As a result, the Energy Department does not know all of the wastes' characteristics.

These high-level wastes will remain radioactive for centuries, and the department is working on ways to convert them to more stable forms. At the Idaho site, a calcining facility heats liquid high-level waste to convert it to a dry powder, which is more stable and lower in volume. Direct human contact with the waste is still dangerous, however, and dry waste can be easily dispersed. High-sodium wastes cannot be converted because they clog the spray nozzles in the calciner.

At the three other sites where fuel was reprocessed, the acidic wastes were neutralized, then stored in carbon steel tanks. The department intends to mix these sludges, saltcakes, and liquids with molten glass (in a process known as vitrification), then pour the glass into metal cylinders. The Energy Department is building two vitrification facilities. One is a $2 billion plant at the Savannah River Site, which has been plagued by delays and cost overruns; the other is a smaller plant at West Valley, New York.

Transuranic Waste

Plutonium production also created "transuranic" waste, which is a term used for any material that contains significant quantities of plutonium, americium, or other elements whose atomic weights exceed that of uranium. Transuranic waste includes everything from the chemicals used in crafting plutonium metal to the air filters, gloves, clothing, tools, and piping used in the plant.

Accidents have also generated transuranic waste. There were a number of fires at Rocky Flats that generated thousands of drums of transuranic waste, much of which was shipped to the Idaho Laboratory for storage.

The nuclear weapons complex has about 100,000 cubic meters—enough to fill half a million 55-gallon drums—of transuranic waste, much of which was put in "temporary storage." Some temporary containers have corroded and need to be repackaged and relocated.

"High-level wastes will remain radioactive for centuries, and the [Energy] department is working on ways to convert them to more stable forms."

Thousands of drums were left exposed to the elements, and as a first step they have now been placed on covered concrete or asphalt pads. Other transuranic wastes remain in earth-covered berms that were expected to hold them for only a few years.

New storage facilities must be built, and corroding or leaking drums will have to be encased in clean metal containers. But these steps are temporary; these wastes are destined eventually for geologic storage.

Because of their long-lived radioactivity, transuranic wastes must be permanently isolated from the environment and from contact with people. . . .

Low-Level Waste

Low-level waste is a catchall term for waste that is neither high-level, transuranic, spent fuel, or mill tailings. It includes rags, clothing, contaminated equipment, waste created by decontamination efforts, construction debris, filters, and scrap metal. Most low-level waste is packaged in drums or boxes and buried in shallow pits or trenches. Approximately 3 million cubic meters of waste have been disposed of in this manner.

But low-level wastes continue to be generated in the process of site cleanup and the management of other wastes. Eighty percent of newly generated waste is low-level.

Newly generated low-level waste is disposed of in a way that meets safety standards, and it does not pose a significant threat to the environment. But low-level waste was not always disposed of so carefully. Some older disposal sites have already been excavated and the waste repackaged. Other disposal sites are now being evaluated. . . .

Hazardous and Mixed Wastes

Legally, "hazardous" waste contains certain chemicals or exhibits dangerous characteristics like ignitability or corrosivity. These wastes must be handled in compliance with the Resource Conservation and Recovery Act (RCRA). Some states have additional laws governing dangerous chemical wastes.

The Energy Department's hazardous wastes resemble those produced by many private companies. They include organic solvents, sludges from degreasing operations, and heavy metal from unrecycled batteries.

Like many private companies, the Energy Department has often failed to take adequate care in handling, storing, treating, or disposing of hazardous wastes. The result is substantial environmental contamination. In some cases, stored waste is discovered for which no records are available; these "unknowns" are particularly difficult to manage. For the most part, however, Energy ships hazardous chemical wastes to private vendors for disposal.

But unlike most private companies, the weapons complex produced large amounts of "mixed" wastes—wastes that are both radioactively contaminated *and* chemically hazardous. RCRA requires that this otherwise low-level waste be stabilized in preparation for disposal, and Energy must now deal with a considerable backlog.

The department must manage 780,000 cubic meters of mixed waste at 22 sites. New treatment technologies like very-high-temperature plasma furnaces and vitrification are now being considered as well as current treatment methods such as incineration and cementation. It will take many years to develop technologies, build facilities, and treat the backlog.

> *"Transuranic wastes must be permanently isolated from the environment and from contact with people."*

Plutonium

When the plants that manufactured plutonium parts for nuclear weapons—Rocky Flats, Hanford, and Savannah River—were shut down, about 26 tons of plutonium were left in intermediate stages. This stranded plutonium is in a wide variety of forms, from plutonium dissolved in acid to rough pieces of metal to nearly finished weapon parts.

Rocky Flats has about 12.8 metric tons of plutonium, about 6.6 metric tons of it in the form of plutonium metal. Scraps of metal and chemicals that contain plutonium worth recovering were stored in drums and cans. Other unknown amounts of plutonium have collected on the surfaces of ventilation ducts, air filters, and gloveboxes.

Handling plutonium requires care, but the complex conditions at the weapons plants make for an even greater challenge. Radioactivity combined with corrosive acids is slowly destroying some of the plastic bags and bottles plutonium is packed in. Hydrogen gas is accumulating inside some of the sealed cans, drums, and bottles that clutter the aisles and fill the gloveboxes. Bulging and ruptured containers have been found. Both the hydrogen and some of the plutonium could ignite and burn. At Hanford and the Savannah River Site, plutonium is slowly collecting on the bottoms of tanks, where enough of it could produce a criticality event.

> *"Like many private companies, the Energy Department has often failed to take adequate care in handling, storing, treating, or disposing of hazardous wastes."*

Plutonium must be inspected, guarded, and accounted for, and the buildings that house it must be maintained, including ventilation systems, air filters, and fire and radiation alarms. . . .

Suggestions for Disposal

Plutonium "pucks" or "buttons" and other forms of plutonium metal are kept in storage vaults. These forms were stored in metal containers enclosed in plastic bags. In some cases, there are no records of what the packages contain. If it is exposed to air, plutonium can "rust," becoming a flammable powder.

The containers must be opened in sealed "gloveboxes" and the rust brushed off and treated. The metal and powder will then be repackaged separately, without plastic, to prevent this problem from recurring.

Plutonium parts not in operational warheads are stored at various facilities across the country. The supply increases steadily as weapons are dismantled at the Pantex Plant in Texas.

In December 1993, Energy Secretary Hazel O'Leary declassified the fact that the United States had produced more than 100 metric tons of plutonium. The ultimate fate of this material is now under discussion. Because it cost billions to produce, some argue that it should be used to fuel nuclear power plants. Others have suggested that some of it should be used to fuel a new tritium-production reactor. Others contend that neither plan is economical (it would require a new type of plant to fabricate fuel rods using a mixture of uranium and plutonium), and that we should find the safest, fastest, and cheapest way to spoil the plutonium's usefulness in weapons. One proposal is to vitrify it along with high-level waste. Other suggestions include storage in deep geologic repositories or deep boreholes, or disposal beneath the seabed.

Many Cold War weapon builders sincerely believed they were in an all-out struggle for national survival. Careful storage of waste products just didn't seem as important as "winning" the Cold War by building up the nuclear arsenal as rapidly as possible.

Now that the Cold War is over, and with the advantage of hindsight, it is both easy and popular to criticize the bomb-builders' mistakes and deplore their production practices.

But, as the government focuses on cleaning up the weapons complex, it should be remembered that, if the present generation does not ask the right questions or press for carefully formulated decisions about environmental management, it will make its own set of mistakes.

Waste Threatens the World's Seas

by Anne E. Platt

About the author: *Anne E. Platt is a staff researcher at the Worldwatch Institute, an environmental policy organization in Washington, D.C.*

During the last four thousand years, the part of our past that we think of as the history of civilization, human settlements have tended to cluster around land-enclosed seas, rivers, and lakes. People in these settlements have been able to supply themselves with food, security, and community to a degree that would have been far more difficult in the vast inland territories—drylands, mountains, scrub forests, deserts, and steppes—that make up the bulk of the terrestrial world.

Whether it was the ancient Aegeans on the Mediterranean, the Persians on the Caspian, or the Chinese on the Yellow Sea, civilizations rose in places where small boats could exchange knowledge and goods, trade was easily conducted, fish were abundant, and the land was rich with the topsoil carried downstream by rivers.

Highly Valued

For these reasons, the basins of the great seas were also more highly valued than other landforms, and controlling them became central to human notions of security. Security meant military control of homelands and trade routes. It has also meant, increasingly in the past few centuries, control of the water itself—by damming tributaries, digging irrigation ditches, dredging shipping channels and harbors, and constructing breakwaters.

In just the last few decades, however, a new kind of stress has crept into the historic relationship between humans and the seas. While civilizations have continued to develop most rapidly around the coasts and rivers that feed the seas, that growth has accelerated to a point that is now dangerously unstable. Various side effects of human activity that passed unnoticed until the twentieth

From "Dying Seas" by Anne E. Platt, *World Watch*, January/February 1995. Reprinted by permission of the Worldwatch Institute, © 1995.

century have begun to ravage the very qualities that make the seas valuable—depleting both sea-based and land-based food production, fouling the human nest, and evidently even beginning to alter weather patterns for the worse.

Today, most of the world's seas are suffering from a wide range of human-caused assaults, in various lethal combinations: their ecological links to the land blocked by dams; their bottoms punctured and contaminated by oil drilling; their wildlife habitats wiped out by coastal development; and their water contaminated—or turned anoxic—by farm and factory waste. And what fish remain after these assaults are being decimated by overfishing. In the world's most biologically productive and diverse bodies of water, ecosystems are on the verge of collapse—and in some cases have already collapsed. The levels of damage and progress toward protection vary from sea to sea. But in general, compared to the open oceans, semi-enclosed seas tend to be damaged more severely and quickly because water circulation is limited and there is less dilution of pollutants. . . .

There are about 35 major seas in the world, some coastal and some enclosed by land. Of these, four—the Baltic, Mediterranean, Black, and Yellow Seas—illustrate the panoply of ills that now afflict, in varying degrees, all 35. Each of these seven carries different wounds. One, the Black, is a microcosm of them all.

Black Sea: A Sea of Troubles

In ancient times, it was valued for its abundance of fish, its relatively temperate climate, and its strategic location: the city of Constantinople was the gateway between East and West, capital of the Byzantine Empire, and one of the great hubs of human civilization. During the past century, the Black Sea became famous for its beach resorts where wealthy Russians and Ukrainians built their dachas. But in recent decades, this beautiful place has been ravaged. First, and most tragically, there has been the onset of a disease that is now endemic to enclosed or semi-enclosed bodies of water worldwide: an immense excess of marine nutrients. Like a compulsive eater who becomes increasingly obese, immobile, and finally moribund, the Black Sea has been overloaded with nutrients—fertilizer washing downstream from farms, human waste from the cities. The result has been massive eutrophication—a burgeoning growth of algae and bacteria, creating thick floating mats so dense that they block sunlight and destroy the natural ecological balance.

> *"Compared to the open oceans, semi-enclosed seas tend to be damaged more severely and quickly because water circulation is limited."*

To this cancer-like process, other complications have been added. While the Black Sea was serving as a playground for elite Soviets during the Cold War, it was also being used as a convenient sink for all sorts of industrial activity—in an era when Soviet industries were driven by production quotas with little concern for their environmental impact. Toxic pollutants from plants ran uncontrolled down the three main tributary rivers, and growing quantities of municipal waste mingled with industrial and agricultural waste. The contaminated waters weakened the fish populations, which were further destroyed by heavy overfishing.

Oxygen Depletion

In this morass of biological decline, the most visible blight is the vast greenish mass that now lies over much of the water. What was once a rich, diverse ecosystem has been replaced by a monoculture of opportunistic weeds and algae. Gradually, as the dissolved oxygen supply is depleted by the algae and bacteria, the water becomes anoxic—incapable of supporting oxygen-dependent plants or animals. When the algae dies, it settles to the sea bottom, releasing hydrogen sulfide, which is poisonous to animals.

> *"The Danube [River] delivers much of [Europe's] fertilizer runoff, detergent waste, and human sewage."*

A key source of the trouble can be found along a 350-kilometer stretch of northwestern shoreline where three major rivers, the Danube, the Dniester and the Dnieper, drain into the sea. The Danube delivers much of the fertilizer runoff, detergent waste, and human sewage produced by the 81 million people in the Central and Eastern European drainage basin. Each year, it dumps an estimated 60,000 tons of phosphorus and 340,000 tons of inorganic nitrogen on the shallow waters of the Black Sea shelf, which is approximately one-fourth of the sea's entire area.

In the past 25 years, the Danube's concentrations of nitrate and phosphate (stable compounds that form when nitrogen and phosphorus react with oxygen) have increased six-fold and four-fold, respectively. Concentrations from the Dniester, which flows across the Ukrainian breadbasket region, have increased three-fold for nitrate and seven-fold for phosphate since the 1950s. The Dniester has also brought heavy loads of pesticides, after flowing through the fields of Ukrainian and Moldovan farmers. And the Dnieper still suffers from the radioactive fallout of the Chernobyl nuclear disaster in 1986. . . .

Yellow Sea: Heavy Metals

Six thousand kilometers east-southeast, between northern China and Korea, the Yellow Sea suffers its own version of the Black Sea's dysfunctional relationship with its tributary rivers. And here, too, the result has been a disaster for fisheries. But whereas the Black Sea region is moderately populated, the Yellow Sea coastal region is densely populated and growing rapidly. Here, as a result, the decline of fisheries has gone beyond the economic sphere, into overt military confrontation. And here, perhaps more than anywhere else, the fundamental dilemma—and irony—of the human relationship with the seas is illustrated in its simplest form: the more people there are to depend on the seas for food and jobs, the more pollution there is to make those assets scarcer. In China, pollution takes on a broader meaning as well—it includes huge quantities of silt from the intensive farming that takes place on every available hectare of the drainage basin.

> *"Rapid industrialization in [China's coastal] region has occurred with few or no pollution control measures."*

In fact, the Yellow Sea gets its name from the ochre-colored soil that washes down the Yellow River (Huang He) out to the Bohai Sea (the large bay linking Beijing and the Yellow Sea) at a rate of 2.4 billion tons per year. Today, a more accurate name for the Yellow Sea might be the *Brownish-Red Sea*. And the problem with this silt is that it is no longer just topsoil, but is now laced with heavy metals. Just as the sea has absorbed silt for thousands of years, it now absorbs the pollution and wastes from China's rapidly industrializing coastal areas.

Currently, there are more than 400 million Chinese living on or near the coast. With an estimated 40 percent of the industrial plants located along the coast, more workers and their families are tempted to move to coastal areas every year in search of jobs. In fact, of all the migratory movements in the world today, this internal movement of rural Chinese to the coast may be the largest. In 1989, the coastal population density was 312 people per square kilometer. By the year 2000, it is projected to have risen by an additional 62 people per square kilometer.

To keep up with demand for housing and buildings, coastal land that used to be cultivated is now developed at a rate of 3,400 square kilometers per year. This leaves aquatic and terrestrial habitat areas at an even greater disadvantage: not only are they losing ground, but they are being forced to absorb increasing volumes of runoff from more industries and more people. Not surprisingly, the coasts of China and Korea are showing signs of extraordinary stress.

Metals Contamination

Pollution from heavy metals "may be among the highest in the world" in China's coastal areas (including the Yellow Sea, East China Sea, and South China Sea), according to Fan Zhijie of the State Oceanic Administration in Dalian, China, and R.P. Côté of the Dalhousie University School for Resource and Environmental Studies in Halifax, Nova Scotia. One reason is that rapid industrialization in the region has occurred with few or no pollution control measures.

According to the Chinese *Annual of Environment Quality in Offshore of China, 1989*, the Yellow River dumped 751 tons of cadmium, mercury, lead, zinc, arsenic, and chromium, along with 21,000 tons of oil, into the Bohai Sea in 1989. The Yellow Sea itself received more than twice that quantity of heavy metals. This study also found that the greatest concentrations of toxic metals occurred in the top layer of sediment—in some cases more than 1,000 times greater than those in the water.

The contamination is thus heavily concentrated in the seabed where many species live and feed. And indeed, monitoring between 1981 and 1984 showed that the concentrations of cadmium in crustaceans (such as crabs) increased three-fold, while lead and copper in fish and mollusks (such as mussels) increased two- to four-fold. Data from 1989 found that mercury in bivalves (clams and oysters) was over 10 times acceptable levels.

In addition to the contamination flowing in from rivers, the Yellow Sea is being contaminated by atmospheric pollution, particularly from coal-burning plants and smogbound cities, and by direct dumping from coastal industries. The Qingdao Soda Plant on Kiaochow Bay, for example, has dramatically altered the condition of sediments. Chromium levels in sediments near the plant have been recorded at levels as high as 430 mg per kilogram—enough to dramatically discolor a beach near the discharge point. In 1963, 141 types of marine animals—mollusks, crustaceans, echinoderms, and the like—were living in these sediments; by 1988, only 24 remained. By 1995, most of the estuaries, bays, and wetlands bordering the Yellow Sea had been polluted enough to have serious effects on fisheries. . . .

Baltic Sea: Organochlorines

In Scandinavia, the numerous rivers and fiords coming out of Sweden and Norway into the Baltic Sea have a very different look; instead of wending across wide, intensively cultivated and heavily populated valleys like so many of the world's sea-feeding tributaries, they wind through quiet, seemingly pristine forests. But these forests are also the sites—and resources for—another kind of sea-endangering industry: pulp and paper mills. In the 1940s, most of these mills began using elemental chlorine or chlorine compounds to bleach the paper—to make it white enough to satisfy consumers, publishers, and especially advertisers.

The bleaching processes release substantial amounts of organochlorine compounds into the environment. These compounds do not

> *"Some 300,000 to 400,000 tons of chlorinated compounds are released each year—much ending up in the Baltic Sea."*

dissolve in water, but are lipid-soluble and accumulate readily in the fatty tissues of animals and fish. With the pulp and paper industries of Sweden and Finland now accounting for 10 percent of the world's total output, some 300,000 to 400,000 tons of chlorinated compounds are released each year—much ending up in the Baltic Sea.

What happens when these compounds find their way up the food chain into humans and other higher animals has become a subject of intense scientific scrutiny since the late 1980s—with the weight of evidence linking them not only to cancer but to reproductive and endocrine diseases.

Population Declines

Among the early inklings of these effects were reports of die-offs in sea eagles, seals, and minks, first observed on the shores of the Swedish coast in the late 1950s. Since then, these species have suffered severe declines and are now almost extinct. Studies of other species in decline—including both marine mammals and such fish as herring, cod, sprat, and salmon—show that they too contain high levels of organochlorines. Compared to fish in the neighboring North Sea, fish in the Baltic have been found to contain concentrations of these chemicals three to ten times greater.

"The Mediterranean, like the other seas, is being subjected to heavy degradation."

In addition to the population declines or collapses, marine biologists report a disturbing increase in birth defects in populations with high organochlorine levels. Among Baltic gray seals, half the females observed in one study were incapable of breeding because of deformed uteri horns. Among baby seals, eggshell-fragile skulls and skull bone lesions were believed to be caused by the immune suppression effects of exposure to PCBs [polychlorinated biphenyls]. Unfortunately, these trends were not well documented until the late 1980s. Now the effects are so far along and pollution is so great that it is "almost too late to do anything about it," according to Susan Shaw, Executive Director of the Marine Environmental Research Institute in New York City, who works with marine biologists in Sweden.

For epidemiologists, the witches' brew of organochlorines (there are hundreds of these compounds) is trouble enough. But in the Baltic, other ingredients are being added to the brew as well. For years, this sea served as a receptacle for the untreated sewage and industrial wastewater generated by areas under Communist rule, such as Upper Silesia in Poland and Ostrava in the Czech Republic. A 1991 *Ambio* article, for example, indicates that atmospheric metal input is the most important source of metal contamination in the Baltic area. Metal concentrations in the region have increased five-fold over the last 50 years, largely as a result of burning fossil fuels. Fish from many coastal areas are now blacklisted, because they contain too much mercury. But with the sources of Baltic pollution so diffused, it is difficult—with one major exception—to detect and monitor the polluters.

The exception is the pulp and paper mills. In the last few years, the European community has moved to impose new restrictions on chlorine bleaching. How well they succeed may go a long way toward determining the health of the Baltic for future generations—both of marine life and of the people who depend on it. . . .

41

Chapter 1

Mediterranean Sea: Tankers and Tourists

Few seas have played more vital roles in the rise of human civilizations—and the support of their rapidly growing populations over the past four millennia—than the Mediterranean. Providing access to three continents, it played key roles in the rise of Aegean, Egyptian, Phoenician, Greek, and Roman empires, and to the development of historic exchanges of information and culture between places as far-flung as China, Britain, and Ethiopia. Today, it is bordered by 18 countries, all of which are as dependent on the sea as their predecessors were. Yet, the Mediterranean, like the other seas, is being subjected to heavy degradation—with the prospect of irreversible losses to its dependent human communities.

Concern about this degradation began to emerge in the 1960s and 1970s, with a series of tanker spills and severe chemical leaks. The heart of the Mediterranean, the Lake of Santa Gida near Cagliari, Sardinia, was a fertile breeding area for 10,000 water birds. But it was also a repository for mercury effluent from petro-chemical factories. Mercury contamination was so severe in the fall of 1976 that the regional government had to block off the entrance to the lake, remove all the shellfish, and dredge the bottom to remove any traces of the metal.

While marine scientists had warned for many years of marine degradation, it was not until fishers were banned from contaminated waters, beachgoers were forced to go home early, and oil-covered seals and dolphins made the nightly news, that—with tourist revenue at stake—the first actions were taken. Tourism is critical to the Mediterranean economy; each summer, the seasonal population on the sea's coasts almost doubles, adding 100 million visitors each year to the region's more than 160 million residents.

A Regional Plan for Improvement

The Mediterranean is especially vulnerable to pollution because it is a major shipping and transport route between the Middle East and Europe—meaning that there is heavy traffic of oil tankers. It also has naturally low levels of rainfall, nutrients, and species diversity, which, combined with increasing levels of urban and coastal pollution, leave the sea with little leeway. Luckily, in the 1970s, developing and industrialized countries around the region realized that the sea was sick, and for environmental reasons and self-interest they joined together to try to prevent it from getting worse.

"Among the Earth's sea-dependent populations, there appears to be little or no money for marine protection."

In 1975, Mediterranean countries were the first to approve a UNEP [United Nations Environment Programme]-sponsored regional sea program—and today, arguably, the condition of the Mediterranean is not as bad as it would have been without the Mediterranean Action Plan (MEDAP). The first issue MEDAP tackled was marine dumping, in the Barcelona Convention. A Regional Oil

Center was established on Malta in 1976 to provide training, information, emergency management programs, and waste retention facilities in ports. But the problems did not stop: in the 1980s, one-fifth of the world's oil spills occurred in the Mediterranean Sea. . . .

Essential Steps

Among the Earth's sea-dependent populations, there appears to be little or no money for marine protection, or in many cases even for basic sanitation services and sewage treatment. Subsistence fishers, seasonal dockworkers, small-scale farmers, and migrant workers are encountering growing hardship. As resources become scarce and tensions rise, the fishing industry, tourist resorts, oil and gas developers, and shipping facilities are all taking losses.

To reverse these losses will require at least three politically difficult but ecologically essential steps. The first is to reduce and restrict the use of

> *"We need a philosophical change of heart to reconnect ourselves with the seas."*

damaging chemicals: chlorine in paper bleaching, and phosphates, nitrates, and chlorine in detergents and pesticides. These are chemicals that persist in the environment, bioaccumulate in animal tissues, cause direct damage to individual species and entire aquatic ecosystems, exacerbate anoxia, and disrupt the earth's carbon cycle. Banning or limiting their use will allow ecosystems to slowly re-establish their natural equilibrium.

The second step is to secure financial commitments from industrial countries and private companies to invest in basic infrastructure to handle the sewage and waste from cities. This is already being done in the Baltic where Finland, Sweden, Denmark, and Germany are helping eastern Baltic countries to pay for sewage treatment plants. Recently, the European Bank for Reconstruction and Development committed $67 million to construct a sewage treatment plant in Tallinn, the capital of Estonia.

Action and Change

The third, and most critical, step is to secure cooperation—commitment to joint management in lieu of preoccupation with extraction and control—at all levels of community and government. On the international level, an instructive model is the Ronneby Declaration, signed in 1990 by all of the Baltic Sea countries, members of the European Union, and four multilateral banks. This agreement identifies 132 pollution hot spots in the Baltic region, most of them in the former Eastern bloc countries. To clean up the hot spots, a 20-year, $25.6 billion Joint Comprehensive Environmental Action Program underwrites investments in sewage treatment, the refitting of pulp and paper plants, and other pollution control efforts. At the community level, a successful example can be found in the Gulf of Thailand, where several Buddhist and Muslim fishing villages are working with local activists and the U.S.-based Earth Island Institute to close the inner reaches of Kuntulee Bay to pushnets and trawlers. Both of these cases shows how action and change can happen even in the absence of political agreement.

Finally, we need a philosophical change of heart to reconnect ourselves with the seas that have supported our civilizations since the dawn of history. We may not need to restore the seas to their original pristine conditions—that may no longer be possible. But we urgently need to rehabilitate and protect whatever ecological and economic value can still be salvaged.

Pesticides Contaminate America's Drinking Water

by Environmental Working Group

About the author: *The Environmental Working Group is a Washington, D.C., environmental organization that studies concerns such as agriculture, pesticides, drinking water, and toxic waste.*

Beginning on May 15, 1995, a network of environmental organizations began testing tap water for weed killers in cities across the U.S. Corn Belt, in Louisiana, and in Maryland.

Samples were collected every three days from people's homes or offices. Samples collected were sent to the Iowa State Hygienic Lab and analyzed for the presence of atrazine and cyanazine, two of the most heavily used pesticides in all of the United States.

On or about the first day of June and July, larger samples were taken from the same locations and more extensively tested for 11 weed killers and their by-products.

The purpose of the study [*Weed Killers by the Glass*] is to inform the debate and fill current gaps in knowledge about the extent and magnitude of tap water contamination with weed killers, including the severity and duration of peak levels of exposure that routinely exceed federal health standards during the three- to four-month peak runoff period.

The results of these tests reveal widespread contamination of tap water with many different pesticides at levels that present serious health risks.

Herbicides Exceed Health Standards

Major Agricultural Weed Killers Are Routinely Found in Tap Water at Levels That Exceed Federal Health Standards.

EPA's [Environmental Protection Agency] Lifetime Health Advisory (LHA) level for the herbicide cyanazine was exceeded at least once in 18 out of 29 cities (62 percent) with a total population of 4.48 million people, 60 percent of

From the Executive Summary of "Weedkillers by the Glass," a 1995 report by the Environmental Working Group, Washington, D.C. Reprinted by permission.

the population covered in the study. The herbicide atrazine exceeded the Maximum Contaminant Level (MCL) at least once in 13 communities with a total population of 2.98 million people, representing 43% of the cities, and 40% of the population in the study. Cyanazine levels exceeded federal health guidelines in 35 percent of all samples. Atrazine concentrations were above the federal health standards in 17 percent of all samples.

In some cities, herbicides in tap water exceed federal health standards for weeks or months at a time. In Springfield, IL, cyanazine exceeded the LHA in all tap water samples collected between May 27 and June 29. In eight other cities more than half of the samples collected exceeded the atrazine MCL or the cyanazine LHA: Danville and Decatur, IL; Indianapolis, IN; Columbus and Bowling Green, OH; Jefferson City, MO; New Orleans, LA; and Kansas City, KS.

Some samples and locations were severely contaminated. Six samples from Danville, IL, contained cyanazine at levels *more than 10 times* the LHA, and one sample contained cyanazine at *34 times* the LHA. All nine samples with the highest cyanazine concentrations came from Danville, followed by water from Kansas City, KS; Decatur, IL; Fort Wayne, IN; and Omaha, NE.

The highest atrazine concentration—18 ppb [parts per billion], more than 6 times the MCL—was also found in Danville, IL, as were the next five samples with the highest atrazine concentrations. The communities with the next four highest atrazine detections, all above the MCL, were Fort Wayne, IN; Bowling Green and Columbus, OH; and Kansas City, KS.

Weed Killers Were Found in the Tap Water of 28 out of 29 Cities.

Atrazine was found in tap water in 28 out of 29 cities tested (97 percent), cyanazine was found in 25 (86 percent), metolachlor in 19 cities (66 percent), acetochlor in 15 (52 percent), alachlor in 10 cities (34 percent), simazine in four (14 percent), and metribuzin in two cities (7 percent). One of two breakdown products (known as metabolites) of atrazine, desethylatrazine and desisopropylatrazine, was found in 12 communities. The only community where weed killers were not found in the drinking water was Memphis, TN, which obtains its tap water from deep groundwater wells.

"In some cities, herbicides in tap water exceed federal health standards for weeks or months at a time."

Most of these herbicides have been used in agriculture for decades. However, our study also found trace levels of the herbicide acetochlor, a probable human carcinogen, approved for use in 1993.

Average Levels of Weed Killers in Tap Water Exceeded Federal Standards in 13 Cities.

Average cyanazine levels in tap water over the six-week testing period exceeded the LHA in 13 cities with a population of 2.8 million people. Average atrazine levels in drinking water during the same period exceeded the federal MCL in six of these same 13 cities, including Indianapolis, IN; Columbus, OH; and Fort Wayne, IN.

Midwesterners and Children at Risk

People in Many Midwestern Cities Are Routinely Exposed to Many Different Pesticides in a Single Glass of Water.

Tap water from two-thirds of the cities tested contained between four and nine pesticides or pesticide by-products. Current EPA drinking water standards are set one chemical at a time and assume that this simultaneous exposure does not occur.

Two or more pesticides or pesticide metabolites were found simultaneously in the drinking water of 27 out of 29 cities, three or more pesticides were found in 23 cities, four or more pesticides in 21 cities, five or more pesticides in 18 cities, six or more pesticides in 14 cities, and seven or more pesticides or metabolites in the treated tap water of five cities: Ft. Wayne, IN; Muncie, IN; Danville, IL; Columbus, OH; and Bowling Green, OH. In Fort Wayne, IN, nine different pesticides and metabolites—atrazine, cyanazine, metolachlor, alachlor, metribuzin, acetochlor, desethylatrazine, desisopropylatrazine, and simazine—were found in a single sample of tap water collected in June 1995. Three of these pesticides were found at levels above EPA standards. The nine pesticides included two probable human carcinogens, five possible human carcinogens, one pesticide responsible for birth defects, and four pesticides that disrupt the hormone or endocrine system.

> *"We estimate that 45,000 infants in 29 cities drank infant formula reconstituted with tap water contaminated with weed killers."*

Infants and Children Are Exposed to Unsafe Levels and Mixtures of Pesticides in Infant Formula, Juices, and Drinks Reconstituted with Tap Water.

Drinking water standards do not account for the vulnerability of infants to toxic chemicals such as the weed killers found in our tests. Standards also fail to account for the high volume of water young children drink relative to adults.

We estimate that 45,000 infants in 29 cities drank infant formula reconstituted with tap water contaminated with weed killers during the six-week study period. More than 10,000 infants drank infant formula made with tap water with an average atrazine contamination level above the EPA standard for the six-week period. These same 10,000, plus an additional 8,400 infants, drank infant formula made with tap water contaminated with cyanazine at levels above the federal LHA.

An estimated 28,000 infants drank infant formula reconstituted with tap water that was contaminated with at least four and as many as nine pesticides and toxic pesticide by-products during the six-week testing period.

Chapter 1

Inadequate Monitoring and Standards

Federal Drinking Water Monitoring Requirements Are Fundamentally Flawed.

Federal drinking water monitoring requirements provide regulators and public health officials with a fundamentally distorted picture of contamination levels in tap water. Extended periods of exposure to contaminants at levels above federal health standards are not identified by federal monitoring requirements, nor are peak exposures that may exceed these standards by 10-fold to 30-fold or more.

Within the peak contamination period, extended and repeated exposure to weed killers at levels above federal health standards is common in the cities where we tested. Federal monitoring requirements, in contrast, treat all seasons the same and mandate only one sample during each quarter of the year, including the three-month peak contamination period. Even this lone sample can be taken very early in the spring-summer quarter, before herbicides are applied, or very late, after pesticides have largely flushed downstream. A sample taken at either end of this period will not reflect accurately the degree of the contamination.

Moreover, there is *no monitoring requirement* for so-called "unregulated contaminants" such as cyanazine, even though in our testing program cyanazine was found at levels exceeding federal health advisories more often than any other herbicide.

These failings are of particular concern because federal drinking water standards:
- Do not protect the public from extended periods of exposure above the MCL or LHA;
- Do not consider the risks of exposure to multiple herbicides simultaneously;
- Do not explicitly take into account special risks to children;
- Are based on a flawed methodology that does not adequately protect the public from cancer risks.

Actions and statements by many water utility authorities underscore the need to dramatically improve monitoring. The Kansas City, MO, water system will not allow atrazine contamination to exceed EPA lifetime health standards for even one day; to achieve this goal they monitor drinking water daily during peak contamination periods. The American Water Works Association, which represents the majority of water utilities, noted in their comments to EPA on the atrazine special review that "AWWA is concerned with exceedances of *any* MCL at *any* time. . . ."

Conventional Water Treatment Does Not Remove Weed Killers.

Following the release of an October 1994 report by the Environmental Working Group (*Tap Water Blues*),

> *"Congress must strengthen federal pesticide and drinking water laws so that they explicitly protect infants and children."*

many water utilities claimed that the standard water treatment techniques they were using were able to adequately remove herbicides from contaminated source water. This is not the case.

All of the water tested in this study was treated tap water. In most cases, utilities are using only conventional water treatment—chlorination and sand filtration—which does nothing to reduce weed killer levels in water delivered to the community .

The only technology that can adequately remove pesticides once they have contaminated water supplies is the more expensive Granular Activated Carbon. Such water treatment costs are passed on to water customers—the polluters are not billed. Preventing contamination of drinking water with herbicides in the first place, by phasing out the most toxic compounds and reducing use of all pesticides, is the most efficient and effective means of ensuring the safety of our water supplies.

Recommendations for Safety

• Parents in the most contaminated communities should seriously consider alternatives to tap water for infant formula and reconstituted juices or drinks for their infants and children from May 1 through August 30.

• The EPA should require daily monitoring for triazine herbicides with inexpensive immunoassay tests for all surface-water-supplied drinking water systems in the Corn Belt. The monitoring cost is about $1,500 per city; less than 10 cents per person in a city of 20,000.

• The EPA should phase out the use of the triazine herbicides.

• Congress must strengthen federal pesticide and drinking water laws so that they explicitly protect infants and children from acute and chronic effects of these contaminants.

• Absent Congressional action, the EPA should move to set pesticide and drinking water standards to protect infants and children.

When setting drinking water standards to protect infants and children the EPA must strictly follow the recommendations of the National Academy of Sciences report *Pesticides in the Diets of Infants and Children*. At a minimum the EPA must specifically account for contamination of tap water with many different pesticides and metabolites. The agency (1) must explicitly account for additive or synergistic risks that may result from pesticides that act via a similar toxic mechanism or cause a similar toxic effect, (2) it must specifically account for any increased sensitivity or risk associated with infant or childhood exposure to these mixtures of compounds, and (3) it must consider all routes of exposure to the pesticides that an infant or child might encounter.

The Garbage Crisis Is a Myth

by John Tierney

About the author: *John Tierney is a staff writer for the* New York Times Magazine.

As they put on plastic gloves for their first litter hunt, the third graders knew what to expect. They knew their garbage. It was part of their science curriculum at Bridges Elementary, a public school on West 17th Street in Manhattan. They had learned the Three R's—Reduce, Reuse, Recycle—and discussed how to stop their parents from using paper plates. For Earth Day they had read a Scholastic science publication, "Inside the World of Trash." For homework, they had kept garbage diaries and drawn color-coded charts of their families' trash. So they were primed for the field experiment on this May afternoon.

Analyzing Trash

"We have to help the earth," Natasha Newman explained as she and her classmates dashed around the school collecting specimens. Their science teacher, Linnette Aponte, mediated disputes—"I saw that gum wrapper first!"—and supervised the subsequent analysis of data back in the classroom. The students gathered around to watch her dump out their bags on the floor.

"Do you see any pattern as I'm emptying it?" Miss Aponte asked. "Yeah, it stinks."

"Everybody's chewing Winterfresh."

"A lot of paper napkins."

"It's disgusting."

"They're throwing away a folder. That's a perfectly good folder!" "It's only half a folder."

"Well, they could find the other half and attach them together."

Miss Aponte finished emptying the last bag. "We've been learning about the need to reduce, reuse and recycle," she said, and pointed at the pile. "How does all this make you feel?"

From "Recycling Is Garbage" by John Tierney, *New York Times Magazine*, June 30, 1996. Copyright © 1996 by The New York Times Company. Reprinted by permission.

"*Baaaad*," the students moaned.

Miss Aponte separated out two bottles, the only items in the pile that could be recycled. She asked what lesson the students had learned. The class sentiment was summarized by Lily Finn, the student who had been so determined to save the half folder: "People shouldn't throw away paper or anything. They should recycle it. And they shouldn't eat candy in school."

> *"The simplest and cheapest option is usually to bury garbage in an environmentally safe landfill."*

Lily's judgment about candy sounded reasonable, but the conclusion about recycling seemed to be contradicted by the data on the floor. The pile of garbage included the equipment used by the children in the litter hunt: a dozen plastic bags and two dozen pairs of plastic gloves. The cost of this recycling equipment obviously exceeded the value of the recyclable items recovered. The equipment also seemed to be a greater burden on the environment, because the bags and gloves would occupy more space in a landfill than the two bottles.

Obsession with Garbage

Without realizing it, the third graders had beautifully reproduced the results of a grand national experiment begun in 1987—the year they were born, back when the Three R's had nothing to do with garbage. That year a barge named the Mobro 4000 wandered thousands of miles trying to unload its cargo of Long Islanders' trash, and its journey had a strange effect on America. The citizens of the richest society in the history of the planet suddenly became obsessed with personally handling their own waste.

Believing that there was no more room in landfills, Americans concluded that recycling was their only option. Their intentions were good and their conclusions seemed plausible. Recycling does sometimes make sense—for some materials in some places at some times. But the simplest and cheapest option is usually to bury garbage in an environmentally safe landfill. And since there's no shortage of landfill space (the crisis of 1987 was a false alarm), there's no reason to make recycling a legal or moral imperative. . . .

The Evangelist's Alarms

After the litter hunt in Miss Aponte's science classroom, it was time for a guest lecturer on garbage. A fifth-grade class was brought in to hear Joanne Dittersdorf, the director of environmental education for the Environmental Action Coalition, a nonprofit group based in New York. Her slide show began with a 19th-century photograph of a street in New York strewn with garbage.

"Why can't we keep throwing out garbage that way?" Dittersdorf asked.

"It'll keep piling up and we won't have any place to put it."

"The earth would be called the Trash Can."

'The garbage will soon, like, take over the whole world and, like, kill everybody."

Dittersdorf asked the children to examine their lives. "Does anyone here ever have takeout food?" A few students confessed, and Dittersdorf gently scolded them. "A lot of garbage there."

She showed a slide illustrating New Yorkers' total annual production of garbage: a pile big enough to fill 15 city blocks to a height of 20 stories. "There are a lot of landfills in New York City," Dittersdorf said, "but we've run out of space." Showing a slide of Flushing Meadows, a former landfill that's now a park, she asked, "Would you want to live on top of one of these landfills?" The place didn't look too bad, actually, but Dittersdorf explained that toxic threats could be hidden in a landfill. "Have you ever heard of a place called Love Canal? It was an old landfill that belonged to a chemical company, and they sold it to build a school on, and everyone who went to that school got very sick. There was poison in the dirt underneath."

> *"Plastic packaging and fast-food containers may seem wasteful, but they actually save resources and reduce trash."*

A supermarket package of red apples appeared on the screen. "Look at the plastic, the Styrofoam or cardboard underneath," Dittersdorf said. "Do you need this much wrapping when you buy things?"

"*Noooo.*"

Myths of the Garbage Crisis

"Every week," Dittersdorf said, "75,000 trees are cut to make the Sunday *New York Times*." The children were appalled. A few glanced reproachfully at me sitting in the back of the room. I didn't try to justify my—or your—role in this weekly tree-slaying, garbage-generating, earth-defiling ritual. The children were in no mood for heresy. Dittersdorf had masterfully reinforced the mythical tenets of the garbage crisis:

We're a wicked throwaway society. Plastic packaging and fast-food containers may seem wasteful, but they actually save resources and reduce trash. The typical household in Mexico City buys fewer packaged goods than an American household, but it produces one-third more garbage, chiefly because Mexicans buy fresh foods in bulk and throw away large portions that are unused, spoiled or stale. Those apples in Dittersdorf's slide, protected by plastic wrap and foam, are less likely to spoil. The lightweight plastic packaging requires much less energy to manufacture and transport than traditional alternatives like cardboard or paper. Food companies have switched to plastic packaging because they make money by using resources efficiently. A typical McDonald's discards less than two ounces of garbage for each customer served—less than what's generated by a typical meal at home.

Plastic packaging is routinely criticized because it doesn't decay in landfills, but neither does most other packaging, as William Rathje, an archaeologist at the University of Arizona, has discovered from his excavations of landfills. Rathje found that paper, cardboard and other organic materials—while technically biodegradable—tend to remain intact in the airless confines of a landfill These mummified materials actually use much more landfill space than plastic packaging, which has steadily been getting smaller as manufacturers develop stronger, thinner materials. Juice cartons take up half the landfill space occupied by the glass bottles they replaced; 12 plastic grocery bags fit in the space occupied by one paper bag.

Our garbage will bury us. The Mobro's saga was presented as a grim harbinger of future landfill scarcity, but it actually represented a short-lived scare caused by new environmental regulations. As old municipal dumps were forced to close in the 1980s, towns had to send their garbage elsewhere and pay higher prices for scarce landfill space. But the higher prices, predictably, encouraged companies to open huge new landfills, in some regions creating a glut that set off price-cutting wars. Over the past few years, landfills in the South and Middle West have been vying for garbage from the New York area, and it has become cheaper to ship garbage there than to bury it locally.

> *"America today has a good deal more landfill space available than it did in the mid-1980s."*

America today has a good deal more landfill space available than it did in the mid-1980s. Landfills are scarce in just a few places, notably the Northeast, partly because of local economic realities (open land is expensive near cities) but mainly because of local politics. Environmentalists have prevented new landfills from opening by propounding another myth. . . .

Our garbage will poison us. By mentioning Love Canal, Dittersdorf made landfills sound like the Slough of Despond, John Bunyan's [seventeenth-century author of *The Pilgrim's Progress*] dread swamp. But it's not fair to compare modern municipal-trash landfills with Love Canal, an old industrial dump filled with large concentrations of toxic chemicals that seeped into the ground when a school was, stupidly, built on the site. (Even so, it's not clear that any of the schoolchildren were poisoned. Exhaustive scientific studies around Love Canal haven't detected any increase in cancer rates.)

Landfills Are Safe

Today's landfills for municipal trash are filled mostly with innocuous materials like paper, yard waste and construction debris. They contain small amounts of hazardous wastes, like lead and mercury, but studies have found that these poisons stay trapped inside the mass of garbage even in the old, unlined dumps that were built before today's stringent regulations. So there's little reason to worry about modern landfills, which by Federal law must be lined with clay and plastic, equipped with drainage and gas-collection systems, covered daily with soil and monitored regularly for underground leaks.

The small-time operators who ran the old municipal dumps can't afford to provide these safeguards, which is why corporations have moved in, opening huge facilities that might serve half a state, typically in a rural area with few neighbors. It's a prudent environmental strategy and it provides jobs for rural communities, which is why some of them have been competing to attract new landfills. But the availability of landfill space in the countryside has created an awkward situation for cities committed to more expensive alternatives like recycling programs and incinerators. Environmentalists have responded with a mythical imperative. . . .

We must achieve garbage independence. When Dittersdorf told the children that New York City was running out of landfill space, she was technically right. Mayor Rudy Giuliani and Governor George Pataki have promised Staten Island that its municipal landfill will close by the year 2001, and there's no logical place in town to put a new one. But why should the city have to use a local landfill? Why assume that New Yorkers have a moral obligation to dispose of their garbage near home? Most of the stuff was shipped to the city from factories and farms elsewhere. What's wrong with shipping it back out to be buried in places with open land?

New Yorkers' and Americans' Garbage

"I don't understand why anyone thinks New York City has a garbage crisis because it can't handle all its own waste," says James DeLong, an adjunct scholar at the Competitive Enterprise Institute in Washington. "With that kind of logic, you'd have to conclude that New York City has a food crisis because it can't grow all the vegetables its people need within the city limits, so it should turn Central Park into a farm and ration New Yorkers' consumption of vegetables to what they can grow there." Some politicians in other states have threatened to stop the importing of New York's garbage—it's an easy way to appeal to some voters' chauvinism—but in the unlikely event that they succeeded, they would only be depriving their own constituents of jobs and tax revenue.

"By the year 3000 [America's] national garbage heap will fill a square piece of land 35 miles on each side."

We're cursing future generations with our waste. Dittersdorf's slide showing New Yorkers' annual garbage output—15 square blocks, 20 stories high—looked frightening because the trash was sitting, uncompressed, in the middle of the city. But consider a different perspective—a national, long-term perspective. A. Clark Wiseman, an economist at Gonzaga University in Spokane, Washington, has calculated that if Americans keep generating garbage at current rates for 1,000 years, and if all their garbage is put in a landfill 100 yards deep, by the year 3000 this national garbage heap will fill a square piece of land 35 miles on each side.

This doesn't seem a huge imposition in a country the size of America. The garbage would occupy only 5 percent of the area needed for the national array of solar panels proposed by environmentalists. The millennial landfill would fit on one-tenth of 1 percent of the range land now available for grazing in the continental United States. And if it still pains you to think of depriving posterity of that 35-mile square, remember that the loss will be only temporary. Eventually, like previous landfills, the mounds of trash will be covered with grass and become a minuscule addition to the nation's 150,000 square miles of parkland.

America Does Not Have a Garbage Problem

by Richard Shedenhelm

About the author: *Richard Shedenhelm is a library technical assistant at the University of Georgia in Athens and the publisher of* Summa Philosophiae, *a monthly philosophical journal.*

One of the foremost difficulties facing American cities is where to put the refuse generated every day. It is widely thought that the United States is literally burying itself in garbage—producing mountains of waste and running out of places to put it.

The alleged crisis has prompted a renewed interest in incineration, source reduction, composting, and recycling. Recycling has been the most popular, and the most costly. Outside of saving natural resources, saving our landfills is the most frequently cited reason for recycling.

If the crisis mentality that shrouds the issue of landfills is found to be largely a matter of political misinformation and factual error, then we will have uncovered a major misdirection of local, state, and federal policy. An objective examination of refuse generation and management is in order.

Are Americans Producing Mountains of Trash?

A popular idea in public discourse today is that the United States produces an overwhelming amount of trash—so much that our landfills will not be able to handle the quantity. The most eloquent symbol of this viewpoint was the "garbage barge," which in the late 1980s left Long Island and could not find a port or country willing to accept its 3.168 tons of refuse.

The actual data (such as they are) on the amount of municipal solid waste produced present us with more questions than answers. "Municipal solid waste" is defined by Congress's Office of Technology Assessment [OTA] as "solid waste generated at residences, commercial establishments (e.g., offices, retail shops, restaurants), and institutions (e.g., hospitals and schools)." The

From "Are We Burying Ourselves in Garbage?" by Richard Shedenhelm, *Freeman*, April 1995. Reprinted courtesy of the Foundation for Economic Education.

first question concerns the matter that is being quantified. For instance, an EPA [Environmental Protection Agency] report published in 1990 states that during the years 1960 through 1988 American commercial and residential refuse amounted to 156 million tons, i.e., 3.47 pounds per person per day. This statistic for refuse did not include the 13 percent of discards that were recycled. Many studies of solid

"A typical McDonald's discards less than two ounces of garbage for each customer served."

waste generation rates are unclear about their definition of "waste," e.g., whether automobile bodies, ash from industrial boilers, industrial waste, construction, and demolition debris were included in their analysis. (According to William Rathje, an archaeologist who has spent over two decades investigating actual landfill contents, construction and demolition debris represents about 12 percent by volume of a typical landfill.)

Part of the difficulty results from the methodology employed. One popular method of estimating the quantity of solid waste is the "materials-flow" approach. As indicated in [OTA's] *Facing America's Trash*, this technique estimates solid waste generation without any actual measurement at the points of generation (households, offices, stores) or disposal (landfills, incinerators, recycling facilities). Instead, this method makes assumptions about such things as the lifetimes of products, recycling rates, and the effects of imports and exports. One difficulty of this approach, as Rathje and Cullen Murphy observe, is that certain counterfactual assumptions tend to be made about product durability. For instance, one study that used the materials-flow approach simply assumed that major household appliances have a useful life of 20 years, after which time they are thrown away. In fact, appliances such as washing machines and refrigerators last much longer in low-income households and as a source of parts no longer carried by dealers.

A second question regarding the data of solid waste generation is one of temporal perspective. The earlier-cited figure of daily per capita solid waste generation (3.47 pounds per day) covered the period after 1960. Not taken into account is the greater waste per capita generated in previous ages. According to Rathje and Murphy, there were over three million horses living in cities at the turn of the twentieth century. Each one produced at least twenty pounds of manure daily. Hundreds of thousands of these horses died each year and had to be disposed of. In addition, over twelve hundred pounds per year of coal ash (for cooking and heating) from each American had to be gotten rid of.

Trash Per Capita

Historian Martin Melos found that between 1900 and 1920 Manhattan residents generated an annual average of 160 pounds of garbage, 1,230 pounds of ashes, and 97 pounds of rubbish. The total comes to 1,487 pounds, per capita,

17 percent higher than the above-cited 1,267 pounds allegedly produced by each American annually between the years 1960 through 1988.

According to figures from the American Public Works Association and the Environmental Protection Agency, as late as 1939 cities like Newark, New Jersey, and Austin, Texas, reported annual per capita discards of garbage, ash, and rubbish 20 percent greater than the refuse of the average American in 1988. True, affluence may cause more discards (since in one sense affluence *means* there are more things per capita to eventually discard). But along with a higher standard of living come phenomena such as "light-weighting," where the producers of a commodity (e.g., plastic cola bottles and aluminum cans) find a way to produce the same service with less material. As Judd Alexander [author of *In Defense of Garbage*] observes, fast-food restaurants also help decrease waste: a typical McDonald's discards less than two ounces of garbage for each customer served.

Affluence may also induce *less* waste of food. Rathje and Murphy found that due to packaging, U.S. households produce a third less garbage than households in Mexico City (even after correcting for family size). The main reason for this difference is that a greater percentage of food in Mexico City is bought "fresh" (i.e., unpackaged), resulting in a larger volume of spoilage and more refuse.

> *"The modern landfill has a system to collect and process leachate and manage the methane gas generated by organic decomposition."*

The news about waste generation is not all bad. As [Gonzaga University economic professor] Clark Wiseman points out, between 1960 and 1970 municipal solid waste grew at an annual rate of 3.2 percent. Between 1970 and 1986, the annual growth rate declined to 1.7 percent (with the amount entering landfills growing by only 1.0 percent). This rate is far less than the growth rate of the consumption of goods and services.

A few cities have actually kept track of the solid waste disposed over certain periods of time. According to Harvey Alter of the U.S. Chamber of Commerce, Los Angeles had an unchanged per capita generation of solid waste disposal (by weight) between 1967 and 1976. He also concludes that for the nation as a whole, municipal solid waste generation was almost constant on a per capita basis.

Are Landfills Not Being Built Fast Enough?

The data for landfill openings and closings are similarly ambiguous. To begin with, a modern landfill is not a "dump"—a distinction with more than semantic characteristics. A dump was basically an open pit, but the modern landfill has a system to collect and process leachate and manage the methane gas generated by organic decomposition. It has a clay and plastic lining, and is covered over daily with about six inches of dirt.

The modern landfill is a complex system with a lifetime much shorter than its predecessors. The majority of sanitary landfills are designed for approximately ten years of operation. Hence, in any five-year period, half of these close. We are not necessarily in any "landfill shortage" just because in 1989 we could say that "by 1995, . . . half of our nation's landfills will be closed," according to the National Solid Wastes Management Association. Like the five-day stock of Cheerios on the store shelf, an *inventory* of landfills is all that is economically necessary, not ready-and-waiting landfills for the next one hundred years.

> *"The notion that modern America is especially wasteful is demonstrably wrong."*

The question could arise, however, whether landfills are being built fast enough to replace the ones that close down. To begin to address this issue, we should note that the "landfill problem" exists only in certain parts of the United States, and not in the country as a whole. For instance, Wiseman estimated that at the current rate of solid waste generation, the nation's solid waste for the next 500 years could be buried in a single landfill 100 yards deep, 20 miles to a side. In almost every state, there is no physical or environmental constraint on the building of sanitary landfills. In New York state, a study found 200 square miles of land capable of environmentally safe landfills. Less than 10 percent of that area is needed to serve the entire state for the twenty-first century. If there is an impediment to siting new landfills the cause cannot be physical but instead political. Specifically, the NIMBY (not-in-my-back-yard) problem has kept many jurisdictions from siting new landfills. In addition, some states with lower landfilling costs have tried to ban the importation of other states' refuse.

Despite the "crises" in landfilling for certain areas of the United States (most notably the Northeast and Florida), there is reason for hope. In the long run, environmentally safe, private landfill space may open up to meet areas facing high tipping fees (the per-ton charges at landfills for garbage trucks to leave their load of refuse). For example, Alexander recounts how the tipping fees in the Northeast began to skyrocket in the late 1980s because of a rash of landfill closures by state officials. By the summer of 1992, the tipping fees began to plummet due to the competition of private landfill companies. These companies had responded to the sharp increase in tipping fees by buying the land and permits needed for new landfills.

Conclusion

The crisis mentality has distorted judgment of waste disposal. The notion that modern America is especially wasteful is demonstrably wrong, both in terms of the last decades as well as the last 100 years. The idea that our landfills are literally "running out" is even less credible. If in the twenty-first century major portions of the United States really need to export their refuse to other states, a "gold mine" for refuse burial does exist: South Dakota. This state is geologically, economically, and politically almost ideal for massive municipal solid waste management: much of the western portion of the state consists of cretaceous shales, much of the land is unsuitable for anything except grazing, and the area is in general sparsely populated (hence unlikely to suffer a lot of NIMBY resistance). Should such an alternative become necessary, the most efficient form of transportation would probably be by rail—which is already one of the cheapest forms of waste transport.

So, in the matter of a few years, any "shortage" of landfills (as reflected in higher tipping fees) can bring about the opening of new landfill space. Landfill space is an economic resource, and if we consistently regard it as such we can view the present situation as analogous to the oil crisis of the 1970s.

America's Garbage Problem Is Improving

by Norm Crampton

About the author: *Norm Crampton, author of* The One Hundred Best Small Towns in America, *is the executive director of the Indiana Institute of Recycling in Terre Haute.*

In 1990, lots of Americans were worried about garbage. Taking it out was no longer a mildly pleasurable act of household cleansing. For many of us, toting the trash to the curb had become a big guilt trip.

Forecasts of disappearing dump space had us down in the dumps. A tidal wave of trash was about to bury us under our wasteful lifestyles, or so we thought at the time. The cover story on the Nov. 27, 1989, issue of *Newsweek* was typical: "BURIED ALIVE . . . An Environmental Crisis Reaches Our Doorstep."

Here we are years later, and things look pretty tidy, garbage-wise. What happened to the "crisis?" Did we solve it or did it just go away? The answer is, some of both.

Reforming Wasteful Ways

In fact, there really wasn't a garbage crisis in the first place—we weren't running out of garbage dumps. We were running out of badly managed, poisonous, small, local dumps, and most of them have now closed. But the hyped-up shortage of dump space led us to reform some wasteful ways. Since 1990 we have:

- Learned how to recycle, cutting a big slice out of the old household garbage load.
- Nudged manufacturers to package products in less material and use more recycled ingredients.
- Cheerfully told check-out clerks to skip the bag for small purchases.
- Started to pay our full, fair, household share for garbage service—a sharp spur to waste reduction.

Yet we're reluctant to take credit for our efforts, possibly because garbage

From "We're Winning the Garbage War" by Norm Crampton, *American Legion Magazine*, January 1995. Reprinted by permission of the publishers.

bulletins often aren't so optimistic. They are saying, if we've really reformed and are winning the garbage war, what about those reports telling us we are producing more garbage than ever before?

For instance, in 1970, total U.S. garbage divided by population equaled 3 pounds per person per day. In 1990, total U.S. garbage divided by population equaled 4 pounds per person per day.

That may look like business as usual in "The Throwaway Society," but it's not, according to Marge Franklin, president of a Kansas firm that tracks "municipal solid waste"—the technical term for all our household leftovers. Franklin says that the total garbage figure also includes things we recycle.

There's evidence of change in Delaware, for one place. N.C. Vasuki, head of the Delaware Solid Waste Authority, says garbage production in his state on a per-person basis peaked in 1989 and has been declining since 1991. Recycling is the reason.

It's easy to understand why we became nearly hysterical about garbage a few years ago. We had seen the infamous "Garbage Barge" sail port to port looking for a dump. And other environmental matters were clamoring for attention and action—acid rain, ozone depletion and global warming.

The Spread of Recycling

But garbage was something we could understand. And the front line of defense against garbage—recycling—was kids' play. In fact, in many households kids brought the lessons home from school and taught their parents.

Recycling has spread like wildfire. One survey reports 101 million Americans—up 24 million in a year—now receive curbside collection of their old newspapers, advertising mail, empty food and beverage containers, cardboard boxes and the like. At last count there was curb service in 6,678 cities and towns. That's a huge increase compared to about a thousand programs in 1990.

During the same period, garbage dumps—landfills, as they are called by the pros—dropped from 8,000 to less than 4,400. But that reduction may not be as startling as it seems. At any given time, it's fairly accurate to say that half the dumps will close in five years. Just as cars wear out and are replaced, dumps fill up and are replaced.

"There really wasn't a garbage crisis in the first place—we weren't running out of garbage dumps."

The decline in total dumps is mainly a result of tough new federal regulations that have padlocked a large number of leaky old sites. The new dumps are environmentally much better and bigger. That is one reason why Ed Repa, the research director at Environmental Industry Associations, believes total dump space has remained fairly constant since 1990.

The big change with dumps is they are getting farther away: Seattle, an outstanding recycling city, loads its nonrecyclable leftovers on a garbage train for shipment 325 miles to a disposal site in eastern Oregon.

But the best news, perhaps, is that Americans may really have reformed and given up their garbage-spreading ways. Recycling programs are here to stay. They're hugely popular with the public, and industry has invested an estimated $15 billion so far in gearing up to handle recycled raw materials.

You hear less about the success of recycling these days, experts say, because it has become a routine part of so many households and communities.

> *"Package 'lightweighting'. . . conserves natural resources and cuts transportation costs."*

Yet prices for recycled materials are shaky. The problem is simple: supply—large and growing larger— is chasing demand, which is small, but gaining. Thus, supplies of old newspaper, plastic jugs and other items periodically pile up. Pete Grogan, former president of the National Recycling Coalition, isn't worried. He points out that recyclables, like all commodities, will have their ups and downs in price.

A better indicator is how recycling is reducing the other GNP—the "Gross National Pile." In 1989, recycling reduced 9 percent of it. In 1995, according to best estimates, recycling will have reduced our garbage by 19 percent, including yard wastes such as grass, leaves and brush.

Better Packaging

And the buying public has let manufacturers know it wants products packaged with the least amount of material. Many Americans blame "excessive packaging" for a lion's share of the garbage crisis. Perhaps rightly so. Containers of all kinds, from cardboard boxes to toothpaste tubes to plastic "bubble" packs, make up at least a third of America's trash.

And industry has responded. For instance, plastic milk jugs are thinner, and it takes more aluminum cans to make a pound. Both are examples of package "lightweighting" that conserves natural resources and cuts transportation costs.

The message hits the breakfast table on cereal boxes labeled, "Carton made from 100 percent recycled paper," with the added technical information: "Minimum 35 percent postconsumer content." Some of the 35 percent is made from the old newspapers we're recycling at home.

But there are skeptics who argue that consumers haven't really changed, that many of us talk a tougher garbage game than we play. Pollsters, for example, know that Americans exaggerate when asked how much they recycle. And while we say we prefer products that reduce waste, we seem to buy products for other reasons, like price or convenience.

For instance, when the garbage crisis was at a fever pitch in 1990, Clorox Co. was worried about its Pine-Sol brand of household cleaner after competitor Procter & Gamble came out with a Spic and Span bottle made of 100 percent recycled plastic.

Chapter 1

"We immediately panicked. There goes our market share," recalls Terrence Bedell, environmental packaging manager at Clorox. But there was no need to worry. "We never saw one single share point of difference between our products," he says.

The Hot Issue

If the choices made in supermarkets have nothing to do with garbage, then why do so many Americans tell pollsters that garbage is the most important environmental issue?

Judd Alexander, author of *In Defense of Garbage*, has an answer. To him, garbage *is* very personal stuff. Everybody has it in their homes. They live with it every day. And that turns each of us into a garbage expert.

Bill Rathje is a University of Arizona archaeologist who digs up landfills to discover what garbage tells us about America. He says the garbage crisis began with "the absolutely visceral symbol of 'The Garbage Barge.' People really can imagine being buried in garbage."

But Rathje thinks Americans are smarter now. He believes the "crisis" of 1989 has been reduced to a manageable "problem" in 1994. "More and more people in the environmental community are beginning to come to that same conclusion."

Pesticides Do Not Contaminate America's Drinking Water

by Max Schulz

About the author: *Max Schulz is the managing editor of* Forbes MediaCritic, *a quarterly magazine covering American journalism.*

Don't drink the water north of the border, either.

That's the message from Fenton Communications, the public-relations firm that cooked up the alar apple scare in 1989. Working with a savvy environmental research group, Fenton has been waging a new campaign claiming the nation's tap water is laced with dangerous levels of cancer-causing pesticides. The point, as one water treatment specialist in the Midwest put it, is "to scare the hell out of people." Fenton appears to be achieving that end, thanks to a docile news media.

Sounding Alarms

On August 17, 1995, the Environmental Working Group (EWG), a non-profit environmental research organization, convened a press conference in the nation's capital where it released *Weedkillers by the Glass*, a study of tap water samples collected in 29 mostly midwestern towns and cities by various environmental organizations. The study sounded alarms: Ordinary drinking water is contaminated with deadly pesticides, and the federal regulations designed to protect the public are being flouted regularly. These cancer-causing agents don't just threaten weeds. Everybody— children especially—is at risk.

Scary stuff, as readers and viewers quickly learned. The *New York Times*'s story began, "Tap water in the corn belt is dangerously contaminated with agricultural weedkillers . . . according to a study released today." CBS reporter Frank Currier gravely told viewers that the issue was "too hot to ignore—the risks even harder to swallow." His report featured one concerned mother who

From "Spin Cycle" by Max Schulz, *Forbes MediaCritic*, Winter 1996. Reprinted by permission of *American Heritage* magazine, a division of Forbes, Inc., © Forbes, Inc.

only feeds her baby daughter formula mixed with bottled water. "I just don't want my kids getting sick—or dying."

Not surprisingly, stores in towns all over the Midwest reported runs on bottled water, and local water treatment plants were deluged with calls from worried citizens. There was, however, a problem the press failed to detect: The organization had distorted the interpretation of federal water safety standards so that it appeared there was massive contamination of midwestern drinking water. The EWG, in other words, had manufactured the scare.

The group's report focused on two of the most heavily used pesticides in agriculture, atrazine and cyanazine, reporting that the highest concentrations of each and the most "severe contamination" found anywhere were in the tap water samples taken in Danville, Illinois. There, according to *Weedkillers*, atrazine was "found in 100 percent of 16 tap water samples [and] 88 percent of samples were above the federal health standard." As for cyanazine, "94 percent of samples were above the federal health advisory."

According to the report, the average concentration of atrazine in Danville water samples was 8.71 parts per billion (ppb). The report also noted that the federal standard (known as the Maximum Contaminant Level, or MCL) for atrazine is 3 ppb. The natural inference was that the water in Danville and other places mentioned in the EWG report with similar concentrations of atrazine was unsafe by federal standards. That was the message conveyed by *New York Times* correspondent Dirk Johnson, who wrote that at 18 of the 29 test cities, "the levels exceeded federal safety standards."

The Real Story

The story the media did not discover is that the MCL of 3 ppb is not the safety threshold for spot samples, such as those examined by the EWG study, but for lifetime exposure, which is measured annually. As it happens, the Environmental Protection Agency (EPA) calculates the MCL by taking the *average* of quarterly samples throughout the year. This average cannot exceed 3 ppb.

> *"The organization had distorted the interpretation of federal water safety standards so that it appeared there was massive contamination of midwestern drinking water."*

The idea is that if your drinking water averaged no more than 3 ppb of atrazine over the course of a lifetime, you wouldn't be in any danger.

How much is 3 ppb? One midwestern water treatment specialist said it amounts to "about one ounce [of herbicide] in 2.6 million gallons" of water. Furthermore, an EPA official concedes there is as much as a 1,000-fold margin of safety built in to the safety standards—which might even seem to render meaningless negligible differences in the numbers.

The press gave the Environmental Working Group a pass on another aspect of its report. The group took samples only during the growing season—May and June—when agricultural runoff leaves the highest concentrations of pesticide residue in drinking water. Concentrations are far lower at other times of the year. Though this fact was mentioned in press accounts, no context was provided. Namely, the EPA itself recognizes that samples with more than 3 ppb of atrazine are likely to be found in May and June.

> *"EWG's samples were taken only during a short period when they knew the concentrations of cyanazine would be high."*

The press also missed another angle to the story. The EPA, which issues the standards focusing on average lifetime concentrations, is also concerned about health effects from short-term, high exposure. In 1988, the EPA issued a set of short-term Health Advisory Levels (HALs), which deal with instances where individual samples show high levels of atrazine. These HALs were under review in 1995 to see if they should be updated.

Omitted Information

The HALs are the more important measure of crisis levels, and the EPA has set a number of them for atrazine. This information is found nowhere in the EWG report, nor in the press accounts. The one-day and the 10-day HALs for children are 100 ppb. The longer-term (seven years) HAL for children is 50 ppb. For adults, the longer-term HAL is 200 ppb. Alarm should set in when concentrations of the pesticide reach or break these levels. But the highest concentration of atrazine the EWG found anywhere was 18 ppb in Danville. In the 29 towns and cities the EWG tested, only six had an average concentration—during the peak growing season, mind you—greater than the 3 ppb MCL. Danville, with its 8.71 reading, was one, and the five other locations had averages ranging from 3.04 to 3.69 ppb.

The press did little better in its treatment of cyanazine, the other herbicide chiefly targeted by the EWG. No MCL has yet been set by the EPA for cyanazine, though it has issued a set of HALs similar to those for atrazine. In the absence of a legal standard like the MCL for atrazine, the EPA has also established a lifetime health advisory level (LHA) for cyanazine of 1 ppb. (DuPont, the largest producer of cyanazine, has agreed to phase out production by 2002, though it still maintains the herbicide is safe.)

Weedkillers by the Glass assumed that any sample of water with a concentration of cyanazine above 1 ppb exceeds the LHA. This was the case, the study said, in 35 percent of the samples. But the LHA is figured to deal with average lifetime exposure, and the EWG's samples were taken only during a short period when they knew the concentrations of cyanazine would be high.

The EWG failed to note the other health advisory levels for cyanazine: one-day and 10-day HALs for children (100 ppb) and longer-term (seven years)

HALs for children (20 ppb) and for adults (70 ppb). The numbers the EWG published for cyanazine levels are not nearly so scary when considering these other Health Advisory Levels—the ones the EWG did not mention.

Evidently, that didn't matter to the Associated Press's Joe Hebert. After observing from the report that atrazine levels exceeded federal standards, he wrote, "Concentrations of

> *"The drinking public would have been better served by the media watchdogs if the press had raised a few questions."*

cyanazine, another suspected carcinogen, were too high at least once in 18 communities." Too high? According to the Environmental Working Group, certainly, but not according to the EPA's own health advisory levels. But there was no way to know that from reading the AP account.

Not Critical Enough

To be sure, the material addressed by the EWG study is complicated, even stultifying. But that's all the more reason the press should have viewed it with a critical eye, especially since the EWG report had not been independently peer-reviewed, as all formal scientific studies are.

As it happened, the media did approach *Weedkillers by the Glass* with some degree of skepticism at the press conference. It just didn't show up in media accounts. Televised on C-SPAN, the press conference featured a number of tough, probing questions. One reporter asked whether the report is unnecessarily alarming because it focused on "peaks" rather than on the average readings for pesticides. Another brought up the point made by the Ohio Farm Bureau Federation that the EWG is not a scientific organization and *Weedkillers* was not a scientific study. EWG President Kenneth A. Cook responded that the Ohio Farm Bureau isn't a scientific organization, either, but that he would never say it shouldn't participate in the debate. Other questioners repeatedly asked where the real evidence of danger was, if any.

The appropriate skepticism that surfaced at the press conference disappeared in the days that followed as one national news outlet after another uncritically reported the EWG claims about contaminated tap water.

Fenton's Scare Tactics

Fenton Communications is best known for manufacturing the notorious scare in which it publicized a report by another environmental advocacy group claiming that the pesticide used to treat apples was deadly. Aided by celebrity activists like Meryl Streep, the 1989 report received mega-coverage. That report was not peer-reviewed either, and in subsequent months its claims would be successfully debunked. But not before it caused a nationwide panic and wrenched the apple industry. Apples were banned from school lunches and removed from grocery stores. "It was most embarrassing for the media," says Dr.

Elizabeth Whelan, President of the American Council on Science and Health. "They were manipulated and used."

Now Fenton is using its skill at spinning the media to drum up another crisis. Under Fenton's direction, the Environmental Working Group sponsored a number of press conferences in places like Danville, Illinois, where it has even taken out newspaper ads asking, "How many pesticides did your child drink last summer?" But how much of a crisis really exists?

The answer may be found in a question posed by Craig Cummings of the Consumers Illinois Water Company, which controls Danville's drinking water. "These tests they took were in June saying the levels were way too high. But they held onto them and didn't disclose them until the August press conference. Why didn't they call us if they had that genuine concern? We would have investigated. If they were valid, we could have treated the problem. They held onto them and used the numbers for maximum fear appeal."

Why didn't they call, indeed. The drinking public would have been better served by the media watchdogs if the press had raised a few questions like that.

Chapter 2

Is Toxic Waste a Health Hazard?

Chapter Preface

Recycling has become a ritual in many households. Recyclers routinely save aluminum cans, plastic bottles, newspapers, and other items for curbside collection or delivery to a neighborhood recycling center. More popular than ever, recycling saves between 19 to 24 percent of America's trash from being landfilled or incinerated. In fact, the rate of office paper recycling has reached 36 percent, and nearly half of all newspapers are now recycled.

Despite the increase in recycling, there is much debate about its cost-effectiveness. Many cities' recycling programs do not pay for themselves and require subsidies to keep operating. San Jose, California, for example, loses $5 million a year on its curbside-recycling program. According to *Waste Age* magazine, in 1994 the states spent more than $250 million to subsidize recycling. Environmental consultant Barbara J. Stevens writes, "In virtually every community, adding a curbside-recycling program increases costs." Michael J. Engelbart, a resource recovery manager for Milwaukee's sanitation department, adds, "I don't know if recycling ever will really make money. The object is to do it in the most cost-effective way."

However, recycling advocates point to success stories such as Seattle, where 90 percent of residents and 80 percent of businesses participate in curbside recycling. From 1988 to the end of 1995, Seattle saved $12.1 million by paying contractors to process recyclables instead of dumping them in landfills. Other cities are streamlining similar operations. In Houston, New York, and Pittsburgh, dual-compartment trucks collect and compact both garbage and recyclables, thus eliminating separate pickups. According to advocates, recycling not only costs less than landfill disposal, but making products from recycled material also uses less energy than manufacturing products from virgin materials.

As communities seek to recycle a greater percentage of trash, debate about whether recycling programs can save money promises to continue. The authors in the following chapter debate the effectiveness of recycling.

Dioxin Is Extremely Hazardous to Humans

by Brian Tokar

About the author: *Brian Tokar is the author of* Earth for Sale *(South End Press, 1997) and* The Green Alternative *(New Society Publishers, 1992). He teaches at the Institute for Social Equality and Goddard College, both in Plainfield, Vermont.*

In even the briefest visits, it is clear that Louisiana is a land of extremes. It is a shorter trip than many people realize from the uninhibited multicultural melting pot of downtown New Orleans to the run-down suburbs where the Ku Klux Klan has only recently shed its white robes for business suits. From there, all along the Mississippi River some 85 miles upstream to the state capital of Baton Rouge, is a place known to locals as Cancer Alley. At one time the meandering bayous of song and legend were all that interrupted the lush cypress and maple swamps of southern Louisiana. Today, it is a nightmare landscape of oil refineries, chemical plants, and plastics factories, a region with the highest cancer rate in the U.S. It is the main reason why Louisiana leads the nation in emissions of toxic chemicals, toxic industrial accidents, and childhood cancer.

Dioxin is probably the single most toxic chemical consequence of all of Louisiana's—and the world's—industrial excess. First discovered as a by-product of the manufacture of herbicides such as 2,4-D and Agent Orange, dioxins (actually a group of 75 similar compounds) are formed whenever certain common organic chemicals come into contact with chlorine at high temperatures. Waste incinerators are common sources of dioxins, which form when paper, wood, and vinyl-based plastics are burned together. So are pulp and paper mills, cement kilns, and many other industrial facilities. Dioxins have been found to cause cancer in laboratory animals at concentrations of only a few parts per trillion, a fact widely used by activists to press for more stringent regulation of incinerators and other industrial sources.

In 1991, paper manufacturers and other industries pressured the EPA [Environmental Protection Agency] to undertake a systematic reassessment of the toxicity

Brian Tokar, "Campaigning Against Dioxin," *Z Magazine*, May 1996. Reprinted with permission.

of dioxins, confident that the data could be found to justify a weakening of dioxin-based regulations. But while there may be a paucity of definitive data on human cancers caused by dioxins, a much more urgent series of findings emerged from these studies. Not only can dioxins and a wide variety of related substances cause cancer at extremely minute doses, but they have widespread damaging effects on the reproductive, immune, and nervous systems of people and animals. Dioxins, PCBs [polychlorinated biphenyls], dibenzofurans, and a variety of chemically related pesticides are now widely recognized as "environmental hormones," which mimic the actions of vital molecular messengers in all living cells, and send systematically incorrect messages to every cell in every organ system of the body.

> *"Dioxins . . . have widespread damaging effects on the reproductive, immune, and nervous systems of people and animals."*

At doses already found in the fatty tissues of people all over the world, dioxins and related endocrine disrupters can alter levels of sex hormones, impair immune system function ("chemical AIDS" is a name given to dioxin in some quarters), reduce sperm counts, disturb fetal development—especially the proper development of sex organs—and increase the likelihood of learning disabilities. A wide range of behavioral abnormalities, including abnormal sexual behaviors, have been observed in laboratory animals exposed to minuscule doses of dioxin. People who live near pesticide plants and chemical waste sites report locally high rates of birth defects, infant cancers, and children showing signs of puberty before age five. Fish and wildlife in the Great Lakes and other areas impacted by chemical industries demonstrate thyroid dysfunction, decreased fertility, malformed and underdeveloped sex organs, metabolic and behavioral abnormalities, and impaired immune systems, among other symptoms. Average sperm counts of men living in the U.S. have fallen 50 percent since 1975, and while the link to dioxin may not yet be certain, no other family of chemicals is nearly as damaging or as pervasive.

People living near incinerators receive the highest doses of dioxin, which persists in fatty tissue for many years, but up to 90 percent of human dioxin exposure comes from food, particularly meat, fish, and dairy products. Native peoples, such as the Inuit of northern Canada who largely survive on subsistence fishing and hunting, have high doses of dioxin in their bodies even though they live hundreds of miles from any identifiable dioxin source, and African Americans have, on average, a third more dioxin in their tissues than others in the U.S. Recent findings suggest that even human breast milk is now a significant source of infant exposure to dioxin.

Unifying Movements

In March of 1996, Baton Rouge was the site of a gathering of nearly 600 antitoxics and environmental justice activists, who met to plan a coordinated strategy against the growing threat of dioxin to public health and the environment. The Third Citizens Conference on Dioxin and Other Synthetic Hormone Disrupters was a landmark event in the development of a people's movement against this growing toxic onslaught. Since 1991, activist conferences on dioxin have been organized every few years to raise awareness about the nature of the dioxin threat and translate recent scientific findings into more widely accessible terms. In 1996, people representing a wide variety of regional and national organizations agreed that the time for action had come, that there is now a sufficient base of common knowledge and experience among people across the country to mount a coordinated campaign to eliminate these pervasive chemical poisons once and for all.

Over 550 people attended the three-day conference in Baton Rouge, exceeding organizers' expectations nearly three times over. There were people whose communities had survived, and often won, long-term battles against toxic industries, waste dumps, and incinerators, and those from communities desperately seeking evacuation from toxic hazards. Activists from Greenpeace and the Native Forest Network were a visible presence, along with those from the Southern Organizing Committee, which has revived the spirit of early civil rights struggles in communities throughout the South in the name of environmental justice and combating environmental racism.

Many Delegations

There were delegations from several native communities, organized under the umbrella of the Minnesota-based Indigenous Environmental Network, as well as representatives from Canada, Mexico, Britain, and Russia. The Citizens Clearinghouse for Hazardous Waste, which was founded by former Love Canal [a Niagara Falls, New York, neighborhood contaminated by chemical wastes] resident Lois Gibbs and now boasts a network of 8,000 local groups nationwide, was a key presence, as were Vietnam veterans' groups, issue-oriented networks such as the Silicon Valley Toxics Coalition, and movement-oriented scientists such as Peter Montague of the Environ-

> *"Since 1991, activist conferences on dioxin have been organized every few years to raise awareness about the nature of the dioxin threat."*

mental Research Foundation and Paul and Ellen Connett. The Connetts' *Waste Not* newsletter has offered an important clearinghouse for anti-incinerator activists for well over a decade.

A significant majority of the participants were women, some 40 percent were from the South, and another 40 percent had experienced a battle with breast cancer, either themselves or in support of a family member. "Everybody is affected by dioxins and endocrine disrupters, no matter what campaign they are working on," explained Gary Cohen, a member of the conference organizing committee and former director of the Boston-based National Toxics Campaign Fund, "so there is a way of uniting people around the health impacts and the worst corporate actors that gets beyond the old turf issues that used to divide us." This unity-in-diversity was reflected in an impressive array of voices at the conference.

The conference program also reflected the increased sophistication and political development of anti-toxics activists, the fruits of a movement that has been evolving steadily for over 15 years since Love Canal first became a household name. Along with new scientific findings and international political developments regarding dioxin, panels addressed the primary importance of environmental justice, strategies for allying with chemical workers, the need to challenge corporate power and the development of economic as well as technological alternatives.

"Nearly 300 waste incinerators have been halted by grassroots activists in the U.S. since the mid-1980s, or 4 out of every 5 that have been proposed."

At the same time, there was a realistic understanding of the difficulties inherent in this kind of alliance-building work. "You can't just show up in southwest Atlanta and talk to people about dioxin when they're more afraid of getting killed by the police," explained Vernetta Perkins, one of the many spokespeople for the conference's youth caucus, and a young veteran of the movement against discriminatory school tracking in Selma, Alabama, in the early 1990s. Outside the official proceedings, some activists expressed disappointment about the lack of labor representation at this conference. While the Oil, Chemical and Atomic Workers [OCAW] were a visible presence at previous, more technically oriented dioxin conferences, they had declined to participate this time in a gathering with an explicitly abolitionist agenda. OCAW's long-standing call for a "workers' superfund" for retraining displaced chemical workers was one proposal that was endorsed to deflate persistent myths of an inherent conflict between job creation and environmental protection. Alternative economic development strategies, such as the Sustainable America efforts that have been springing up in Milwaukee and other cities, were also discussed as important models for the future.

Stopping the Poison

Strategy groups in nine different areas will form the basis for a long-term coordinated organizing effort to stop the poisoning of communities and ecosystems. Topics for strategy sessions focused on specific sources of dioxin contamination, as well as particular constituency groups that can work together to further the anti-dioxin campaign. Some of the specific focuses included:

• Getting chlorine out of the pulp and paper industry: Chlorine bleaching of paper leads to dioxin in mill waste, as well as from the incineration of paper packaging. Discussions centered on the need to make demands for chlorine-free paper as centrally visible as the demand for recycled paper. Many forest activists at the conference welcomed the focus on pulp and paper, as vast acres of forest, especially in the South, are now being devastated by this industry's insatiable demand for wood chips and pulp, both for domestic production and shipping overseas.

• Halting all forms of incineration: Nearly 300 waste incinerators have been halted by grassroots activists in the U.S. since the mid-1980s, or 4 out of every 5 that have been proposed. However, incineration of hazardous waste and medical wastes remains the technology of choice in many areas of the country. Activists left the conference with the sobering news that the long-fought incinerator built to burn dioxin- and PCB-contaminated soil in Times Beach, Missouri, had just received its operating permit. However, people affirmed their commitment to a renewed campaign of outreach and direct action, including an effort focused on mothers concerned about dioxin in breast milk.

• Phasing out all uses of PVC: Polyvinyl chloride (PVC), generally known simply as vinyl, is the end use of over a third of all the chlorine used in industry today. Used in everything from food packaging and fabrics to plumbing and automobile interiors, PVC has become a leading source of dioxin exposure due to both incineration and accidental fires. It is also laden with extremely toxic additives used as stabilizers, softening agents, fire retardants, and biocides. Often the chlorine use of last resort, PVC may be the key to efforts to eliminate dioxin by minimizing chlorine use in industries worldwide. Many communities in Germany, Switzerland, and the Scandinavian countries have implemented partial bans on PVC in buildings and food packaging, an effort which Greenpeace, among others, is trying to spread to the U.S. as well.

> *"Chemical workers have become an 'indicator species' for the effects of dioxin exposure."*

Other groups focused on getting dioxin out of food, coordinating efforts of sympathetic scientists and health workers, and developing tools and strategies to help poisoned communities. A group focusing on chlorine use in manufacturing and cleaning addressed workplace hazards and related health concerns, pointing out that chemical workers have become an "indicator species" for the effects of dioxin exposure (Tom Goldtooth of the Indigenous Environmental Network had earlier described native peoples in similar terms). A strategy group on communicating dioxin issues to the public and media discussed ways to address key constituencies such as students, parents, churches, pediatricians, and artists.

Corporate Disinformation

The participants' understanding of the nature of corporate misinformation campaigns regarding dioxin and related issues was raised by the presence of

John Stauber, co-author of the highly acclaimed *Toxic Sludge Is Good for You: Lies, Damn Lies and the Public Relations Industry*. Stauber described how the multibillion-dollar PR [public relations] industry works in cooperation with an increasingly monopolized mass media to spread myths of corporate benevolence. With poisoned food and water as a leading public concern nationwide, according to even the Republican Party's own polls, corporate myths reinforced by the media play a key role in keeping people passive. This lesson was brought home two days after the conference when the *New York Times*' Tuesday science section

> *"Today's activists are more often facing the long-term consequences of toxic industries in their communities."*

featured a blatant attempt to discredit Dr. Theo Colborn's new book *Our Stolen Future*, which was praised by many conference participants as an important and highly accessible scientific work on the effects of dioxin and other hormone-disrupting chemicals.

Overall, the conference demonstrated the growing sophistication and deepening political commitment of anti-toxics activists in recent years. In the 1980s, anti-toxics activists were often dismissed as "NIMBY's [not in my backyard]," those who simply wanted to keep a particularly distasteful project or land use out of their own backyard. Organizers in middle-class and more affluent communities were especially willing to abandon their organizations once a particular battle had been won and an undesirable project had been moved elsewhere. Today's activists are more often facing the long-term consequences of toxic industries in their communities.

The Bigger Picture

"There's more than just one problem in these communities," explained Lois Gibbs, who led the campaign for evacuation of residents from Love Canal in the early 1980s, directs the Citizen's Clearinghouse, and is now the principal author of the encyclopedic activists' guide *Dying from Dioxin* (South End Press). "Once they get involved, they realize everything is connected and can see the bigger picture that includes their health, their schools, the economy, and everything else." "We're trying to create a world view in which activists can wage long-term campaigns which embody environmental justice, economic justice, a clear analysis of corporate power and an understanding of the international dimensions of this issue as well," added Gary Cohen. "We are seeing the development of a politicized, educated mass movement."

The participants' commitment to integrating environmental and social justice was put to the test on the last day of the conference. A group of Cherokee activists from North Carolina had gone out for an early breakfast at a Shoney's restaurant in a nearby mall. Not only were they refused service, but they were charged for food they never had the opportunity to eat. As the conference's closing session was underway, dozens of people teemed out of the conference halls for a spirited, spontaneous mile-long march to the offending Shoney's restaurant. When the Cherokee delegation received an apology and a full refund from Shoney's management, in full view of local TV cameras, it was an important lesson to everyone present in the possibilities and the joys of solidarity. Defeating the chemical industry will be a much longer battle, but everyone left Baton Rouge with a feeling that victory may be in sight.

Toxic Waste Disproportionately Contaminates Minority Communities

by Dorceta E. Taylor

About the author: *Dorceta E. Taylor teaches environmental sociology at Washington State University in Pullman.*

Hazel Johnson lives in Atgeld Gardens, a predominantly black housing project on Chicago's Far South Side. She refers to the neighborhood of 10,000 residents as a "Toxic Doughnut" because the homes are encircled by landfills, factories and other industrial sites that emit toxic and/or noxious fumes. West of the Doughnut, the coke ovens of Acme Steel discharge benzene into the air, to the south is Dolton's municipal landfill, to the east is Waste Management's landfill, and to the north lie beds of city sewage sludge. There are 50 abandoned hazardous dump sites within a six-mile radius of the neighborhood. The toxic stew around the Doughnut is so potent that Illinois inspectors aborted an expedition in one of the dumping lagoons when their boat began to disintegrate.

Illness was common in the area, but it wasn't until her husband died of lung cancer and other family and friends became ill that Hazel wondered if the death and illnesses were linked to the environment. She surveyed 1,000 of her neighbors and was astounded at the number of cancers, birth deformities, premature deaths, skin rashes, eye irritations, and respiratory illnesses that they reported. Hazel and the group she founded, People for Community Recovery (PCR), contacted the City of Chicago about the findings and urged them to investigate the illnesses. The City conducted a controversial study that found high rates of cancer among African Americans on Chicago's South Side, but did not investigate whether the rate was higher than that for African Americans elsewhere, or

Dorceta E. Taylor, "Environmental Justice: The Birth of a Movement," *Dollars & Sense*, March/April 1996. Reprinted by permission. *Dollars & Sense* is a progressive economics magazine published six times a year. First-year subscriptions cost $18.95 and may be ordered by writing to *Dollars & Sense*, One Summer St., Somerville, MA 02143.

whether the health effects were related to the toxins in the area.

Dissatisfied with the findings, PCR commissioned its own study, and persuaded the federal Agency for Toxic Disease Registry to do a health study. Meanwhile, because the neighborhood was not connected to Chicago's water supply system, residents suspected that some of the health problems were caused by contamination of their well water. PCR lobbied for and obtained a hookup to municipal water pipes. Then, after discovering that Waste Management wanted to expand its landfill, PCR staged a series of protests (with the help of Greenpeace) that blocked the expansion.

Community Activists

The Toxic Doughnut is but one of many environmentally hazardous areas where poor and working-class people make their homes. Community activists in the burgeoning "environmental justice" movement have given names like "Street of Death," "Cancer Alley," and "Death Valley" to similar areas.

Organizations such as the Sierra Club, Audubon Society, Wilderness Society, and Nature Conservancy focus much of their attention on wildlife and wilderness preservation, and attract a mostly white, upper-middle-class following. In contrast, environmental justice groups recruit a broad coalition of working- and middle-class activists from various racial backgrounds. Such organizations focus on toxic contamination, occupational safety, and the siting of noxious and hazardous facilities.

> *"The Toxic Doughnut is but one of many environmentally hazardous areas where poor and working-class people make their homes."*

Groups whose members are people of color, on which this viewpoint focuses, are a vital component of the environmental justice movement. They have brought national attention to environmental racism (when people of color suffer disproportionately from health hazards) and environmental blackmail (when communities are forced to choose between protecting their health or losing their jobs). Until people of color made these terms commonplace in environmental circles, more traditional environmental activists paid little attention to policies that led to grave impacts on minority communities.

Environmental Racism

There is ample evidence that the operations of the Environmental Protection Agency (EPA) and other federal and state agencies have had discriminatory impacts on communities of color. A 1992 *National Law Journal* study, for example, found that fines for hazardous waste violations under the Resource Conservation and Recovery Act varied greatly between white and minority areas. On average, companies were charged $336,000 for violations in white neighborhoods, but only $55,000 in minority neighborhoods. Similar imbalances held for violations of other environmental laws.

The study also showed that the EPA waited longer to evaluate whether dangers in minority areas should be placed on the National Priorities List of "Superfund" sites, and once evaluated, the agency was less likely to place such sites on the list. One reason is that EPA's "Hazard Ranking System" scores sites individually, so that it fails to take into account the cumulative effects of having several hazardous sites near a poor community. And even for those designated, it took less than 10 years to clean up sites in white neighborhoods, but between 12 and 14 years for sites in minority areas.

> *"During a 20-year period in King and Queen County, Virginia, all the landfills were placed within one mile of communities that were at least 95% African American."*

The courts have also responded badly to environmental justice cases. Even when communities have shown that there is a discriminatory pattern of siting facilities, the courts contend that simply proving discriminatory impact is not enough. To win a suit, communities must prove that the offending corporation or agency *intended* to discriminate when they made siting decisions.

Examples abound. In Houston, six out of eight municipal incinerators were placed in predominantly African American communities. During a 20-year period in King and Queen County, Virginia, all the landfills were placed within one mile of communities that were at least 95% African American. But in both cases, the courts ruled against the communities which brought lawsuits over these issues.

A Viable Movement

This failure of government to protect people of color in the face of increasing environmental threats, along with the dismissive attitude of corporate decision-makers, led to the growth of the environmental justice movement. Also important has been dissatisfaction by grassroots activists with the agenda of mainstream environmental organizations. Some of these are direct-action–oriented groups like Greenpeace and Earth First! that focused their attention primarily on whales, nuclear disarmament, and forest preservation. Others are legal, technocratic, and lobbyist-oriented associations like the Natural Resources Defense Council and the Environmental Defense Fund.

Although many organizations formed during the 1960s and 1970s began as grassroots groups critical of the reform agenda of the pre-1960s environmental organizations, most eventually adopted similar agendas and lost their close ties to the grassroots. Like their predecessors, these associations lacked racial and social class diversity and failed to adopt an environmental justice agenda.

Filling the vacuum, people of color environmental justice organizations have grown rapidly in recent years—despite the failure of the mainstream to recognize them. As late as 1994 only five people of color groups were listed in the Conservation Directory, and none were listed in the Gale Environmental Sourcebook. Yet in the same year, the People of Color Environmental Groups Directory contained over 300 such organizations.

Roots of Struggle

Organizations devoted to combatting environmental racism emerged out of struggles for social, political, and economic justice. Native American groups, for example, contending with the erosion of cultural values and treaty rights, have used these issues to call attention to the environmental hazards on their reservations. In one case, the Navajos living near Rio Puerco, New Mexico, face increased health risks from the numerous uranium mines around them, which contaminate their drinking water and animals. As a result, the Navajos have developed a strong environmental justice agenda.

Many African American associations and leaders have their roots in the Civil Rights movement. Some, like the Gulf Coast Tenants Association (GCTA), which was founded to improve housing conditions for Blacks, have taken on environmental justice agendas. Working in and around "Cancer Alley," the 90-mile stretch running along the Mississippi River from Baton Rouge to New Orleans, and home to about one-fourth of the chemical manufacturing plants in the United States, the GCTA constantly communicates with communities in which chemical spills and "accidental" releases of toxins are routine. These communities have high rates of cancers, birth defects, spontaneous abortions, infant mortality, and respiratory illnesses.

Latinos in the farmworker movement have made the link between labor and environmental justice struggles into a key organizing tool. Farmworkers in California and other parts of the South and West, through their participation in the United Farm Workers union, have launched successful grape boycotts and focused the nation's attention on the harmful effects of pesticides. They have documented illnesses from pesticide poisoning, including death, infertility, birth defects and miscarriages, and respiratory infections.

Similarly, Asian Americans concerned about immigrant rights and hazardous working conditions in the computer and garment industries have formed environmental justice groups. These include the Asian Women's Advocates and the Santa Clara Center for Occupational Safety and Health, both in California.

> *"[California farmworkers] have documented illnesses from pesticide poisoning, including death, infertility, birth defects and miscarriages, and respiratory infections."*

Throughout the United States, environmental justice groups are now able to mobilize many people and to raise questions about environmental racism in corporate decision making, government policies, and within the environmental movement itself. They are increasingly effective at disrupting the status quo on the siting of dangerous facilities. As a result, many are taking notice of these organizations and are either incorporating them into the environmental dialogue, or attempting to discredit their claims and destroy their credibility. We can expect continued struggle in the years ahead.

Sewage Sludge Fertilizer Endangers Human Health

by Joel Bleifuss

About the author: *Joel Bleifuss is a senior editor for* In These Times, *a bi-weekly liberal magazine.*

These days a home gardener hoping for a bumper crop can walk into the local nursery and pick up a bag of the multipurpose Milorganite. "Natural organic fertilizer," the bold-faced hype proclaims. The fine print explains: "This product meets 'Exceptional Quality' standards as defined by the EPA [Environmental Protection Agency]." But in 1993 that same fine print warned: "Should not be used on food crops . . . most natural organic fertilizers contain trace amounts of heavy metals."

Sewage Fertilizers

What's up? Milorganite hasn't changed. It's the same old shit, or, more precisely, sludge from the Milwaukee municipal sewer system. Nor has there been any change in the composition of the other leading municipal sewage fertilizers: Houston's Hou-actinite, Los Angeles' Nitrohumus and Chicago's Nu-Earth. But there is one difference. These products have all undergone linguistic detoxification. Sewer sludge, which was once considered hazardous waste and judged too dangerous to be used on food crops, has been deregulated by the EPA and redefined as an agricultural fertilizer. And fertilizers, as marketable products, are exempt from the laws that govern the disposal of hazardous waste. In effect, the EPA has found a way to make the waste problem that once plagued 15,000 publicly owned sewer plants disappear, at least in name.

Each year about 4 million metric tons of municipal sludge—about half of the total produced annually in the United States—are dumped on farm land. That sludge is derived chiefly from human excreta and from the water wastes of 130,000 industrial plants. Typically, municipal sewer sludge contains PCBs [polychlorinated biphenyls], dangerous pesticides such as chlordane, chlori-

From Joel Bleifuss, "Nightmare Soil," *In These Times*, October 16, 1995. Reprinted with permission.

nated compounds such as dioxin, heavy metals such as arsenic and lead, viruses such as Hepatitis A, eggs of parasitic worms, etc. Cornell University's Toxic Chemical Laboratory tested 50 municipal sludges and found that two-thirds contained asbestos. "You test it and you find so much—dioxin, PCBs, DDT, asbestos—it's an endless list," says Cornell toxicologist Donald Lisk. "Urban sewer sludge is a huge problem."

In fact, according to the *Archives of Environmental Contamination and Toxicology*, of 30 municipal sludges analyzed in 1983 only seven were considered suitable for land application. The sludge from the other 23 plants contained elevated levels of one or more heavy metals, such as lead and cadmium. But that was using the older, more stringent standards.

Redefining Waste

The EPA began the linguistic detoxification of sewage sludge in 1984, when it issued a beneficial sludge use and disposal policy that permitted the controlled use of treated sewage as fertilizer. In 1993, new regulations governing this sludge policy were written into "Part 503" of the Clean Water Act. These regulations, which in the sludge community are referred to as "503," further redefined the waste, deeming it "clean" enough for unrestricted use in America's gardens and fields.

This transformation occurred, not because the sludge was suddenly cleaner—though better treatment methods have helped to lower the concentrations of some heavy metals—but because the EPA raised the limits of acceptable exposure to some pollutants so that most of the nation's sludge could be classified as "clean."

For example, the new regulations increased the amount of lead that can be applied annually via fertilizer sludge from 111 pounds of lead per acre to 267 pounds per acre. The arsenic level was raised from 12.5 pounds per acre to 36 pounds per acre. The allowable amount of mercury jumped from 13.4 pounds per acre to 50 pounds per acre. And the amount of chromium permitted ballooned from 472 pounds per acre to 2,672 pounds per acre. In fact, under 503, sludge sold as fertilizer can be so contaminated with toxins that, according to the EPA, such sludge cannot be legally landfilled.

> *"Sludge sold as fertilizer can be so contaminated with toxins that, according to the EPA, such sludge cannot be legally landfilled."*

503 regulates only 21 carcinogenic pollutants found in sludge. These include 10 heavy metals, but not the other 15 inorganic priority toxins on the EPA's Superfund [a waste cleanup program] list. As for the permitted level of dioxin in sludge, the EPA was waiting to finish its never-ending dioxin reassessment before setting sludge limits for that poison. Germany, by contrast, has sharply curtailed the use of sludge fertilizer due to the danger posed by dioxin.

In effect, 503 circumvents the 1984 hazardous waste amendments to the Solid Waste Disposal Act, which regulate the dumping of sewage sludge. The regulations also stipulate that no person, corporation or government body may be held liable for any damages caused by the use of sludge fertilizer.

Health Concerns

The EPA admits that when drawing up 503 it did not take into account the possible impact of sludge contaminants seeping into the water supply and leaching into the soil. Nor has the EPA examined how sludge fertilizer might affect wildlife. Of particular concern are animals that eat worms. Earthworms, not surprisingly, contain a lot of dirt and also accumulate heavy metals in their body tissue.

But earthworms aren't the only animals that can be contaminated with dangerous levels of heavy metals. In setting sludge safety standards for humans, the EPA assumed that children can safely absorb 10 micrograms of lead per deciliter of blood. The Centers for Disease Control and Prevention, however, estimate that levels as low as 10 micrograms of lead will permanently lower a child's IQ. Further, the EPA's risk assessment compounds this problem by assuming that food grown with sludge fertilizer will be evenly consumed by the total population. But that is certainly not the case for families who exponentially increase their exposure by using unlabeled sludge fertilizers on their home gardens.

> *"The EPA . . . failed to explore how the land-dumping of millions of tons of contaminated sludge will pollute groundwater."*

Nor did the EPA evaluate multiyear applications of sludge fertilizer and the resulting toxic buildup of those pollutants, such as heavy metals, that stay in the soil without decomposing. . . .

In drafting 503, the EPA also failed to explore how the land-dumping of millions of tons of contaminated sludge will pollute groundwater. Of particular concern are the wells upon which rural residents depend. The agency realizes there is a risk. In 1986, when 503 was still on the drawing board, the EPA declared: "Low concentrations of a pollutant such as arsenic are a significant risk if that sludge is to be landfilled or land farmed. . . . A potential for contamination of surrounding or underlying soil and/or groundwater does exist from disposal of sludge containing pollutants." But those concerns seem to have been discarded in the EPA's detoxification of sludge.

Ignoring Threats to Safety

The EPA is also ignoring the threat to public safety posed by biologic pathogens that enter sludge through human and animal excrement. In 1989, the EPA documented the presence of 25 infectious agents in sewage sludge: five bacteria (including Salmonella), nine viruses (including Hepatitis A), five intestinal worms (such as tapeworms and hookworms), five protozoa (one of these, Cryptosporidium, killed 100 people in Milwaukee) and one fungi (Aspergillus, which also can be fatal). According to the EPA, "If sewage sludge containing high levels of pathogenic organisms or high concentrations of pollutants is improperly handled, the sludge could contaminate the soil, water, crops, livestock, fish and shellfish."

Two Grades of Sludge

Because of the dangers from human and animal pathogens, the EPA, when writing 503, divided sludge fertilizer into two grades, A and B. Grade A, considered an "exceptional quality" fertilizer by the EPA, is heat-treated to reduce disease-bearing organisms. The use of grade A fertilizer is totally unregulated. It can be freely applied on all lawns and human-food crops. Grade B fertilizer, because it has not been heat-treated, is only allowed on above-ground crops such as wheat and corn. Despite these gradations, the exceptionally pure grade A has just as many chemical contaminants as grade B does.

And, ironically, the heat-treating responsible for grade A's "exceptional quality" is an ineffective method of killing bacteria, viruses and parasite eggs. According to a 1992 study by a group of University of Arizona soil scientists, present sludge-treatment methods do not effectively kill human pathogens. The researchers concluded: "Significant numbers of pathogens exist in sludge even after stabilization and treatment. If these pathogens can remain viable for extended periods of time, groundwater sources beneath sludge disposal and land application sites may become contaminated. . . . Once in groundwater, they may travel significant distances from the site. . . . Viruses [which can survive in the ground for months], because of their small size, probably have the greatest potential of all pathogens for actually reaching groundwater and being transported from the site."

New York City's Tainted Sludge

Sludge from New York City is particularly infected with human pathogens. Eleven of New York's 14 sewage-treatment plants are not up to modern treatment standards. Half were built in the 1930s. In addition, the city does not know how many industries discharge waste into the municipal sewer system. City environmental officials regulate only 1,090 industrial plants, and estimate that there might be another 2,000 that are unregulated.

New York City's waste is so contaminated that the state's Department of Environmental Conservation will

> *"The exceptionally pure grade A [sludge] has just as many chemical contaminants as grade B does."*

not allow it to be applied on land in New York. The sludge is also too dirty for Pennsylvania or Ohio. So, New York City had to go further afield to find a state willing to take some of its sludge. To help in this quest, the city hired a Long Island firm, Merco Joint Venture Co.

In 1992, Merco set its sights on southwestern Oklahoma. Understandably, the rural citizenry were not pleased at the prospect of becoming the Big Apple's pay toilet. Joseph Maness, an environmental physiologist at Southwestern Oklahoma State University in Weatherford, helped lead the successful effort to block Merco. In 1992 testimony before the Oklahoma state legislature, Maness argued that the EPA's policy of promoting the spreading of sludge over land "is not so much to benefit land, but rather to benefit sewage-treatment plants faced with the problem of disposal of millions of tons of sludge."

> *"New York City sewer sludge spread over the Arizona farmland contained coliform bacteria from human feces at levels 33.5 times higher than the federal limit."*

After being defeated in Oklahoma, Merco went to take a dump in the unregulated fields of Arizona. In this frontier state, it found a landowner, Ronald Bryce, who was willing to spread 41,000 tons of NYC sludge over his farms. Reporter Keith Bagwell chronicled what went down in a series of stories in Tucson's *Arizona Daily Star*. The first shipments of New York City sludge contained petroleum hydrocarbons that were 14 to 22 times as great as the state cleanup level for tainted soil. These hydrocarbon pollutants included the potent carcinogens benzene, toluene and xylene. In addition, New York City sewer sludge spread over the Arizona farmland contained coliform bacteria from human feces at levels 33.5 times higher than the federal limit. "That sounds more like untreated sludge," the EPA's sludge inspector, Laura Fondahl, told Bagwell in 1994. Fondahl, who is based in San Francisco, is charged with the impossible task of monitoring the sludge produced and dumped in Arizona, California, Nevada, Hawaii, and Guam.

But the most popular dumpsite for New York City sludge is Sierra Blanca, Texas, a poor, largely Hispanic community whose surrounding countryside is receiving 225 tons of New York sewage a day. When Michael Moore lampooned this outrage during an August 2, 1994, segment of *TV Nation*, Merco filed a $33 million lawsuit against show backer Tristar Television, segment reporter Roy Serkoff, local activist Bill Addington and EPA whistleblower Hugh Kaufman. On the show, Kaufman had characterized Merco's operation as an "illegal haul and dump operation masquerading as an environmentally beneficial project." The company denies all charges.

The run-up to the trial was followed closely by *Sludge*, the sewage industry's biweekly newsletter. *Sludge*'s August 1, 1995, issue reports that the EPA's Office of the General Counsel refused a subpoena to testify in the case. As *Sludge* explains, "Federal agencies are allowed to turn down subpoenas if deemed not in the government's best interest."

EPA's Curious Practices

Certainly the best interests of EPA officials would not be served if the general public were to realize what is going on. In 1989, the EPA came out with its proposed 503 regulation. During the public comment period that followed, industry officials came out in force to challenge the proposed rules. In an effort to settle the dispute, the EPA turned to Terry Logan, a professor of soil science at Ohio State University who, in 1984, had helped invent the concept of "clean sludge." In 1989, Logan served as co-chair of the Land Practices Peer Review Committee, which recommended that 503's proposed regulations be made less stringent. As Logan was rewriting 503 he was also serving as a board member of and consultant to N-Viro International Corp. Using a process invented by Logan, this Ohio-based company mixes sewage sludge with cement-kiln dust to make fertilizer. Logan currently serves as president of Pan-American N-Viro, Inc., an N-Viro subsidiary that was created to market this waste-disposal process to Latin America. Another consultant to N-Viro is former EPA chief William Reilly, who receives $2,000 a month for his services. During Reilly's tenure, N-Viro won an award from the agency for "outstanding technology development contributing to enhanced beneficial use of municipal wastewater sludge."

In fact, the EPA financially supports the very industry it is supposed to regulate. The agency issues grants to the Water Environment Federation (WEF), a trade and lobbying organization formerly known as the Federation of Sewage Works Associations. This coalition of sewer operators has consistently opposed federal attempts to clean up the nation's water. According to *Sludge*, the WEF supported the Clean Water Act reauthorization bill devised by the House Republicans because "the legislation would reduce [sludge] quality by relaxing federal pre-treatment standards."

A Cleaner Term for "Sludge"

This curious conflict of interest was discovered by John Stauber, founder and editor of *PR Watch*. In 1994, Stauber and writer Sheldon Rampton were trying to come up with a catchy title for a book they were writing on the public relations [PR] industry. Inspired by a Tom Tomorrow cartoon, they hit upon the name "Toxic Sludge is Good for You." They then found out that the WEF was about to launch a campaign to convince the public of exactly that.

> *"The EPA financially supports the very industry it is supposed to regulate."*

That campaign is being headed by Alan Rubin, the man who spearheaded the EPA's sludge-fertilizer disposal program. Rubin is on "loan" from the EPA to the WEF. The April 1994 *Environment Today* reported that Rubin will "serve as cheerleader for a joint EPA-WEF sludge education campaign. Recalcitrant states, wary lenders and other foot-draggers are the effort's chief targets."

At Rubin's side will be the best flacks money can buy. In 1992, the EPA awarded the WEF a $300,000 grant to promote the use of sludge fertilizer. In turn, the federation hired the services of Powell Tate, the Washington PR firm born from the union of former Jimmy Carter press secretary Jody Powell and George Bush aide Sheila Tate.

Documents obtained by Stauber through Freedom of Information Act requests include Powell Tate's re-

> *"Sewage sludge is . . . a low-priority issue for national environmental organizations."*

search findings and proposed communications plan. (The EPA, which has released only a few documents, is withholding internal memos and other materials that chronicle the creation of this strange alliance. Stauber plans to go to court to obtain them.) According to the documents released, the cornerstone of the Powell Tate strategy is to promote the WEF's new name for sludge: biosolids.

"The negatives of the term 'sludge' are overwhelming," notes the Powell Tate communications plan. But the necessary rehabilitation, according to the firm, is being obstructed by EPA employees who refuse to get with the program. "The EPA's use of the term 'sewage sludge' instead of 'biosolids' may neutralize the agency's efforts to gain widespread acceptance of the term biosolids," warns Powell Tate. "The research suggests that emphasizing the clear differences between biosolids and sludge will be critical to WEF's ability to increase audience acceptance of biosolid's land application. . . . Achieving this goal will be markedly more difficult as long as sludge and biosolids are perceived as interchangeable or even similar products." According to Powell Tate, sludge fertilizer should ideally come to be viewed as "a vitamin pill for the earth."

Manipulating the public's perception of sludge was one of the central topics at the annual WEF conference in Kansas City in 1995. Powell Tate PR specialist Charlotte Newton advised WEF conferees to marginalize critics of biosolids. "Attack them in a way that does not demonize them," she said. "Do it in any way that does not make [their doubts] their fault. . . . You can't play to those who act weirdest."

A Low-Priority Issue

But what PR tactics can't accomplish, budget cuts might. *Sludge* reports that the EPA has plans to dismantle its "biosolids" program. Michael Cook, the director of the EPA's Office of Wastewater, said the agency is "considering ways of greatly simplifying"—in other words, gutting—a planned evaluation of sludge dumping's ecological impact. "I think everyone agrees sewage sludge is a low priority for the agency," he said.

Sewage sludge is also a low-priority issue for national environmental organizations. The Washington-based groups have been reluctant to challenge land-based sludge dumping. After winning hard-fought battles to curtail the disposal of sludge through ocean dumping and incineration, many organizations feel they do not have the energy to take on this issue—especially since that would involve an attack on the EPA, the very agency that environmentalists fear might be eliminated altogether by the [Republican-dominated] Congress.

However, the news is not all bad. On a county-by-county level, sludge dumping can be stopped. The commissioners of Rappahannock County, Virginia, have successfully stopped the use of sewage as fertilizer. Despite being challenged by three farmers who had been hired to spread sludge on their fields by BioGro, a subsidiary of Waste Management, Inc., the ban has been upheld in higher courts.

Seeking a Real Solution

And a growing number of environmentalists believe there are viable technologies available that promise real—rather than linguistic—solutions to sludge pollution. For the past 22 years Abby Rockefeller has been studying the sludge problem. These days she is devoting her share of the family fortune to finding a solution. Rockefeller, as president of Clivus Multrum, Inc., of Cambridge, Massachusetts, markets composting toilets, which are one of the on-site, sewer-avoiding technologies that can upgrade failing septic systems. She also heads the ReSource Institute for Low Entropy Systems, a group that is working in poor communities in Latin America, teaching people economical ways of managing resources, including "so-called human waste and so-called wastewater."

"We need to make the public understand what is going on," she says. "In the '70s, Sweden used sludge on land, and some of that land is now totally out of use. Because you can't control what people and industries pour down the drain, the toxicity of the sludge is unpredictable. Nor is it enough to keep industry out of the sewer system, since many household materials presently on consumers' shelves are largely toxic. But people don't know this because the EPA and some of the major environmental groups like the Natural Resource Defense Council and the Environmental Defense Fund [tacit supporters of the EPA's sludge-fertilizer policy] have kept their mouths shut on the subject. I had thought I could get support from environmental groups, but I was being naive."

Rockefeller is more hopeful that grassroots groups such as Neighbor to Neighbor, which in the late '80s and early '90s waged a successful boycott against Salvadoran coffee growers, may adopt the sludge issue as part of a major consumer consciousness-raising effort.

"It does no good to talk about the lesser of two evils," she says, referring to those environmental groups that believe land-based dumping is preferable to incineration or ocean dumping. "They are all equally bad. Sludge is a waste, and letting people swim in it or breathe it is no worse than letting people eat it."

Chemical Contamination Affects Wildlife

by Gerald A. LeBlanc

About the author: *Gerald A. LeBlanc is an associate professor at North Carolina State University's Department of Toxicology in Raleigh.*

The year 1995 marked the 25th anniversary of both the U.S. Environmental Protection Agency and Earth Day. The inception of both institutions signified the need to temper anthropogenic stresses on the environment or face unsettling consequences. Decades of environmental abuse culminated in the 1960s when public perception of the repercussion of unabated environmental pollution was heightened by Rachel Carson's [author of *Silent Spring*] graphic depictions. The pressing environmental problems of the 1960s were blatant. Among the most significant of problems were chemical and sewage discharges making aquatic resources unsuitable for human use and habitation by aquatic organisms, and the use of pesticides, which posed a significant threat to nontarget species. In response, the Clean Water Act was instituted in 1972 to regulate waste discharge and to ensure that high water-quality standards were maintained. The Federal Insecticide, Fungicide and Rodenticide Act (FIFRA) was amended three times during the 1970s to provide safeguards against pesticide-mediated harm to human and environmental health. Such legislation provided the foundation upon which a sound and reasonable national environmental policy was established. This policy has resulted in significant improvement in environmental quality concurrent with population and economic growth. The success of the environmental protection policies of the United States is best exemplified when environmental quality of the United States is compared to that of industrialized countries of the former Soviet bloc and other countries where such policies were never significantly instituted.

With the current movement toward the reduction of government size and spending, the issue is often raised as to whether environmental legislation and

From Gerald A. LeBlanc, "Are Environmental Sentinels Signaling?" *Environmental Health Perspectives*, October 1995. Reprinted by permission.

supporting research programs could be relaxed without intolerable consequences. Major fish and wildlife kills due to chemical waste discharge and improper pesticide usage are now largely relegated to distant memory. If one accepts the thesis that fish and wildlife species serve as sentinels for the protection of human health from environmental contaminants, then human health must also be adequately protected from the adverse health effects of pollution. Such logic supports the contention that environmental legislation and research need not be expanded and could perhaps be relaxed. However, not factored into this argument is that, while the flagrant environmental problems of the 1960s have

> *"Fish and wildlife species serve as sentinels for the protection of human health from environmental contaminants."*

been addressed, more subtle, though no less beguiling, environmental threats may persist. Central to this issue is the question, are environmental sentinels currently signaling the existence of such environmental hazards?

Toxicant-mediated endocrine disruption is one example of a toxicological hazard currently presenting itself in the environment. Endocrine-disrupting effects of environmental pollutants were first recognized while investigating mechanisms responsible for reproductive failure among some bird species exposed to organochlorine pesticides. The observation that exposure to some chemicals can lead to reproductive failure led to the promulgation of regulations under FIFRA and subsequently expanded to nonpesticide chemicals under the Toxic Substances Control Act requiring that the effects of chemical exposure on the production of viable offspring be determined. Such tests, conducted in standard test species of birds, fish, mammals, and invertebrates, involve chronically exposing the parent organisms to various concentrations of a chemical, then assessing the number of viable offspring produced. With fish, only subchronic testing, involving the assessment of the effects of the chemical on survival and growth of larval fish, is initially required. Assessments of reproductive toxicity are mandated only if the no-observed-effect level established during the subchronic toxicity test is greater than 1/10 the expected environmental concentration of the chemical. Retrospective assessments have shown that such approaches will adequately protect the environment against most chemicals. However, unique toxicological properties of some chemicals can result in undetected toxicity using these protocols. Endocrine-disrupting chemicals can be among these undetected toxicants because they may 1) elicit effects on the developing fetus that are not manifested until the mature organism enters its reproductive stage, 2) elicit specific biochemical/physiological changes that affect an organism's reproductive capacity without affecting survival and growth as measured during subchronic testing, or 3) adversely affect endocrine processes characteristic of some species but absent in those surrogate species used in toxicity testing. Many pesticides, industrial chemicals, and wastes are among the toxicants that elicit such effects.

Effects on Shore Birds

Shore birds such as gulls and terns typically produce broods of two or three eggs. Ornithologists began observing in the 1970s that broods of five or six eggs were not uncommon. This abnormal clutch size was found to be due to multiple females sharing a nest. This female-female pairing appeared to be due to a deficiency in reproductively competent males. Laboratory investigations demonstrated that exposure to [the insecticide] DDT feminized male gulls during embryonic development. Further, incidence of female-female pairing was higher in environments with significant DDT contamination. Thus, abnormal breeding behavior in these birds appeared to be due to reproductive deficiency in males caused by embryonic exposure to environmental pollutants. This observation is not only of historical relevance, as female-female pairing of terns has been noted recently in areas contaminated with polychlorinated biphenyls (PCBs).

Female Poeciliidae fish inhabiting areas receiving pulp mill effluent have been observed to undergo masculinization. Most obvious is the modification of the anal fin in affected females to a gonopodiumlike structure (used by males for sperm transmission). Exposure to exogenous androgens [male sex hormones] has been shown to cause similar masculinization, and androgens generated by the action of bacteria on phytosterols present in the effluent are presumed to be responsible for this effect. Fish exposed to paper and pulp mill effluent can also experience altered steroid hormone titers, impaired gonad development, and reduced fecundity. Such effects, specific to reproduction, would not be detected in subchronic toxicity tests.

Propiconazole is a member of the imidazole-derivative class of fungicides. A common characteristic of these chemicals is their ability to inhibit enzymes responsible for steroid hormone biosynthesis and induce enzymes involved in steroid hormone metabolism. A consequence of this effect is severe reductions in some steroid hormone levels. This specific and potent effect has led to the consideration of some imidazole-derivatives for use as a male contraceptive. Propiconazole, which is used as an agricultural fungicide, shares these properties and thus has the potential to compromise reproductive success of chronically exposed organisms. These effects would not be detected in a subchronic toxicity test that did not evaluate reproduction. The Ecuadorian shrimp industry has called for a moratorium on the use of propiconazole for fear that it is responsible for the demise of shrimp populations.

> *"Exposure to [the insecticide] DDT feminized male gulls during embryonic development."*

Sex Characteristics

Tributyltin has been used extensively for more than 20 years as an antifoulant in marine paints. Tributyltin has been identified as the causative agent responsible for imposex in many marine mollusk populations. Imposex is the imposition of sex characteristics of one gender onto another (a form of pseudohermaphrodism). In the case of tributyltin-exposed mollusks, females develop a penis, vas deferens, and in severe cases, seminiferous tubules. Affected females can be rendered infertile because the vas deferens blocks the release of eggs from the oviduct. The mechanism responsible for this effect has not been conclusively established, but it seems to involve the neuroendocrine regulation of sexual differentiation. Tributyltin can cause imposex at low part per trillion concentrations and has caused the extinction of some affected populations. Certain mollusk species may be particularly sensitive to the effect of tributyltin owing to unique aspects of sexual differentiation in these organisms. Intersexuality also has been observed in some crustacean populations in the vicinity of sewage discharge, though causality has not been established. Peri- and neonatal exposure of rodent models to a variety of environmental chemicals including 2,3,7,8-tetrachlorodibenzo-*p*-dioxin, PCBs, mirex, chlordecone (kepone), dieldrin, aldrin, chlordane, and atrazine has shown that these chemicals are capable of eliciting a variety of perturbations in the sexual differentiation of mammals.

All Is Not Well

Thus, it would appear that environmental sentinels are indeed signaling us that all is not well. Although the major environmental problems of the 1960s may have been successfully dealt with, we are faced in the 1990s with new problems to surmount. Speculation remains as to whether human health issues such as increased incidence of breast cancer, prostate cancer, testicular cancer, endometriosis, birth defects in the male reproductive tract, and reductions in sperm count may be associated with the existence of endocrine-disrupting chemicals in the environment. Toxicity testing requirements for environmental chemicals must be expanded to consider effects that may go undetected using current guidelines. . . .

Many strategies exist that could improve our ability to detect endocrine-disrupting chemicals and identify exposure dosages at which effects are elicited. Further research is needed to better define such experimental approaches and validate their utility. Ultimately, testing requirements will need to be expanded to ensure the detection of endocrine-disrupting effects of environmental chemicals; environmental legislation must be strengthened to ensure protection against these and other chemicals that elicit subtle, yet devastating, effects. Legislators must be made aware that the absence of dead fish and wildlife is not justification for the relaxation of environmental legislation and supporting research. The deleterious consequences of chemicals in the environment continue. You just have to look a little harder to see them.

Dioxin Is Not Hazardous to Humans

by Joseph L. Bast, Peter J. Hill, and Richard C. Rue

About the authors: *Joseph L. Bast is president of the Heartland Institute, a research organization that studies state and local public policy problems. Peter J. Hill is a senior associate with the Political Economy Research Center, a Bozeman, Montana, think tank that focuses on environmental and resource issues. Richard C. Rue, a former senior policy analyst and vice president of the Heartland Institute, is the senior vice president of the American Life League, a pro-life organization in Stafford, Virginia.*

In recent years, exposure to mercury, lead, dioxin, asbestos, some kinds of pesticides, vinyl chloride, polychlorinated biphenyls (PCBs), and other man-made chemicals has been identified as a real or hypothetical threat to wildlife and sometimes to human health. The environmental movement helped to identify these risks and campaigned to have the offending chemicals banned or regulated. This "watchdog" activity is an important role that environmentalists can perform.

Unfortunately, the environmental movement often has shown poor judgment in deciding *what should be done* once it has sounded an alarm. In particular, the movement too often calls for action before sufficient research is available, and for bans on products or evacuations of communities when alternative forms of regulation or inexpensive cleanup measures would produce better results at lower costs. Nowhere are these mistakes more common than in the movement's reaction to toxic chemicals. In fact, as we will show in this viewpoint, these mistakes have been elevated to the status of deliberate tactics—a "new paradigm"—by Greenpeace and similar organizations that dominate the environmental movement's response to chemical threats. . . . The "new paradigm" claims that traditional rules of scientific research and policy making don't apply to chemical hazards. . . .

From *Eco-Sanity* by Joseph L. Bast, Peter J. Hill, and Richard C. Rue (Lanham, MD: Madison Books); © 1994 by The Heartland Institute. Reprinted by permission of Madison Books.

The Dioxin Scares

Many Americans became aware of the "toxic waste crisis" during the late 1970s and early 1980s, when television stations and newspapers gave extensive coverage to the plight of residents of Love Canal, a neighborhood in Niagara Falls, New York. Part of the community, including a school, had been built during the 1950s directly above a hazardous waste dump, operated by Hooker Chemical Co., that had been closed and sealed with clay years earlier.

The Love Canal "crisis" began with the discovery that possibly toxic chemicals, including dioxin, were leaking into basements and escaping into the air. Lois Gibbs, a resident of Love Canal, blamed her son's epilepsy on the waste and launched a campaign to have government agencies condemn and buy homes in the Love Canal area. At one point, she and fellow residents held two EPA [Environmental Protection Agency] officials hostage, attracting the attention of media and higher government officials.

In 1978, limited evacuations of the site began. In 1980, President Jimmy Carter approved the temporary relocation of 2,500 residents at an eventual cost of some $35 million for relocation and cleanup, and another $20 million in loans and grants.

Around the same time, dioxin was causing a panic in Times Beach, Missouri, where dioxin-contaminated waste oil had been sprayed on streets and fields to control dust. High concentrations of dioxin killed horses kept in an arena near Times Beach, and two children became ill after playing in the area. Fearing that floods in 1982 might carry the dioxin into homes and water supplies, the community was evacuated at a cost of some $33 million. A soil cleanup program is underway with an expected cost of $200 million.

Dioxin was also a contaminant in the herbicide Agent Orange, used in Vietnam from 1965 to 1970. Thousands of military veterans exposed to Agent Orange during combat participated in lawsuits against the U.S. government alleging a wide range of illnesses caused by exposure to dioxin.

"The Love Canal 'crisis' began with the discovery that possibly toxic chemicals, including dioxin, were leaking into basements and escaping into the air."

The environmental movement jumped on dioxin with both feet. Ralph Nader, Ronald Brownstein, and John Richard, in a Sierra Club book titled *Who's Poisoning America?*, claimed that "three ounces of dioxin can kill more than a million people." Samuel Epstein, in two books also published by the Sierra Club (*The Politics of Cancer* and *Hazardous Wastes in America*), and Lewis Regenstein, author of *America the Poisoned*, warned repeatedly that Love Canal was only the tip of a toxic waste iceberg threatening the country.

Into the 1990s, environmentalists stayed close to the dioxin issue, demanding that a zero discharge policy be adopted by the EPA regarding fumes from solid waste incinerators and effluent from paper mills and other factories.

What We Know About Dioxin

True to the "new paradigm," environmentalists sounded alarms and called for complete bans on dioxin before research established that it endangered human health. Subsequent research has found that dioxin is, at worst, a very weak human carcinogen. Research continues into the effects of dioxin on endocrine and reproductive systems, but these effects also appear to be small or nonexistent. (In 1994, the EPA prepared a report on dioxin that alleged adverse effects on human immune systems while calling for further research.)

Studies of the health of Love Canal residents have failed to find any association between chronic illness and exposure to dioxin or other toxic chemicals. A panel named by the Governor of New York and chaired by Dr. Lewis Thomas, chancellor of Memorial Sloan-Kettering Cancer Center, reported, "As a result of this review, the panel has concluded that there has been no demonstration of acute health effects linked to exposure to hazardous wastes in the Love Canal site." The New York State Department of Health reported,

> *"Research has found that dioxin is, at worst, a very weak human carcinogen."*

"Blood testing, which was designed to screen for liver and kidney abnormalities, leukemia, and other blood diseases, showed no patterns of excess abnormality. . . . None had clinical evidence of liver disease. . . . Cancer incidence was within normal limits." And regarding birth defects, "Efforts to establish a correlation between adverse pregnancy outcomes and evidence of chemical exposure have proven negative."

Studies of the residents of Times Beach, Missouri, also have failed to discover any adverse effects of dioxin on health. Vernon N. Houk, who as director of the National Center for Environmental Health at the Centers for Disease Control had urged the evacuation of Times Beach, said in 1991 that he regretted his decision. "I would not be concerned about the levels of dioxin at Times Beach," he told an international conference on health. If dioxin is a human carcinogen, "it is, in my view, a weak one that is associated only with high-dioxin exposures." The American Medical Association, shortly after the Times Beach buyout, voted to "adopt an active public information campaign . . . to prevent irrational reaction and unjustified public fright and to prevent the dissemination of possibly erroneous information about the health hazards of dioxin."

Soldiers and Industrial Workers

The health of military veterans exposed to Agent Orange also has been closely studied. Ben Bolch and Harold Lyons report:

Repeated studies have failed to show a greater incidence of ailments among

98

soldiers who were exposed to [Agent Orange] and who have blood concentrations up to seven times higher than soldiers not exposed to the chemical. . . . Indeed, a series of studies released in 1991 reported "no relationship between Agent Orange-related dioxin and cancer of any kind, liver disease, heart disease, kidney disease, immune system disorders, psychological abnormalities, or nervous system disease."

The National Institute of Occupational Safety and Health has evaluated the health of industrial workers exposed to dioxin levels *fifty times as high* as the exposure received by Vietnam veterans. These workers have shown no increase in cancer risk.

Summarizing this and other research in 1991, Dr. Renate D. Kimbrough, then with the Office of the Administrator of the EPA, wrote: "Thus far, no convincing human evidence exists that suggests a causal positive association between the exposure to PCBs, PCDFs [polychlorinated dibenzofurans], and PCDDs [polychlorinated dibenzodioxins] and a higher incidence of cancer." In November 1992, Houk updated this summary and foreshadowed EPA's growing interest in dioxin's possible effects on endocrine and reproductive systems:

High-dose exposure [to dioxin] has some effect on male/female hormone-like activity. There is no evidence that this is associated with any recognized disease in humans. No convincing evidence exists for the association between dioxin exposure in humans with premature mortality, chronic liver disease, immune disease, cardiovascular disease, neurologic disease, adverse reproductive outcomes, or any other disease, excluding diabetes and cancer. High-dose exposure may be weakly associated with diabetes. This remains to be clarified but does not seem to be a major determinant for the development of diabetes. High-dose exposure, as evidenced by chloracne and very high serum levels (up to 600 times the background level) may result in a small (under 2) increased risk for the category of "all forms of cancer combined" when the population is observed beyond the twentieth year after exposure. Low-dose exposure (absence of chloracne) or lower serum levels of dioxin (up to 60 times background) has not been demonstrated to be associated with increased cancer risk.

The effects of low-level exposure to dioxin on human health have been studied, and no convincing evidence of harm has yet been found. Populations that have been exposed to hundreds of times the amount of dioxin as the average person have had their health carefully monitored for nearly twenty years; no unusual incidence of cancer or other illnesses has been reported. The chemical that many environmentalists consider to be the most deadly of all is not, after all, a serious threat to human health.

Why We Were Wrong About Dioxin

Why were so many environmentalists wrong about dioxin? Lewis Regenstein had claimed in 1983 that "dioxin can cause severe adverse health effects, and death, at the lowest doses imaginable." This statement was accurate, *but only with regard to guinea pigs.* Laboratory experiments have found that extremely small amounts of dioxin can kill guinea pigs . . . but hamsters require a dose *1,900 times as high* before suffering the same mortality rate. Other laboratory animals require injections 300 to 500 times as high, and *human* exposure to much higher levels has not been found to have negative effects beyond a temporary skin condition called chloracne.

Regenstein and many others made the elementary mistake of *relying on laboratory animal experiments to predict carcinogenesis in humans.*

> *"The chemical that many environmentalists consider to be the most deadly of all is not, after all, a serious threat to human health."*

The opponents of dioxin also relied on poorly conducted epidemiologic studies that *mistook correlation for causation.* For example, a survey of Love Canal residents conducted by Dr. Beverly Paigen, a biologist, was widely reported as showing high levels of association between exposure to toxic chemicals and chronic health problems. But when the Thomas panel examined the Paigen report, they found it to be

> based on largely anecdotal information provided by questionnaires submitted to a narrowly selected group of residents. There are no adequate control groups, [and] the illnesses cited as caused by chemical pollution were not medically validated. . . . The panel finds the Paigen report literally impossible to interpret. It cannot be taken seriously as a piece of sound epidemiological research.

A small number of similarly small-scale, unreplicated, and unreliable epidemiologic studies are cited repeatedly in the literature of Greenpeace and the newsletters and fundraising letters of mainstream environmental organizations. The fact that these studies are too small and too flawed to form the basis of scientific proof is unimportant, according to the rules of "new paradigm" thinking. Together with discredited laboratory animal studies, they constitute a "weight of evidence" that dioxin is a serious threat to human health and must be entirely removed from all air and water emissions. In the brave new world of radical environmentalism, nothing more is necessary to ban a product.

The Toxic Threat to Minorities Is Exaggerated

by Christopher Boerner and Thomas Lambert

About the authors: *Christopher Boerner and Thomas Lambert are fellows at the Center for the Study of American Business at Washington University in St. Louis.*

Eliminating "environmental racism" has fast become one of the premier civil rights and environmental issues of the 1990s. Over the past 15 years, what began as a modest grassroots social movement has expanded to become a national issue, combining environmentalism's sense of urgency with the ethical concerns of the civil rights movement. According to "environmental-justice" advocates, discrimination in the siting and permitting of industrial and waste facilities has forced minorities and the poor to bear disproportionately the ill-effects of pollution compared to more affluent whites. What's more, advocates contend, the discriminatory application of environmental regulations and remediation procedures has essentially let polluters in minority communities "off the hook."

To remedy this perceived imbalance, policy-makers in Washington have mounted a full-court press. On February 11, 1994, the Clinton Administration issued an executive order on environmental justice, requiring federal agencies to demonstrate that their programs and policies do not unfairly inflict environmental harm on the poor and minorities. The order also creates an interagency task force to inform the president of all federal environmental-justice policies and to work closely with the Environmental Protection Agency's Office of Environmental Equity as well as other government agencies to ensure that those policies are implemented promptly. In addition to the president's executive order, Congress has debated several separate bills designed to guarantee environmental equity. These proposals would affect the location of industrial facilities.

Questions and Answers

With charges of racism, discrimination, and social negligence being bantered about, discussions of the environmental-justice issue are often passionate and, oc-

Christopher Boerner and Thomas Lambert, "Environmental Injustice." Reprinted by permission of the authors and the *Public Interest*, no. 118, Winter 1995, pp. 61–82; © 1995 by National Affairs, Inc.

casionally, inflammatory. Behind the emotion, however, two critical questions arise: does the existing evidence justify such a high-level commitment of resources to environmental-justice claims; and what reasonable steps should society take to ensure that environmental policies are fairly enacted and implemented?

Contrary to conventional wisdom, the answers to these questions are neither simple nor readily apparent. While it certainly seems noncontroversial to assert that environmental officials ought to enforce existing laws equally, the question of siting and permitting reforms is not unambiguous. Before approving additional regulations on facility siting and permitting, policy-makers would be well advised to assess candidly both the quality of the existing environmental-racism research as well as the likely costs and benefits of proposed solutions to this problem. Only with such a critical eye can legislators be certain that the measures ultimately enacted are both cost-effective and successful in addressing the equity concerns of minority and low-income communities.

> *"Congress has debated several separate bills designed to guarantee environmental equity."*

Evidence of Racism?

The call for environmental justice first surfaced during the late 1970s with the work of grassroots organizations such as the Mothers of East Los Angeles and Chicago's People for Community Recovery. While ostensibly formed to combat specific local environmental problems, each of these groups seemingly shared one unifying belief: that the poor and minorities are systematically discriminated against in the siting, regulation, and remediation of industrial and waste facilities. Through social and political protest, these neighborhood groups aggressively challenged local developments they considered undesirable, becoming an effective voice for the concerns of inner-city residents. In the absence of detailed empirical research, however, the evidence for these organizations' claims of discrimination remained largely anecdotal. As a result, their influence on policy was limited. Not until several studies appeared to substantiate their assertions did the movement gain national attention.

The first major attempt to provide empirical support for environmental-justice claims was conducted by Robert D. Bullard, a sociologist at the University of California, Riverside, in the late 1970s. Examining population data for communities hosting landfills and incinerators in Houston, Texas, Professor Bullard found that while African Americans made up only 28 percent of the city's population, six of its eight incinerators and fifteen of its seventeen landfills were located in predominantly African-American neighborhoods. The presence of these facilities, he suggests, not only makes black Houston the "dumping grounds for the city's household garbage," but also compounds the myriad of social ills (e.g., crime, poverty, drugs, unemployment, etc.) that already plague poor, inner-city communities.

While limited in scope, Professor Bullard's research has helped shape the policy debate surrounding environmental justice. His Houston study played a central role in one of the first, though unsuccessful, legal cases involving environmental discrimination, *Bean v. Southwestern Waste Management Corp.*, and forms the basis for two often-cited books, *Invisible Houston* and *Dumping in Dixie*.

The second widely discussed study examining community demographics near commercial waste Treatment, Storage, and Disposal Facilities (TSDFs) was conducted by the U.S. General Accounting Office (GAO) in 1983. The purpose of the study was to "determine the correlation between the location of hazardous waste landfills and the racial and economic status of surrounding communities." Examining data from four facilities in EPA Region IV (Southeast region), government researchers found that the populations in three of the four surrounding areas were primarily black. African Americans comprised 52 percent, 66 percent, and 90 percent of the population in those three communities. In contrast, African Americans made up no more than 30 percent of the general population of the states involved. In addition, the study found that the communities hosting waste facilities were disproportionately poor when local poverty levels were compared to state averages.

More Studies

The third, and most often cited, empirical study was published in 1987 by the Commission for Racial Justice (CRJ) of the United Church of Christ. The CRJ study had two important components: an analytical survey of commercial waste TSDFs and a descriptive analysis of uncontrolled toxic waste sites. Both statistical studies were designed to determine the extent to which African Americans and other minority groups are exposed to hazardous wastes in their communities. By using population data (based on five-digit zip codes) as well as information gathered from the U.S. Environmental Protection Agency (EPA) and other sources, CRJ researchers isolated three variables: the percent of minority population, mean household income, and mean value of owner-occupied housing.

"While limited in scope, Professor Bullard's research has helped shape the policy debate surrounding environmental justice."

The CRJ study revealed a correlation between the number of commercial waste facilities in a given community and the percentage of minority residents in that community. Specifically, the CRJ found that the percentage of "nonwhites" within zip codes with one waste plant was approximately twice that of zip codes without such a facility. For areas with more than one waste plant, the percentage of minority residents was on average three times greater than that of communities with no facilities. Critically, the United Church of Christ found that race was statistically more significant than either mean household income or mean value of owner-occupied housing. This suggested that race was a more likely determinant of where noxious facilities were located than socioeconomic factors. Combined, these results led the CRJ to conclude that there are "clear patterns which show that communities with greater minority percentages of the population are more likely to be the sites of commercial hazardous waste facilities."

> *"Staten Island—home of the nation's largest landfill—is considered a 'minority' community even though over 80 percent of its residents are white."*

A final study which deserves mention was published by the *National Law Journal* (NLJ) in September 1992. Unlike the research discussed above, which focused on the location of industrial and waste facilities, the NLJ study examined racial disparities in EPA enforcement and remediation procedures. The findings indicate that significant disparities exist in the fines levied against polluters in white communities and those in minority areas. Likewise, the study found that EPA took longer to clean up waste sites in poor and minority communities than in more affluent neighborhoods. The NLJ researchers concluded that "the federal government, in its cleanup of hazardous sites and its pursuit of polluters, favors white communities over minority communities under environmental laws meant to provide equal protection for all citizens."

Research Flaws

While the studies discussed above have been widely cited by environmental-justice advocates, all suffer from serious methodological difficulties. The first major criticism of the present research centers on the definition of the term "community." Defining minority communities as any area where the percentage of nonwhite residents exceeds the percentage found in the entire U.S. population means that a community may be considered "minority" even if the vast majority of its residents are white. Based on this methodology, for example, Staten Island—home of the nation's largest landfill—is considered a "minority" community even though over 80 percent of its residents are white. In fact, Staten Island is the "whitest" of New York City's five boroughs.

Another instance of this is evident in a *National Law Journal* study which ranked communities according to percentage of white residents. The term "white community" was used to refer to the top quartile of all affected communities, while "minority community" referred to the bottom quartile. Interestingly, the "whitest" of the "minority communities" had a higher percentage of white residents (84.1 percent) than the general population of the United States, which is 83.1 percent white.

A second, but related, problem is that these studies ignore population densities. Merely citing the proportion of minority or low-income residents in a given host community does not provide information about how many people are actually exposed to environmental harms. For example, given that blacks presently comprise approximately 16 percent of the nation's population, a host community of 1,000 residents, 20 percent of whom are black, would be considered "minority," while a host community of 6,000 residents, 15 percent of whom are black, would not. By overlooking population density, the studies fail to point out that more blacks (900 versus 200) would be exposed to the pollution in the second, "non-minority" community, than in the first.

Broad Geographics

In addition to the problems associated with proportionality and population density, the environmental justice studies cited above often define the affected area in geographic terms that are too broad. Much of the prior research is based on zip-code areas, which are frequently large units established by the U.S. Postal Service. As a result, the data likely suffer from what statisticians call "aggregation errors." That is to say, the studies reach conclusions from the zip-code data which would not be valid if a smaller, more consistent geographic unit were examined. A study released by the Social and Demographic Research Institute at the University of Massachusetts, Amherst (UMass), confirms that an analysis of census tracts—small geographic units with relatively fixed boundaries—yields strikingly different results.

The UMass study compared the social and demographic characteristics of census tracts that contain commercial TSDFs with those tracts that do not have TSDFs. Contrary to conventional wisdom, the UMass researchers found that the percentage of minorities living in neighborhoods with commercial facilities is no greater than in areas without such facilities. Indeed, in the 25 largest metropolitan areas studied, commercial hazardous-waste facilities are slightly more likely to be in industrial neighborhoods with a lower percentage of minorities and a *higher* percentage of white working-class families. According to Douglas L. Anderton, director of the UMass project, "We looked at smaller neighborhood areas and found that facilities are more often located in census tracts that are white working-class industrialized neighborhoods. Even other census tracts nearest to those with facilities had no higher percentage of minorities." The

> *"Commercial hazardous-waste facilities are slightly more likely to be in industrial neighborhoods with . . . a* **higher** *percentage of white working-class families."*

results of the UMass study—the most comprehensive analysis of environmental justice to date—cast serious doubt on many of the research claims of proponents of environmental justice.

A third flaw in the existing environmental-justice studies is that they imply rather than explicitly state the actual risk presented by commercial TSDFs.

While the research attempts to disclose the prevalence of commercial-waste plants in poor and minority communities, there is no corresponding information about the dangers associated with living near such facilities. The regulatory requirements regarding the building and operation of industrial and waste facilities in the United States are among the most stringent of any industrialized country in the world. These requirements, along with the voluntary efforts of industry, significantly reduce the noxious emissions of commercial-waste plants and other facilities.

Unsubstantiated Health Effects

Moreover, health risks are a function of actual exposure, not simply proximity to a waste facility. The environmental-justice advocates' claims of negative health effects are not substantiated by scientific studies. In fact, many of the legislative proposals to combat environmental inequities may result in greater harm to minority and poor residents than the emissions from noxious facilities themselves. By reducing the incentives for businesses to locate in poor and minority areas, these measures may exacerbate local problems of poverty and unemployment—conditions far more unhealthy than the minute risks associated with waste disposal facilities and industrial plants.

Finally, existing research on environmental justice fails to establish that discriminatory siting and permitting practices caused present environmental disparities. While the studies match the location of industrial and waste facilities with the current socioeconomic and race characteristics of the surrounding neighborhoods, they do not consider community conditions *when the facilities were sited.* Furthermore, they fail to explore alternative explanations for higher concentrations of minority and low-income citizens near undesirable facilities. Thus, none of the studies prove that the siting process actually caused the disproportionate burden that poor and minority communities purportedly now bear.

Wastewater and Sewage Sludge Are Safe for Use on Cropland

by National Research Council

About the author: The National Research Council is part of the National Academy of Sciences, a Washington, D.C., organization founded by Congress as an official adviser to the federal government on scientific and technical matters. The council's Committee on the Use of Treated Municipal Effluents and Sludge in the Production of Crops for Human Consumption produced a 1996 report on the use of wastewater and sludge on cropland, from which this viewpoint is excerpted.

The use of treated municipal wastewater effluent for irrigated agriculture offers an opportunity to conserve water resources. Water reclamation can also provide an alternative to disposal in areas where surface waters have a limited capacity to assimilate the contaminants, such as the nitrogen and phosphorus, that remain in most treated wastewater effluent discharges. The sludge that results from municipal wastewater treatment processes contains organic matter and nutrients that, when properly treated and applied to farmland, can improve the physical properties and agricultural productivity of soils, and its agricultural use provides an alternative to disposal options, such as incineration, or landfilling.

Treatment for Reuse

Land application of municipal wastewater and sludge has been practiced for its beneficial effects and for disposal purposes since the advent of modern wastewater management about 150 years ago. Not surprisingly, public response to the practice has been mixed. Raw municipal wastewater contains human pathogens and toxic chemicals. With continuing advances in wastewater treatment technology and increasingly stringent wastewater discharge requirements,

Reprinted with permission from *Use of Reclaimed Water and Sludge in Food Crop Production.* Copyright 1996 by the National Academy of Sciences. Courtesy of the National Academy Press, Washington, D.C.

most treated wastewater effluents produced by public treatment authorities in the United States are now of consistent, high quality. When treated to acceptable levels or by appropriate processes to meet state reuse requirements, the effluent is referred to as "reclaimed water." Sewage sludge can also be treated to levels that allow it to be reused. With the increased interest in reclaimed water and the promotion of agricultural use for treated sludge, there has been increased public scrutiny of the potential health and environmental consequences of these reuse practices. Farmers and the food industry have expressed their concerns that such practices—especially the agricultural use of sludge—may affect the safety of food products and the sustainability of agricultural land, and may carry potential economic and liability risks.

Reclaimed water in the United States contributes a very small amount (probably much less than one percent) of water to agricultural irrigation, mainly because the extent of the practice is limited both by regional demands and the proximity of suitable agricultural land to many municipal wastewater treatment plants. Most reclaimed water goes towards various nonpotable urban uses such as irrigating public landscapes (parks, highway medians, lawns, etc.), air-conditioning and cooling, industrial processing, toilet-flushing, vehicle-washing, and construction. Irrigation of residential lawns and/or gardens with reclaimed water is becoming increasingly popular where dual plumbing systems to facilitate water reuse have been installed; however, this report concentrates on agricultural uses of reclaimed water, and not residential use.

Sludge Disposal

Sewage sludge (or simply, "sludge") is an inevitable end product of modern wastewater treatment. Many of the organic solids, toxic organic chemicals, and inorganic chemicals (trace elements) are removed from the treated wastewater and concentrated in the sludge. An estimated 5.3 million metric tons per year dry weight of sludge are currently produced in the United States from publicly owned treatment plants. This amount will surely increase as a larger population is served by sewers and as higher levels of wastewater treatment are introduced.

> *"Much of the cropland that receives sludge is used to grow hay, corn, and small grains for cattle feed, and public acceptance generally has been favorable."*

Sludge disposal has always represented a substantial portion of the cost of wastewater management. Over the past 20 years, restrictions have been placed on certain sludge disposal practices (e.g., ocean dumping and landfill disposal), causing public wastewater treatment utilities to view the agricultural use of sludge as an increasingly cost-effective alternative. Currently, 36 percent of sludge is applied to the land for several beneficial purposes including agriculture, turfgrass production, and reclamation of surface mining areas; 38

percent is landfilled; 16 percent is incinerated; and the remainder is surface disposed by other means.

The Midwest has a long history of using treated sludge on cropland. Much of the cropland that receives sludge is used to grow hay, corn, and small grains for cattle feed, and public acceptance generally has been favorable. In Madison, Wisconsin, for example, the demand for sludge as a soil amendment exceeds the local supply. With ocean disposal of sludge no longer allowed, New York City and Boston—among other coastal cities—ship much of their sludge to other parts of the country. A portion of the sludge produced in the Los Angeles Basin is transported to a large farm near Yuma, Arizona.

> *"When reclaimed water or sludge is used on fields producing food crops, the public health must be protected."*

If all the municipal sludge produced in the United States were to be agriculturally applied at agronomic rates, it would only be able to satisfy the nitrogen needs of about 1.6 percent of the nation's 1,250 million hectares (309 million acres) of cropland. About one quarter of this cropland is used to grow food for human consumption, of which 2 percent grows produce crops that can be consumed fresh. Thus, in a national context, the amount of food crops produced on fields receiving sludge would remain very small. . . .

A Benefit to Soil

In February 1993, the U.S. Environmental Protection Agency (EPA) promulgated *Standards for the Use or Disposal of Sewage Sludge* (Code of Federal Regulations Title 40, Parts 257, 403, and 503, and hereafter referred to as the "Part 503 Sludge Rule"). This rule builds on a number of federal and state regulations that aim to reduce pollutants entering the municipal waste stream through source controls and industrial pretreatment programs that have reduced the levels of contaminants in the sludge as well as in the final effluent. The Part 503 Sludge Rule defines acceptable management practices and provides specific numerical limits for selected chemical pollutants and pathogens applicable to land application of sewage sludge. In this context, sewage sludge—traditionally regarded by many groups as an urban waste requiring careful disposal—is now viewed by the wastewater treatment industry, the regulatory agencies, and participating farmers as a beneficial soil amendment. . . .

Irrigation of food crops with treated municipal wastewater has been effectively and safely practiced in the United States on a limited scale. The public has generally accepted the concept of wastewater irrigation as part of larger and more comprehensive water conservation programs to reclaim wastewater for a variety of nonpotable uses. Where reclaimed water has been used for food crop production, the state standards for wastewater treatment and reuse, along with site restrictions and generally good system reliability, have insured that food crops thus produced do not present a greater risk to the consumer than do crops irrigated from conventional sources.

The beneficial reuse of municipal sludge has been less widely accepted. Federal regulations are designed to assure that sludge application for the production of food crops does not pose a significant risk from the consumption of foods thus produced. However, the parties affected by these reuse programs—local communities, crop growers, food processors, and the consumer—remain concerned about the potential for exposure to contaminants, nuisance problems, liability, and adequacy of program management and oversight. Sludge management programs based on agricultural sludge use can involve many potentially responsible parties, and can cross agency, state, and federal jurisdictional boundaries. Therefore, municipalities, public utilities, crop growers, and food processors must be able to provide well-managed and reliable programs that address, and are open to, community, business, health, agronomic, and environmental concerns.

Protecting Public Health

Municipal wastewater contains a variety of pathogenic (infectious) agents. When reclaimed water or sludge is used on fields producing food crops, the public health must be protected. This can be achieved by proper wastewater or sludge treatment and site management that reliably reduces the pathogens to acceptable levels.

There are no federal regulations directly governing the use of municipal wastewater to irrigate crops. However, EPA provided guidelines for reclaimed water quality and its use for crop irrigation in its 1992 *Guidelines for Water Reuse.* There are currently 19 states that regulate the practice by setting criteria for reclaimed effluent quality, such as microbiological limits or process standards; crop restrictions; or by waiting periods for human or grazing animal access or before crop harvest. State regulations vary; some require very high-quality effluents to reduce the concentration of pathogens to levels acceptable for human contact prior to irrigation. Others depend on the use of crop restrictions and site limitations, thus allowing required time for pathogens to decrease to acceptable levels. In general, modern wastewater

> *"There have been no reported outbreaks of infectious disease associated with . . . reclaimed water or sludge applied to agricultural land."*

treatment procedures incorporate monitoring and technical redundancies that provide system reliability and protection against exposure to pathogens.

The strategy for regulating pathogens in the agricultural use of sludge is similar. The Part 503 Sludge Rule requires the use of either Class A pathogen criteria, in which the sludge is considered to be safe for direct public contact, or Class B pathogen criteria, in which site and crop restrictions are required.

Ensuring the Safety of Sludge

Class A (safe for public contact) microbial standards or process standards for sludge appear to be adequate for public health protection. The Part 503 Sludge Rule allows for direct testing of pathogens (bacteria, viruses, and helminths), and the use of salmonella or fecal coliform testing as alternative indicators to determine Class A sludge quality. The prescribed methods for the testing of salmonella are of questionable sensitivity. Until such time as more precise methods are developed and accepted, the present test for salmonella should not be used as a substitute for the fecal coliform test; rather, it should be run in concert with that test or in situations in which the fecal coliform results are in question, such as may happen under some operating conditions. The salmonella test is less precise because of the relatively low numbers of salmonella present compared to fecal coliform.

Restrictions on the use of Class B sludge require allowing a suitable length of time for die-off of helminth ova, which can be transmitted to humans via improperly cooked, contaminated meat. The control of helminth parasites is achieved largely through public health education (e.g., the need for thorough cooking of meat) and government meat inspection, as well as controls over applications of wastewater and sludge to land. Based on a review of U.S. studies, the Part 503 Sludge Rule requires a 30-day waiting period before cattle can graze on Class B sludge-amended fields. An investigation in Denmark indicates that the beef tapeworm (*Taenia* sp.), one of the helminth group, may survive in sludge-treated fields for up to one year. Although the evidence comes from a single study, there is reason to believe that the length of the waiting period for grazing following sludge application to pastures needs to be re-examined.

> *"Most trace organic chemicals present in sludge are either not taken up or are taken up in very low amounts by crops after sludge is applied to land."*

There have been no reported outbreaks of infectious disease associated with a population's exposure—either directly or through food consumption pathways—to adequately treated and properly distributed reclaimed water or sludge applied to agricultural land. Reports and available epidemiological evidence from other countries indicate that agricultural reuse of *untreated* wastewater can result in infectious disease transmission. The limited number of epidemiological studies that have been conducted in the United States on wastewater treatment plant workers or populations exposed to various reclaimed water or treated sludge via land application projects indicate that exposure to these materials is not a significant risk factor. However, the value of prospective epidemiological studies on this topic is limited because of a number of factors, including a low illness rate—if any—resulting from the reuse practice, insufficient sensitivity of current epidemiological techniques to detect low-level disease transmission, population mobility, and difficulty in assessing actual levels of exposure. . . .

Trace Elements and Organic Chemicals

Potentially harmful chemicals (largely, trace elements and persistent organics) become concentrated in the sludge during the wastewater treatment process. Following repeated land applications, trace elements, except for boron, will accumulate in the soil to, or slightly below, the depth of sludge incorporation. The persistent organic chemicals degrade over time in soils. Degradation rates are dependent on the chemical in question and on soil properties.

The Part 503 Sludge Rule for the agricultural use of sludge sets criteria for concentrations of 10 trace elements in sludge: arsenic, cadmium, chromium, copper, lead, mercury, molybdenum, nickel, selenium, and zinc. The rule is based on a risk-assessment approach that considered the effects of these trace elements and organic chemicals of concern on crop production, human and animal health, and environmental quality. Except for cadmium, these trace elements are not ordinarily taken up by crop plants in amounts harmful to human consumers. EPA regulations for cadmium in sludge are sufficiently stringent to prevent its accumulation in plants at levels that are harmful to consumers.

> *"As long as agricultural use of treated sludge is in keeping with current regulations and acid soils are agronomically managed, no adverse effects are anticipated."*

In deriving pollutant loading rates for land application of sewage sludge, EPA considered 14 transport pathways and, in all cases, selected the most stringent value as the limit for each pollutant. For the 10 regulated inorganic pollutants, the most stringent loading rates were derived from pathways that involved a child directly ingesting sludge or from pathways involving effects on crops. This resulted in significantly lower pollutant limits than would have been the case had they been set by human food-chain pathways involving human consumption of food crops, meat or dairy products. Therefore, when sludges are applied to land according to the Part 503 Sludge Rule, there is a built-in safety factor that protects against human exposure to chemical contaminants via human food-chain pathways.

Available evidence indicates that most trace organic chemicals present in sludge are either not taken up or are taken up in very low amounts by crops after sludge is applied to land. The wastewater treatment process removes most of these organic chemicals, and further reduction occurs when sludge is processed and after it is added to soil. Consequently, only negligible quantities of toxic organic chemicals from municipal wastewater systems will persist in soils for an extended period. Recent studies suggest that plant tissues may absorb volatile toxic organic chemicals from the vapor phase of volatile compounds; however, the aeration that occurs during treatment of wastewater and during many sludge treatment processes removes most of the volatile organic chemicals at the treatment plant. . . .

Marketing Sludge Products

In addition to its use on agricultural land, sludge can be marketed and distributed to the public for home gardening and landscaping purposes. EPA has used the term "Exceptional Quality" (EQ) to refer to sludge that meets specified low pollutant and pathogen limits and that has been treated to reduce the level of degradable compounds that attract vectors. EQ sludge is a product that required no further regulation. EPA allows sludge that is sold or given away to the public to exceed the EQ chemical pollutant concentrations with the stipulation that prescribed application limits not be exceeded. However, there is little assurance that the home gardener or landscaper will either be aware of or be able to follow these requirements, nor is there a method for tracking the disposition of sludge marketed to the public. Allowing sludge with less than the highest quality chemical pollutant limits to be used by the public opens the door to exceeding regulatory limits, and thereby undermines the intent of Part 503 and public confidence in the law. Recommendation: The Part 503 Sludge Rule should be amended to more fully assure that only sludge of exceptional quality, in terms of both pathogen and chemical limits, is marketed to the general public so that further regulation and management beyond the point of sale or giveaway would not be necessary. . . .

Treated Municipal Sludge

Municipal sewage sludge is a source of nitrogen and phosphorus in crop production. The addition of organic matter through successive sludge applications improves the physical properties and productivity of soils. When used at agronomic rates for nitrogen and phosphorus, sewage sludge can usually satisfy crop requirements for many other nutrients as well, with the possible exception of potassium. EPA's Part 503 Sludge Rule specifies the annual and cumulative loadings of trace elements in sludge-amended soils, and, based on currently available information, these limits are adequate to protect against phytotoxicity and to prevent the accumulation of these elements in crops at levels harmful to consumers.

"Regulatory mandates . . . must be funded and implemented to be meaningful safeguards."

Because repeated sewage sludge applications lead to accumulations of trace elements in soil, concern has been expressed over possible adverse effects associated with the use of sludge on soils that are acidic or may become acidic. However, as long as agricultural use of treated sludge is in keeping with current regulations and acid soils are agronomically managed, no adverse effects are anticipated. The Part 503 Sludge Rule is based on approximately 20 years of research and experience in applying sewage sludge to cropland. While this has provided an adequate knowledge base for developing the regulations, continued monitoring of trace elements in soils over longer time periods is desirable.

As in all farm operations, proper management is needed to avoid the buildup of nitrates. Typically, sludges comprise approximately 1 to 6 percent organic and inorganic nitrogen on a dry weight basis. The soluble inorganic forms are immediately available to plants, but the organic forms must first be mineralized to plant-available forms. For sludge to be efficiently used as a source of available nitrogen, the mineralization of organic nitrogen must be taken into account to avoid overfertilization and potential leaching of excess nitrate-nitrogen into ground water.

> *"Established numerical limits on concentration levels of pollutants added to cropland by sludge are adequate to assure the safety of crops."*

Most sludges supply more than enough phosphorus to satisfy crop needs when applied as a source of nitrogen. In certain soils, available phosphorus may be excessive, particularly where animal manure is plentiful and where impacts to surface water quality are of concern. In these situations, soil phosphorus levels should be monitored and sludge application rates be adjusted to correspond to crop phosphorus rather than nitrogen needs.

Heavy metals are not mobile in soils, and their transport to ground water as a result of sewage sludge application at agronomic rates is unlikely. Likewise, toxic organic compounds in sludge are not likely to contaminate ground water because their concentrations are low, because they are volatilized or biodegraded in soils, or because they are strongly sorbed to soil particles. Because of predictable pathogen die-off and because of the immobilization of microorganisms on sludge and soil particles, the risk of transporting viruses, bacteria, and protozoa to ground water due to sludge application is negligible as long as sludge is properly treated and applied to or incorporated into unsaturated soils. As with all agricultural soil amendments, sludge use must be managed properly to avoid contamination of surface or ground waters. . . .

Other Regulations and Institutional Controls

From a regulatory perspective, it is important to remember that EPA's Part 503 Sludge Rule augments a wide array of existing institutional programs and controls over the disposition of municipal wastewater and sludge. For example, federal and state regulations govern the handling and treatment of toxic waste and the protection of surface and ground waters. These regulatory mandates appear adequate to manage most of the risks associated with land application, but they must be funded and implemented to be meaningful safeguards.

Sludges that do not meet beneficial use criteria standards as defined by the Part 503 Sludge Rule must be disposed of according to federal and state regulations as applicable. Both the general public and state and local regulators should be aware that the Part 503 Sludge Rule is not the only control over agricultural use of sewage sludge. Recommendation: Management of sludge for beneficial use should be more visibly linked to existing regulations governing its disposal. Program credibility may be improved and public concern reduced if federal, state, and municipal regulators clearly assign authority to local governments for responding to any reports of adverse consequences related to beneficial use of sludge, such as ground water contamination, odor, attraction of vermin, or illnesses. The public should be aware that state and local units of government have the necessary regulatory authority to take corrective actions against parties who have violated rules and guidance.

Negligible Risk

In summary, society produces large volumes of treated municipal wastewater and sewage sludge that must be either disposed of or reused. While no disposal or reuse option can guarantee complete safety, the use of these materials in the production of crops for human consumption, when practiced in accordance with existing federal guidelines and regulations, presents negligible risk to the consumer, to crop production, and to the environment. Current technology to remove pollutants from wastewater, coupled with existing regulations and guidelines governing the use of reclaimed wastewater and sludge in crop production, are adequate to protect human health and the environment. Established numerical limits on concentration levels of pollutants added to cropland by sludge are adequate to assure the safety of crops produced for human consumption. In addition to health and environmental concerns, institutional barriers such as public confidence in the adequacy of the regulatory system and concerns over liability, property values, and nuisance factors will play a major role in the acceptance of treated municipal wastewater and sewage sludge for use in the production of food crops.

Chlorine Is Not a Health Hazard

by David Rothbard and Craig Rucker

About the authors: *David Rothbard is the president and Craig Rucker is the executive director of the Committee for a Constructive Tomorrow (CFACT), a Washington, D.C., organization that promotes free-market and safe technological solutions to consumer and environmental concerns.*

When the subject is man's best friend, you're likely to hear a lot of conflicting opinions. Some point to the stately Great Dane, others to the lovable Beagle, and still others leave dogs off the list completely and instead hold aloft such dandies as the golf club, the riding lawnmower, and the remote control. One thing you probably won't hear mentioned, however, is chlorine, and that's a shame, because given its incredibly wide range of benefits, it should at least rank up there next to Rover.

Chlorine's Importance

Every time you turn on your tap, whiten your socks, fill a prescription, or diaper your baby's bottom, chlorine is helping to brighten your day. It is found in such diverse products as teflon, compact discs, birth control pills, photographic film, sofa cushions, linoleum, and lawn chemicals. It is used in 85% of all pharmaceuticals, 96% of all pesticides, purifies 98% of all U.S. drinking water, and directly affects 1.3 million American jobs. Chlorine is so important, in fact, it is used in 60% of all chemical transactions which amount to 40% of our total gross national product.

With MVP [most valuable player] numbers like those, it's hard to imagine anyone would attempt to completely strike out its use. Nevertheless, some are claiming we must do just that because they say the consequences of not banning chlorine are too severe. Liberal environmental groups led by Greenpeace, the National Wildlife Federation (NWF), and the Canadian-based Pollution Probe are actually calling for "zero discharge" of the chemical. And nowhere have their efforts been more intense than in the region of the Great Lakes.

From "Anti-Chlorine Crusade Fouls Great Lakes Region" by David Rothbard and Craig Rucker, *CFACT Citizen Outlook*, March/April 1994. Reprinted with permission.

Testing the Waters

For over 25 years, many environmental extremists have looked to the Great Lakes as one of the best opportunities to pursue their militant anti-chemical campaign. Their most notable early achievement was the 1978 expansion of the Great Lakes Water Quality Agreement to include the "virtual elimination" of "persistent" toxic chemicals, so named because they do not break down rapidly in the environment. Since responsibility for deciding how to interpret and carry out this difficult agreement fell to the International Joint Commission (IJC)—a body established in 1909 to resolve boundary water disputes between the U.S. and Canada—the Greens [environmental activists] began a decade-long mobilization to not only get the agency in gear on existing chemical targets, but also to broaden the list to ultimately include the all-important element of chlorine.

These efforts began to pay off at the IJC's 1989 biennial meeting in Hamilton, Ontario. There, where according to commission staff member Mike Gibertson the Greens dominated the gathering, they succeeded in establishing an IJC task force that would draft the strategy for sunsetting various toxics. In 1991, they scored another major victory when they convinced the commission to include chlorine on the list of chemicals to be X'd out. And although loud protests from industry kept the chemical off the task force's final October '93 report, the enviros retained their momentum in February 1994 when the IJC reaffirmed its earlier commitment to the banning of chlorine. Now, with the IJC firmly planted in the Green camp, the battle is in full rage.

"Just Get Rid of Them!"

At the heart of the chlorine controversy are complaints about the chemical's effects on the environment and human health. Foremost, the Greens say human activities such as incineration, paper production, water purification, and pesticide use are resulting in dangerous amounts of toxic chlorine compounds being formed in the environment. They further claim these compounds, known as organochlorines, can persist in the ecosystem for as much as one hundred years and can thus build up, or bioaccumulate, in living tissue and pass from one organism to another. Since animals farther up the food chain are more susceptible to being KO'd by such persistent chemicals, the Greens sound their loudest alarm about chlorine's impact on such species as birds, whales, and people.

"Chlorine is so important . . . it is used in 60% of all chemical transactions which amount to 40% of our total gross national product."

So convinced are they of chlorine's devastating impact that Tim Eder, a spokesman for NWF, sees no room for compromise. "When it comes to organochlorines," he stated in an interview with *Citizen Outlook*, "you don't make them, produce them, or dispose them . . . you just get rid of them!"

Chapter 2

Apocalypse Not

Despite such bold certainty, basic science and some real-world observations are casting a long shadow on the Greens' claims. To begin with, there are literally thousands of different kinds of organochlorines and despite environmentalist assertions to the contrary, many, like chloroform and methylene chloride, are produced by nature. Even "persistent" chlorine by-products like dioxin and PCBs [polychlorinated biphenyls] are often naturally produced by forest fires and volcanoes.

> *"Even the most persistent chlorinated organic compounds are far more degradable than generally thought."*

As for breaking down in the environment and in living tissue, scientists from the respected [Canadian] CanTox group in Ontario say even the most persistent chlorinated organic compounds are far more degradable then generally thought. In the Great Lakes, for instance, levels of PCB and dioxin have dropped dramatically since their use was curtailed—a drop of fifteen fold in just 20 years. And fish, which had PCB levels of as much as 40 parts per million (ppm) in the 1970s, are commonly found today with a meager level of 1 ppm and rarely exceed 2 ppm.

With regard to wildlife, the enviros point to several species they say are being harmed. But if that's so, their numbers, according to the U.S. Fish and Wildlife Service, do not reflect it. Bald eagles, one of the Greens' favorite "victims," have been on the rebound for more than two decades, and the Great Lakes just happens to be among their strongest habitats. In 1973, there were an estimated 345 pairs in the region, but today that number has burgeoned to 1,449. Trout numbers in the area also continue to remain healthy while a frequently mentioned bird known as the double-crested cormorant, which numbered just 157 nests in the region in 1977, has now exploded to an estimated 11,439. Beluga whales, often cited to elicit public sympathies, aren't even on the threatened, never mind endangered, species list. And as for seagulls, any Great Lakes boater or fisherman can tell you there's little danger of the area running out of them any time soon.

A Lack of Evidence

Finally, concerning the chemical's impact on human health, there have never been any known real-world fatalities caused by organochlorines. Environmentalists, in fact, have been able to produce only one report of any scientific interest that links chlorine's use to physical human harm. This report, known as the "Jacobson" study, postulates a connection between birth defects and the consumption of contaminated Great Lakes fish by pregnant mothers. The study, however, has been roundly rejected because it included no chemical analysis or legitimate demographics of the individuals surveyed and came up with only a statistically insignificant 2 out of 36 positive tests that showed any link.

118

Unfortunately, this lack of convincing evidence to show any damaging effects has not slowed down the drive to ban chlorine. Even the Bill Clinton Administration called for the creation of a "national strategy for substituting, reducing, or prohibiting the use of chlorine" as part of [a renewed] Clean Water Act. Such a move, however, would carry huge costs in money, and maybe even in lives. The Charles River Associates group of Boston pins the cost of chlorine substitutes, in the cases they are available, at $91 billion, or $1,500 a year for a family of four. And with countries such as Bolivia and Peru experiencing a cholera epidemic following their decision to stop chlorinating their water, the cost in human health could also be real and severe. The chlorine ban is one product of environmental extremism we can ill afford to swallow.

Chapter 3

Is Recycling Effective?

Chapter Preface

Garbage and waste disposal is a significant and unavoidable concern in America. Approximately 80 percent of municipal solid waste—largely paper, food, yard waste, metals, plastics, and glass—is sent to landfills. The remainder is either recycled or incinerated. From 1978 to 1996, the number of operating landfills declined from approximately twenty thousand to three thousand. According to Environmental Protection Agency estimates, by the year 2008 only one-third of these will be available to accept the approximately 160 million tons of trash dumped annually.

Closures of filled landfills have increased concerns that landfill space is dwindling, particularly in populous and congested regions such as the Northeast. Furthermore, in many instances plans to construct new landfills have been thwarted by community protests and opposition. According to ReThink Paper, an environmental organization that advocates environmentally sound paper consumption, "Unfortunately, to be at all economical, landfills must be situated near areas where people live. And that's the rub. Nobody wants to live near a landfill." ReThink Paper contends that the landfill space problem will become more critical as existing landfills reach capacity and close.

Other observers disagree that a landfill space problem exists. According to the National Solid Waste Management Association, the number of states with more than ten years of remaining landfill capacity has increased from twenty-nine in 1991 to thirty-eight in 1995. Moreover, some experts argue that only a minimal amount of space will be needed to accommodate future waste. A. Clark Wiseman, an economics professor at Gonzaga University, calculates that the amount of land needed to store America's trash for the next one thousand years equals a rectangular area forty-four miles on each side and one hundred twenty feet deep, occupying one-tenth of one percent of U.S. land.

Garbage disposal and landfill space are important issues in an industrial society such as America's. Whether garbage and waste is inundating the nation and harming public health is the focus of the following chapter.

Recycling Can Benefit Businesses

by Laura M. Litvan

About the author: *Laura M. Litvan is a former senior writer for the monthly magazine* Nation's Business.

Aquapore Moisture Systems Inc. seems appropriately based in Phoenix, the Arizona city named after the mythological bird that arose from its ashes: The goods that roll off Aquapore's production lines are made from recycled scrap materials.

The 130-employee company makes a variety of garden hoses from worn-out tires, and this use of these recycled materials has helped Aquapore products wind up on the shelves of environmentally conscious retailers such as Home Depot.

Moreover, in 1992 the company decided to take its commitment to recycling an important step further by forming a team of employees to fashion a comprehensive in-house recycling program. Today that program touches everything from white office paper to large clumps of rubber scrap that were once discarded after the manufacturing process but are now recycled into still more garden hoses.

The new effort is adding to Aquapore's bottom line, with reuse of rubber scrap alone saving the company about $9,000 a month. The savings result from lower disposal costs and from a reduction in the amount of raw materials the company must buy, says marketing manager Kerry LePage, who led the employee team that set up the program.

Reduce and Recycle

Aquapore is one of a growing number of small and midsized businesses exploring ways to reduce solid waste and recycle whatever they can. Once viewed mostly as an altruistic way to do one's part for the environment, recycling now appears to be catching on as a way to cut costs, industry consultants say.

Laura M. Litvan, "Gold from Garbage." Reprinted by permission, *Nation's Business*, July 1995. Copyright 1995, U.S. Chamber of Commerce.

In addition, recent improvements in the market for recycled materials could bolster the trend. The market had been lackluster in recent years as mandatory household curbside recycling programs spurred a glut of cast-off materials. But now, sellers of recyclable materials are finding their positions more favorable.

In 1994, prices for old newspapers, aluminum cans, white office paper, used plastics, and other materials

> *"For companies in the services sector, the typical challenge is to reduce paper use."*

rose for the first time in several years, according to the Environmental Industry Association, in Washington, D.C. And prices for recyclable materials will probably continue to rise, says Philip Bailey, director of marketing development for the National Recycling Coalition, a Washington, D.C., organization that tracks developments in recycling.

Generally, however, the real payoffs still lie elsewhere, according to managers at several companies with recycling programs. In interviews, they indicated that the most cost-effective programs couple recycling with a comprehensive plan to eliminate waste before it occurs.

The considerations for companies vary widely according to their operations, says Steve Hammer, president of Hammer Environmental Consulting, in Brooklyn, New York. Hammer's small-business recycling consultancy is assisting the U.S. Environmental Protection Agency with a voluntary waste-reduction program for industry.

For example, for companies in the services sector, the typical challenge is to reduce paper use, because white office paper and computer paper typically account for 60 to 80 percent of waste in an office setting, Hammer says. Manufacturing companies, meanwhile, should pay particular attention to ways to reuse or recycle waste that results from manufacturing processes, he says.

What's most important, Hammer says, is that you "focus on whatever the biggest part of your waste stream is. Don't worry about two-sided photocopying if you have a million wooden pallets going out the back door."

Aquapore's experience underscores the benefits a company can derive from such focus. The firm's environmental team examined every area of company operations to find opportunities for waste reduction and recycling. It decided the most important things to address were the chunks of tire rubber—typically more than 30,000 pounds a month—left over from the hose-manufacturing process.

To reuse that waste, the company purchased a $20,000 machine that grinds rubber scrap into small pieces that can be used to make more hoses, LePage says. "Now, we don't have any waste from our production process."

Reducing Paper Waste

In Cherry Hill, New Jersey, Jeffrey Lucas is focusing attention on his biggest problem, the proliferation of office paper at Needleman Management Co., a property-management firm. Lucas has made it a mission to reduce paper waste at the 16-employee office since joining the firm as vice president in 1994, and he has already achieved savings.

Lucas says he was astounded by paper waste in the office when he arrived. For example, when one of the 400 tenants in office buildings managed by Needleman would call to request repairs, Needleman employees would fill out a work order in triplicate. Because only one copy of the order was required, the employees would immediately throw the two bottom copies into the trash.

Lucas quickly purchased one-page forms for work orders, and he wound up getting a year's supply for about 8 percent of the cost of the triplicate forms.

He also pushed workers in his office to begin sharing documents instead of making multiple copies, and employees have stopped using cover sheets for faxes. The white office paper that is used is now collected in recycling bins. "The first thing we always ask is, 'Do we need this?'" Lucas says.

For its efforts, Needleman Management saves on trash-collection costs, which have been steadily rising across the country in recent years. Whenever the company disposes of the contents of a regular trash bin, fees for landfill disposal, called "tipping fees," raise the price of collection to $300, Lucas says. The company pays only $40 for removal of an equivalent amount of white paper. Lucas' goal for 1995 was to save $3,000 by shifting more of the company's refuse away from local landfills to recycling facilities.

The Market for Recyclables

One of the biggest deterrents to recycling has been an overabundance of recycled materials, which far outstripped demand for them. The number of mandatory local recycling programs has soared in recent years, from about 600 nationwide in 1986 to about 6,000 today, says Bailey of the National Recycling Coalition. But there weren't enough companies using those materials to make new goods, which kept the prices for items that businesses might recycle, such as white office paper, relatively low, he says.

Now, however, the situation appears to be changing slowly. More manufacturers have invested in equipment that allows them to use recycled materials. Paper companies, for example, increasingly are investing in "de-inking" machines, which allow them to process used paper for reuse. Such manufacturing changes are driving the improvements in the market for recyclables, says Robert Garino, director of commodities at the Institute of Scrap Recycling Industries, in Washington, D.C.

The notion of trash as a commodity gained impetus in 1994 when the Chicago Board of Trade launched a national electronic bulletin board, called the Recyclables Marketplace, which links buyers and sellers of recycled glass and plastics.

"It's become a real win-win solution," says Bailey. "Recycling is where business and the environment meet."

Curbside Recycling Is Effective

by John F. Ruston and Richard A. Denison

About the authors: *John F. Ruston is an economic analyst and Richard A. Denison is a senior scientist for the Environmental Defense Fund, an environmental public interest organization in New York City.*

Recycling conserves energy. Much less energy is needed to make recycled materials into new products compared to beginning the process again with new, "virgin" raw materials. By recycling a ton of materials in a typical curbside recycling program, at least $187 worth of electricity, petroleum, natural gas and coal are conserved, even after accounting for the energy used to collect and transport the materials. In other words, the energy conserved through recycling is about five times as valuable as the average cost of disposing of trash in landfills in the U.S. . . .

Curbside recycling programs can be economically competitive with landfilling and incineration, and can become much more efficient. This is not a matter of theory, but is supported by actual experience in U.S. cities.

Landfilling and incineration are relatively expensive in the more densely populated parts of the nation, and markets for recovered materials are booming. For example, average U.S. prices paid by newsprint recycling mills for old newspapers, the material collected in the greatest quantity in curbside recycling programs, rose from $28 in January 1994 to $112 in January 1995. While market prices for recyclable commodities will always fluctuate, the underlying structure of the market for at least one material, recovered paper, has fundamentally shifted. Prices for recovered paper are expected to remain reasonably high through the rest of the 1990s.

Economic Advantages

In combination, these factors offer a significant economic "credit" to recycling programs. For example, with high market prices for recovered materials,

From pages 20-25 of "Advantage Recycle," a 1995 Environmental Defense Fund report by John F. Ruston and Richard A. Denison. Reprinted by permission of the Environmental Defense Fund. For more information, write EDF, 257 Park Avenue South, New York, NY 10010.

the Seattle Solid Waste Utility is paying its private recycling contractor that serves the northern half of the city $46 for every ton of material they collect, process and sell. In comparison, the fee that the city pays its contractors for garbage collection is [as of February 1995] $53 per ton, and landfill and rail-haul fees for shipping Seattle's trash to landfill in Oregon are about $46 per ton.

Avoided disposal costs and revenues from sales of materials are often not enough to offset the costs of undertaking a curbside collection program. For all the attention focused on disposal costs, the costs of collection are usually the most expensive part of any residential garbage or curbside recycling service. For example, in Houston, Texas, the landfill tip fee [the fee charged to companies for dumping trash] is $18 per ton. In comparison, trash collection costs $105 per ton, recycling (net of processing and sales of materials) costs $115 per ton, and collection and composting of yard trimmings costs $59 per ton in high-participation neighborhoods. With 90,000 households served by Houston's curbside recycling programs, the comparative costs per household per year for these three programs are $105, $43.50 and $25, respectively.

> *"In dense cities, a recycling collection route may be substituted for a garbage collection route altogether."*

The greatest cost increases due to curbside recycling collection programs result from the duplication of regular trash collection routes with new recycling routes. The solution to this problem is to adjust regular trash collection routes, redesign collection trucks and optimize recycling and garbage collection so that the systems work together efficiently. For example, with less materials to collect at each stop, garbage trucks can travel longer routes, or in dense cities, a recycling collection route may be substituted for a garbage collection route altogether. New York, Houston and a number of smaller towns and cities are also testing fleets of collection trucks that can pick up garbage and recyclable materials simultaneously.

Seeking More Efficient Recycling

Attaining efficiencies like these is not a trivial matter, and will take time and effort. Given the rapid changes in recycling and waste management in the 1980s, it is not surprising that many new programs have not begun to gain such efficiencies. In many cities, however, solid waste management officials are exploring several opportunities for increasing the efficiency of the collection of recyclables:

• *Expand recycling programs, collect more materials.* The opportunities for optimizing the system are greatest when recycling diverts a substantial quantity of materials from the waste stream. On a per-ton basis, effective recycling collection programs cost much less than ineffective ones. The Ecodata consulting firm conducted a survey of recycling and refuse collection costs in 60 randomly selected U.S. cities. This study found that recycling collection costs (exclusive of landfill costs or sales of materials) averaged $282 per ton for curbside programs that diverted less than 10% of wastes, $102 per ton for cities that diverted between 10% and 20%, and $93 per ton for cities that diverted more than 20% of their wastes through curbside recycling (not including yard waste composting). In other words, the cities with relatively

> *"Trucks picking up the refuse and recyclables operate at nearly the same efficiency as the garbage-only trucks used previously."*

high recycling rates had costs almost three times less on average than those with low recycling rates. Other results from the Ecodata study were cited [in a January 19, 1995, *Wall Street Journal* article criticizing curbside recycling], but this major finding was left out.

• *Substitution of garbage collection/optimizing routes.* In communities that have refuse collection more than once a week, recycling and/or yard trimmings collection may be substituted for one of the weekly refuse collections. "Little, if any, increase in household MSW [municipal solid waste] management costs may occur with this substitution," according to Franklin Associates, a consulting firm. There are also opportunities for restructuring routes in more densely populated urban areas, where the limit on the total amount of material collected in a shift is determined by truck capacity and/or how much a person can lift in a day.

• *Collecting trash and recyclable materials using the same truck.* Co-collection is the simultaneous collection of recyclables and refuse in the same truck in order to reduce the number of trips. One type of co-collection is the "blue bag" programs, in which bags of recyclable materials are tossed into the collection truck along with the garbage and later pulled out for sorting. Results with this approach in several cities have been mixed at best. Another type of co-collection uses new, multi-compartment trucks that collect and compact garbage in one compartment and recyclable materials in others. A few cities and towns have achieved substantial savings with this approach. New York and Houston both are testing two-compartment compacting trucks, and towns like Loveland, Colorado, and Visalia, California, are using them exclusively.

• *Adding additional materials.* Efficiencies in regular refuse collection are easier to achieve as recovery rates increase. Yard trimmings and additional grades of paper are both targets for communities that seek to increase their overall recovery rates.

Larger Capacities

• *Bigger trucks.* Regular "packer" trucks compact trash and have capacities in the 23–25 cubic yard range. The early generations of recycling trucks were more expensive to operate because they did not compact materials and were limited in the size of their compartments by how high a worker could lift a bin. These trucks filled up more rapidly and had to go off-route to unload more often. Trucks are now in use with side containers for different materials that mechanically lift and empty into the larger main compartments and have 42–45 cubic yards of usable volume.

• *Larger collection containers.* Some recycling programs give households large rolling carts in which to store their recyclable materials. The use of rolling carts also allows solid waste authorities to automate the collection process and can allow for less frequent pick-ups. For instance, the city of Visalia, California, has developed and patented its own divided 110-gallon cart. Residents put commingled recyclables on one side and refuse on the other. The dual compaction vehicles used for co-collection have been converted to fit the carts. Trucks picking up the refuse and recyclables operate at nearly the same efficiency as the garbage-only trucks used previously. The only additional cost results from the extra stop for dropping off the recyclables. Such containers are also used in Milwaukee.

> *"Drop-off centers can be used as a sole recycling method in rural areas as well as an addition to curbside collection programs."*

• *Scheduling.* With regard to the frequency of collection, programs will optimize collection cost with recovery success. Since recyclables do not decay like garbage, collection does not have to be as frequent. In the southern half of Seattle, for example, residents place all recyclable materials in a large rolling cart (with glass in a separate attached container), allowing for collection once a month.

Education and Incentives

• *Education and promotion.* Increasing participation rates and set-out rates through educational and promotional efforts can decrease the net cost of the collection system.

• *Variable can rates (per-unit waste collection charges).* Providing households with an economic incentive to recycle is an efficient way to increase participation and set-out rates. Currently two main systems are being used: pre-paid tag or sticker systems (e.g., in Tompkins County, New York) and per-can volume-based systems (e.g., in Seattle). Charging generation-driven rates for general garbage collection and lower rates for the collection of recyclables can promote both recycling and source reduction. More than 1,000 cities and towns now use some form of variable rate system.

• *Marketing of materials.* Small towns can work together to gain more leverage in selling their materials in commodity markets and in coordinating transportation. The New Hampshire Resource Recovery Association provides this service for the state of New Hampshire, and the New York State Department of Economic Development has helped establish several regional marketing cooperatives in New York. Montana Recycling, a private business, conducts a similar operation in Montana, Wyoming and parts of South Dakota.

• *Alternative collection methods.* Drop-off centers can be used as a sole recycling method in rural areas as well as an addition to curbside collection programs. They can be used to include additional recyclable materials such as batteries, oil, clothes, tires and appliances which do not appear regularly in the waste stream.

Programs in New Jersey and Seattle

The potential of these types of innovations to reduce the costs of recycling will not be resolved through speculation and hypothesis, but through local action in testing and evaluation. The ultimate savings could be significant. For example, Richard Bishop Consultants conducted a detailed study of 12 curbside recycling programs and three intermediate processing facilities in New Jersey chosen to be representative of the state's mix of programs. The firm found costs in 1990 to be $124 per ton without revenues from the sales of materials and $115 per ton including revenues. The study estimated that improved collection, revenue enhancement, administrative refinements, and changes in strategy and program design could reduce overall costs by 41%.

Seattle provides an example of the positive economics of curbside recycling that are readily achievable in mid-sized American cities. The Seattle Solid Waste Utility has designed its collection contracts with the city's private recycling, composting and waste hauling companies so that these contractors are paid under a formula that accounts for the total tonnage of material collected by each program. The city's contracts also allow it to share in the risk and reward of prices in markets for recyclable commodities, a policy that is now paying off nicely.

In 1994, Seattle achieved a 39% curbside recycling/composting collection rate in its residential curbside program and a 44% recycling/composting rate citywide. Detailed analysis of five years' worth of cost data from the Seattle Solid Waste Utility shows that on a systemwide basis (accounting for the costs of all programs together), the addition of curbside recycling and composting services saved the city approximately $2.4 million in 1994, compared to what the city would have had to spend if it had not implemented curbside recycling and composting in 1989. . . .

Recycling provides a cost-effective source of materials for manufacturers, especially as new plants are built and old ones retool over the medium term. Recycling thus simultaneously creates jobs and reduces the cost of packaging and other materials to consumers. These are both direct economic benefits of recycling programs that accrue to curbside recycling as much as any other type of recycling collection system, and should always be considered in a full analysis.

Families Are Avidly Recycling to Reduce Waste

by Carol Leonetti and Jim Motavalli

About the authors: *Carol Leonetti is a freelance journalist in Connecticut. Jim Motavalli is the managing editor of* E Magazine, *a bimonthly magazine covering environmental issues.*

It's hardly an original observation to say that environmentalism begins at home. But living in harmony with the Earth involves more than just turning up at the clearcutting demonstration and mailing annual dues to Greenpeace. The serious environmentalist is green all the way through, not just on the surface. The four families in this viewpoint have made a deep and personal commitment to reducing, reusing and recycling—in some cases, at the cost of considerable domestic comfort.

We're not trying to make our readers feel guilty here. But these paragons can inspire and instruct us with their stories. They've found ingenious and creative solutions to life's more mundane eco-problems. Anyway, relax. Despite all the hard work, they still seem to be having a pretty good time.

The Crandall-Hanifins of Hopkinton, Rhode Island

The chickens are out back feasting on Friday night's stirfry as the worms under the sink munch the morning coffee grounds. Aaron Crandall, 17, is elbow deep in a bag of potato chips, explaining between mouthfuls how it is that a couple of teenagers and their parents throw out only a 30-gallon bag-and-a-half of trash a month.

It's all in what you generate, he says, looking accusingly at the bag that holds the chips.

It once was that the Crandall-Hanifin family of Hopkinton, Rhode Island, had a much harder time keeping their trash in check. For decades they confined their environmentalism to buying their food in bulk at the co-op they founded and ran, reading magazines second-hand, and buying their wares in wide-mouth bottles that could be used over and again.

From "Seriously Green" by Carol Leonetti and Jim Motavalli. Reprinted with permission from *E/The Environmental Magazine* (July/August 1995). Subscription department, PO Box 2047, Marion, OH 43306. Subscriptions are $20/year.

But a not-so-funny thing happened in the sleepy town in the southwest corner of Rhode Island. In 1992, the Hopkinton landfill shut down. So did the one in nearby Westerly. Townspeople were pitted against each other in the debate over disposal. After much deliberation, the town officials decided that Westerly would build a transfer station for itself. Hopkinton townsfolk could only dispose of their trash in area-sanctioned 30-gallon trash bags that sold for $1.35 apiece at local supermarkets. The money would help pay for costs incurred by the transfer station and would force a direct correlation between what people used and what they paid to get rid of it.

Living as Simply as Possible

The shortage of dump space also prompted major recycling efforts by the area. Where in 1992 the Crandall-Hanifins stockpiled their newspapers for the annual Boy Scout drive, now they keep them in a shed out back for monthly trips to the dump. Magazines go there, too, along with cans, bottles, junk mail, office paper, cardboard and some plastics.

"It's a mindset. You just have to get in the habit," says Crandall's mother, Nancy Hanifin.

Not all people of Hopkinton are as trash-conscious as the Crandall-Hanifin family. Most families of four in the area generate about a 30-gallon bag every three days, says Doug St. Clair, foreman of the Westerly transfer station, who noted that recycling increased more than a third when the town instituted its pay-as-you-dump fee.

But the Crandall-Hanifins are not like most people. They live without running water or electricity in a tiny three-bedroom 250-year-old Cape by an old graveyard on the edge of the woods. Propane gas powers the lights in the kitchen and the refrigerator. The outhouse is, well, outside. An Ashley wood stove in the living room burns all day: heating the water in an old beer keg for the morning's showers, taking the chill out of the nighttime air when the family gathers to watch the black-and-white TV that's powered by the battery in Nancy Hanifin's 1983 Toyota.

> *"We like to live as simply as possible. To me the luxuries complicate things."*

"We like to live as simply as possible. To me the luxuries complicate things," says Brian Crandall, 42, a carpenter, who never ceases to be amazed that people are amazed at the way his family lives.

"A lot of my friends are aghast when they first come here, but I think it's great," says Kally Hanifin, 14, who says it's not so hard, really, to live without a hair dryer and other appliances synonymous with being a teenager. "When you grow up without it, you don't miss it as much." She's curled up on the sofa, sketching, chuckling about the frenzy that took over her community during 1994's numerous winter power outages. At her house, it was business as usual.

In terms of trash, business as usual at the Crandall-Hanifins includes "precycling," opting for the right packaging when shopping—choosing a recyclable plastic milk container instead of a wax one, for example, or opting for recyclable cardboard instead of non-recyclable plastic. And there's less need to worry about food packaging.

With consumption, says Crandall, inevitably comes waste, and the

> *"The Burgers produce three pounds [of garbage] a year."*

Crandall-Hanifins are trying to keep theirs in check. "There's a whole lot that can be done for the environment. You can do something about it or do nothing," Crandall says. "It's an individual choice. We're trying to do what we can."

The Burgers of Whitney Point, New York

Environmental fanatics aren't supposed to have normal suburban three-bedroom homes with all of the modern conveniences, including a dishwasher, microwave and Marantz stereo playing Bob Dylan. Their daughters aren't supposed to be sitting in comfortable armchairs playing Nintendo Gameboys, munching Wise potato chips.

No, they're *supposed* to be shivering in unheated log cabins and living on raw tofu. But the Burger family, residents of this Central New York farming community, defy expectations. Their lifestyle doesn't differ markedly from that of the average American family's. And yet the average American family produces three tons of garbage, or 6,000 pounds, every year. The average citizen jettisons 4.3 pounds every *day*.

The Burgers produce three pounds a *year*. And their little garbage bags—filled with cut credit cards, empty toothpaste tubes, used-up pens and, yes, potato chip bags—are going to the Smithsonian Institution to be put on permanent display, right next to the Enola Gay. They've been in *Good Housekeeping, Seventeen, Garbage* and *Family Circle*. They were on Nickelodeon, PBS, and if Linda Ellerbee's show hadn't been cancelled, they'd have been on her show, too.

Yes, the Burgers are probably the most famous recyclers in America. But you wouldn't expect such people to be so, well, *normal*.

Chris Burger, now a county legislator, says he and his wife, Cindy, were inspired by the first Earth Day, in 1970. "We were both in college, and we were protesting against what the big, bad companies were doing. We started to think about what we as individuals could do to change things. The biggest opportunity was in the waste we were producing."

Recycling Pioneers

In 1970, recyclers were pioneers, without convenient curbside service. "The Boy Scouts took the newspapers, and we had to go directly to a scrap metal dealer for the cans," says Chris. "There were all these big trucks coming in, and our little car. We got some funny looks. We found a glass manufacturing place that would take the bottles. Nobody would take the plastics, but we still separated them out and kept the bags out on the back porch—just so we knew how much we were producing." They weren't famous—yet.

Recycling was doubly hard for the Burgers because they were living in an apartment then. But in 1979, they bought five-and-a-half acres in Whitney Point and moved into a homemade Mongolian yurt on the property while Chris designed and built their ecologically correct house.

By the late 80s, the Burgers were filling their 32-gallon garbage can only six times in a year. They really started getting attention around the 20th anniversary of Earth Day, in 1990.

Jennie Burger, 16, who'd been reading *Nintendo Power* magazine as her parents talked, now perked up. "My friends think it's cool that we're kind of famous. But I don't think of

> *"A store manager . . . wondered aloud to Peeples why anyone would pack their groceries in their own canvas totes."*

saving the Earth every time I brush my teeth. Our family only talks about this stuff when reporters come."

By 1993, the Burgers were producing only a half can of garbage a year. "I was raised to waste not, want not," says Cindy, who works at a local medical office. "When we were growing up they told us never to throw away something that still had some use to it. They toss out paper clips in my office, and I yell at them, 'Hey, that affects the bottom line!' It drives me crazy."

In the greenhouse, where the mylar plastic windows rattle from the strong Central New York winds, is *the* garbage—two small bags, set for national display. Jennie—whose chores include washing and reusing plastic straws and sandwich bags—offers an apology: "She," pointing at Debbie, "really likes these granola bars, and their wrappers can't be recycled." Debbie defends herself. "I tried other ones, but they're not the same." Cindy settles the matter. "We're not into depriving the kids over things like this."

The Burgers are proud of what they've done, and they're not going to stop reducing their already very light tread on the Earth, but they're not going to let it drive them nuts. "It's not like we're thinking about this all the time," says Cindy. "It's integrated into our lives. It's second nature, a habit."

The Peeples of Freetown, Maryland

There was the time Tobi Peeples gathered all the cellophane wrap from a month's worth of cereal and cracker boxes and sent the lot to the Nabisco Company, along with a note complaining about excess packaging.

Nabisco didn't respond.

There was the time a store manager came from behind a counter and wondered aloud to Peeples why anyone would pack their groceries in their own canvas totes when baggers could certainly do a faster and more efficient job packing store-provided plastic bags.

Peeples apologized for the inconvenience and bagged her own groceries anyway.

There was the time a neighbor happened upon Peeples' recycling bags, found months' worth of bottles and cans and accused Peeples of being a lush. Peeples patiently explained she was saving them and would recycle them at the dump. The skeptical neighbor reminded her the dump was more than 20 miles away.

Oh, how times have changed. These days, Peeples puts her recyclables curb-side—bottles and cans one week, mixed papers the next—in a program launched in 1995 in Peeples' hometown of Freetown, Maryland, a farm community just seven-tenths of a mile below the Mason-Dixon line. The program was sparked by a grassroots recycling effort by Peeples and her friends, who met up regularly to deposit their recyclables in huge bins donated by the local food store and picked up by the town for the half-hour drive to the dump.

A Garbage Expert

Now that the recycling program is underway, Peeples has taken her efforts elsewhere—to the compost heap.

"Ask me about compost. I really know my poop," says Peeples, a potter by trade who has become somewhat of a local celebrity for her knowledge of all things garbage. People come up to her in county-sponsored booths at local fairs, foul-smelling piles in hand, seeking advice on what went awry. Grade school teachers ask her to visit their classrooms and to show students how to set up mini-composters at home.

> *"People shouldn't deplete the Earth. I like the idea of not using things up and trashing them."*

Peeples, who has two enthusiastic helpers in Jennifer, 16, and Amanda, 10, says her motivation is simple. "I certainly don't want the new dump to go in the empty field across the street and I'm sure other people don't, either," she says.

Peeples has been making similar statements for the past 25 years, starting from the time she was in the Ecology Club in high school. Then, people thought she was a militant, anti-establishment crusader, she recalls. Now that she's earned the title of "Master Composter," a title bestowed upon her after taking numerous classes on composting sponsored by Baltimore County, people are finally listening to what she has to say.

"It's very gratifying to talk to somebody and see the light go on," says Peeples, 40, a former mail carrier and preschool teacher who has experienced new-found success as a potter. "A lot of people who compost wear a suit and tie Monday through Friday and drive a BMW."

Sara Steck and Steven White of Berkeley, California

If you sent Sara Steck a Christmas card last year, chances are someone else will get it this December. Steck saves the cards that don't have writing on the flip side of the picture. She cuts them at the fold, writes her own message, and sends them out the following year as holiday postcards. "I also use cereal boxes and things for postcards. I hate to throw anything away," says Steck, who has been watching her trash disposal for most of her life.

As a child, Steck, now 39, spent many summers camping with her parents in the Sierra Nevadas. "There you bury your food waste and you carry your trash with you." She still buries her food waste, sort of. It goes out on the back porch in the worm bin, which sits next to similar containers for glass and aluminum. Steck stacks newspapers on the front porch, and collects mixed papers in the kitchen and the second bedroom, which serves as a study for Steck, a teacher, and her fiance Steven White, a woodworker.

Little Trash

Steck has been recycling everything from cans to yard waste in her Berkeley, California, bungalow since she settled there in 1989. The only thing the city doesn't pick up curbside is plastic, so Steck and White try not to buy any.

The current contents of their lone trash bag, which dangles from a nail under the sink and once carried vegetables home from the supermarket: a soy milk carton that's laminated and lined with foil, a plastic seal that covered a cork, paper towels that were used to mop up the cat's hairball, a wax milk carton and assorted plastic wraps.

Steck and White accumulate a bag to a bag and a half of trash a week. The couple buys in bulk at the local natural food store, thereby cutting down on packaging. The plastic bags they bring the food home in get washed and reused during the next trip to the store. Steck and White use canvas bags to tote their groceries home from the supermarket. They bring their coffee bags back to the coffee shop to get refilled, they take cloth lunch bags to work.

"I think that people shouldn't deplete the Earth. I like the idea of not using things up and trashing them," says Steck. "I've never seen a landfill other than in pictures. It's kind of depressing to think about."

Technology Is Improving Plastics Recycling

by Robert Steuteville

About the author: *Robert Steuteville is a senior editor for* BioCycle, *a monthly magazine covering recycling topics.*

Postconsumer plastics recycling is still relatively new. There is a considerable amount of innovation taking place around the country with both processing and product development. Because markets are difficult to predict and impossible to control, plastics recyclers need to focus on manageable portions of the business or operation. These include efficiency, flexibility in feedstock and, in the case of a manufacturer, the competitiveness and quality of the final product. An example of innovation on the processing side can be found at Total Recycling in Boswell, Pennsylvania, a 200 ton/day materials recovery facility (MRF). Total Recycling is using optical technology to improve its manual sort of commingled plastics.

Mixed containers from curbside programs—which Total Recycling has been processing since the late 1980s—are conveyed up to the company's elevated sorting line. A magnet removes ferrous—the only automated sorting equipment on Total Recycling's line. Easily recognizable plastic—HDPE [high-density polyethylene] milk jugs and detergent bottles and PET [polyethylene terephthalate] soda bottles— are then picked off the line manually, followed by aluminum cans, glass and pieces of trash.

Differentiating Plastics

That leaves "other" plastic containers, which is where Total Recycling uses the optical technology. A $120,000 grant was awarded by the Pennsylvania Department of Environmental Protection (DEP), to conduct a year-long study of the Kisspotlight system developed by Frankel Industries of Edison, New Jersey. It markets for $17,500 and utilizes optical dispersion and refractive techniques in various wavelengths to change the appearance of plastic bottles on the picking line, allowing for sorting by resin type.

Robert Steuteville, "Plastics Recyclers Stay on the Cutting Edge," *Biocycle*, May 1996. Copyright by JG Press, Inc. Reprinted with permission.

The Kisspotlight is designed to remove Polyvinyl Chloride (PVC) contamination in PET, a plastics recovery challenge because small amounts of PVC can seriously degrade batches of PET. However, it also aids in differentiating PET-G [glycol] "custom PET" and polystyrene from PET and PVC, explains Sonya Eppley, recycling coordinator for Total Recycling. The unit is six to eight feet long, is waist high, and contains a see-through mesh conveyor where two pickers are stationed, wearing special goggles. The specially dispersed light shines up through the conveyor, giving different resins distinct appearances—i.e. PET soda bottles appear bright as if they were light bulbs, while PVC appears dark blue. According to Henry Frankel, who has a patent on the technology, the goal is to help recyclers improve the quality of their bales, which then reduces the need for additional sorting at later stages in the plastics recovery process. Fewer sorting steps ultimately increase the economic viability of plastics recycling. The system was tested in Total Recycling's MRF and two other facilities in Pennsylvania in 1996, all funded by the DEP grant.

Increasing Value Added

In 1991, Sandhill Plastics Inc. began using a process to make four by eight foot plastic sheeting from unwashed HDPE. "It had kind of a mottled appearance—but it was very functional," says Jim Weber, president of the Kearney, Nebraska firm. The sheeting, as thick as plywood, was used to line manure spreaders, provide flooring for hog pens and serve other agricultural purposes.

With the help of funding from the Nebraska Department of Environmental Quality (DEQ), which Weber used to put together a financial package, the company purchased extrusion equipment. This enabled Sandhill to make higher value sheeting that could be sold into a broader range of markets. It required, however, that Sandhill purchase clean postconsumer HDPE flake. This system left Weber very vulnerable when the prices of plastics skyrocketed in late 1994 and the first half of 1995. At times, Sandhill was paying 45 cents lb. ($900/ton) for feedstock. "I feel very fortunate to have survived, because I saw a lot of people go under," Weber says.

In the fall of 1995, Weber made a second upgrade which will help the company in future market volatility. A $119,000 DEQ grant was provided to purchase a miniwash system and separation tank. Now plastic flake is purchased in the unwashed form, which saves about eight cents/lb. If the price of flake sky-

"Fewer sorting steps ultimately increase the economic viability of plastics recycling."

rockets again, Weber can save even more money by buying plastic in baled form (Sandhill has a grinder at the plant which is currently used to reprocess scrap from the company's manufacturing operation). The bottom line is that the company can process various forms of feedstock, increasing its flexibility.

In 1995, Sandhill processed 700,000 lbs. of HDPE, about evenly split between natural and colored grades. About one-quarter of the company's feedstock is purchased locally in small quantities. The rest is shipped in from western Iowa, where the larger-scale plastics processors are located. These processors, in turn, purchase HDPE collected in both Nebraska and Iowa, Weber says. While Sandhill lost money in 1995, "we've seen a definite increase in profitability in the last quarter," he adds. "Business has rebounded and the margins have returned."

Targeting a New Feedstock

"We market our products as recycled, but that will only take you so far," says Donald Jacobsmeyer, president of Combined Plastics Recycling Inc. of St. Louis, Missouri. "People love to talk about it because it is recycled—but their first question is 'how much does it cost.'" As a result, the two year old company focuses on developing products from mixed plastics that are cost-competitive with the conventional alternatives.

One example is a wheel block for parking lots. A concrete wheel block costs between $13 and $15. "Our plastic wheel blocks cost $16 to $18, but they weigh only 45 lbs. (one quarter the weight of concrete)," Jacobsmeyer explains. "By the time you get the block shipped and installed, ours costs the same or less than the alternative." The challenge is convincing the engineers, planners and property owners that the new recycled plastic product is better than the old concrete variety. One selling point is that plastic doesn't chip or crumble over time like concrete; the product comes with a 20-year guarantee.

In Combined Plastics' latest venture, Jacobsmeyer is utilizing a feedstock that is currently disposed in large quantities—shrink wrap. "That material makes up a large part of what is thrown away at distribution centers and plants," he says. "Every pallet they unwrap is covered in polyethylene. It's no secret that with all the shrink wrap that is thrown away every day, you could make a Mount Everest."

Combined Plastics received a $100,000 grant from the Missouri Department of Natural Resources to purchase grinding equipment to handle shrink wrap. The equipment became operational in early April, 1996. The first loads of material came from grocery chains in the St. Louis area with distribution centers and multiple store locations, Jacobsmeyer says. The company is working out arrangements with haulers to collect the shrink wrap separately. Because it is so lightweight, it is very expensive to haul. "If they are throwing it away anyway, I must show the haulers that it costs the same or less to take it here—that is the trick of the trade," he explains. If the material is free of contamination, no tipping fee is charged.

For collection, an extra container is required at the generator's loading dock. The sources for Combined Plastics feedstock are located in a 60 mile radius around St. Louis. Jacobsmeyer is hoping to get enough material to keep the grinder operating at capacity (processing two to three million pounds/year). A new product is planned using the new feedstock—mail box posts. These L-shaped posts are solid and designed to look like painted four by four wooden posts, he adds.

The Effectiveness of Recycling Is Exaggerated

by Roger Starr

About the author: *Roger Starr is a contributing editor for the* City Journal, *a quarterly publication of the Manhattan Institute, a New York City public policy research organization.*

A week before the 1994 elections, Mayor Rudolph Giuliani received a piece of very good news from the New York City Department of Sanitation, perhaps the last good news he was to receive for quite some time. The department reported that the market for used newsprint (the paper on which newspapers are printed) had become so strong that the city would now receive $10,000 a day for bringing discarded newspapers to wastepaper dealers instead of paying the dealers $10,000 a day for taking papers off the city's hands. The prospective net savings enabled the mayor to reduce the department's annual budget by $5 million a year—a tidy sum, though, in effect, it constitutes less than 2 percent of the department's $326 million budget for waste removal and street cleaning while newsprint constitutes about 8 percent of its total waste stream.

Mayor Giuliani's good news was immediately mistranslated into great news by advocates who demand that recycling be declared the means of first choice for the disposal of garbage, or as the industry terms it, municipal solid waste. The rise in the market price of used newsprint may be permanent, as they suggest, or, as others believe, it may reflect only a not-unusual fluctuation in market demand. In any case, the role of recycling in waste management depends not on what newsprint is worth to the paper industry but on the effectiveness and costs of recycling all other wastes.

Handling the Waste Stream

A report prepared by Franklin Associates and released in September 1994 (on recycled paper) by the environmentally conscious organization Keep America Beautiful, Inc., concluded that the maximum that can be achieved by the year

Roger Starr, "Recycling: Myths and Realities." Reprinted with permission of the author and the *Public Interest*, no. 119, Spring 1995, pp. 28-41; © 1995 by National Affairs, Inc.

2000 in recycling and composting is between 25 percent and 35 percent of the total waste stream. It further stated that an increase to the midpoint estimate, 30 percent, would simply meet the probable increase in the total tonnage of municipal waste in the United States.

The 70 percent of the waste stream that will not be made to disappear by recycling and composting will have to be disposed of by landfilling and incineration or, as it is often described, waste-to-energy production. Paper, more flammable than most materials, has an important role to play in this. Though it does not contain more British Thermal Units than many types of plastic containers in the waste stream, it ignites immediately, helping the plastic to ignite. Thus, the widespread, but misguided, belief among conscientious citizens that recycling is the wave of the future only harms our ability to deal effectively with the entire waste stream.

> *"The 70 percent of the waste stream that will not be made to disappear by recycling and composting will have to be disposed of by landfilling and incineration."*

Paper Chase

In New York, this misconception was fueled even further by Kendall Christiansen, Chairman of the Citywide Recycling Advisory Board, who described the $5 million (annualized) windfall as "not just a home run, but a grand slam." Thus, he introduced his prediction that the city would collect and sell every ton of discarded paper, instead of disposing of it in the Fresh Kills dump on Staten Island or storing it in warehouses. He saw a future in which the Sanitation Department, having learned the value of one waste product, would expand its vision to include every recycling goal under the sun.

While Christiansen's enthusiasm is admirable, the sudden rise in the value of old newspapers requires a second look. Christiansen suggests that new capital investment in plants that recycle old ink-covered newsprint into fresh newsprint is largely responsible for the increased demand for old newsprint. Dr. Harvey Alter, Manager of Resources Policy for the U.S. Chamber of Commerce and an acknowledged national authority on waste disposal, points to other factors. He notes that wide swings in newsprint demand have not been unusual, and that they probably reflect variations in newspaper advertising lineage and circulation figures. Both of these, in turn, reflect seasonal and general economic conditions that are subject to rapid change.

Predicting the future value of secondhand newsprint is a chancy business, and both dealers and municipalities might find themselves in trouble if they make long-range investments in trucks and facilities based on a possible temporary surge in newsprint demand. Above all, newsprint value has little or no bearing on the resale value of other assertedly recyclable materials.

Accurately Appraising the Costs

Jacques Besnainou, a French chemical engineer whose firm, Ecobilan, served as consultant to the European Economic Union, suggests that newsprint reconditioning plants are likely to be sited near paper manufacturing facilities rather than near the cities producing large quantities of used newsprint. He argues that air pollution attributable to the truck transport of used paper products to distant reconditioning plants and the energy requirements of both the transport and the reconditioning process must be taken into account to appraise accurately the social and economic cost or benefit of increasing paper recycling far beyond present levels.

Besnainou also emphasizes a salient characteristic of overstretched efforts to collect widely distributed materials of any kind. Collectors soon discover that what they picked up first were the easy loads: newspapers from the newsstands, printing offices, and major public and private buildings. To continue to increase tonnage level, the collector, whether it is the municipality or a private dealer, must be satisfied with smaller quantities at more widely separated spots, resulting in higher costs and lower profits, if any.

A sound waste-disposal program has to involve three elements: recycling, incineration, and landfilling the incombustible residual materials. A program eliminating too large a portion of the wood-fiber products might require their replacement by much more expensive fuel. Thus, while increased demand for waste paper should help reduce the cost of getting rid of it, that cost saving can be quickly wiped out if, treated as a "merit good," concentrating on paper resale results in upsetting a more economically sound balance of the three major waste disposal disciplines.

"A sound waste-disposal program has to involve three elements: recycling, incineration, and landfilling the incombustible residual materials."

This discussion does not refer to a fourth discipline—reducing the amount of materials that become waste by cutting back on the packaging of consumer items. Though waste-disposal philosophers emphasize the economic beauty of such a discipline, it, if practical at all, is surely not within the control of the municipality in which consumers live and throw away what they do not use.

The Virtue of Recycling?

Although governments in recent years have concentrated their attention on human problems like crime, education, and civil decay, two physical problems—water supply and waste disposal—continue to demand urgent attention.

After establishing the Resource Conservation and Recovery Act, a clumsy and grossly unsuccessful program that was intended to remedy inadequate disposal of urban wastes, the federal government left solid-waste disposal problems mainly to local governments. Cities, whose dense populations make those problems critical, had to find landfill replacements for old garbage dumps that could not meet new, thoroughly justified standards, most of them established by state governments. These standards include procedures for collecting and burning methane gas produced in landfills by rotting organic wastes and for trapping and purifying leachate, the rainwater that penetrates the massed refuse, which poses the danger of bacterial and chemical contamination of groundwater and surface streams. . . .

As public opposition to landfill disposition of urban wastes swelled, major American organizations dedicated to the protection of the natural environment were persuaded that waste-to-energy was simply the proponents' slang for bad old incineration. They remain convinced that the third option—recycling—is not only the most efficient but also the most righteous choice for disposing of municipal waste.

In their view, recycling of refuse into newly usable materials and artifacts is a process free of the threat of toxic chlorine compounds that are produced, even if later destroyed or recaptured by state-of-the-art technology, in the incineration process. These organizations insisted that reusing already existing products, like corrugated cardboard, glass bottles, plastic containers and sheets, newsprint, and cans, rescued from the waste stream and subsequently rehabilitated can be an efficient and economical procedure. It is far less wasteful than simply burying them in the ground.

Finally, the recycling process is given top priority by the environmental organizations and their followers because it involves the citizenry as a whole in a daily or weekly reminder of the importance of environmental protection. Recycling, the organizations insist, enlivens public consciousness and opens new vistas of public participation in the agenda of environmentalism.

> *"The apparent success in reusing some parts of the waste stream enabled recycling advocates to promise unlimited future applications."*

This view—attaching priority to recycling as the key to disposing of municipal waste—became a virtuous cause in which legislators and editorialists found common ground. It also slowly but surely energized entrepreneurs to establish themselves as middlemen between municipalities and existing businesses, like newspaper publishers and plastic-container manufacturers, that are able to reuse materials salvaged from the waste stream. However, reuse is possible only after the materials have been subjected to separation, sorting, cleansing, and sometimes pulverization, in order to make them reusable. These entrepreneurs, who include the wastepaper dealers already mentioned, are market-oriented and may pay the municipality (or the commercial haulers) for the recyclables they beneficiate, demand to be paid for taking them, or refuse to accept them under any circumstances.

The Utility of Incineration

As long as this degree of recycling does not interfere with waste-to-energy or landfilling, or impose noncompetitive costs on the municipality, it is constructive, especially when it eliminates incombustible glass and metals from the waste-to-energy intake. However, a large part of municipal solid waste consists of organic material—discarded foodstuffs—that cannot be reused. The apparent success in reusing some parts of the waste stream enabled recycling advocates to promise unlimited future applications, while considerations like the costs of collection and separation of salvaged items, storage, purification for reuse, and transportation, remain unexamined.

Ordinarily civic leaders and potential candidates for local public office follow the costs of municipal government very closely. They are quick to charge officeholders with unwarranted extravagance, if not graft, when they find that they have chosen programs that could be matched by cheaper alternatives. Yet, municipal and state legislators and administrators—except for those actually charged with the job of getting rid of the wastes or regulating the private haulers who

> *"A very large part of the municipal waste stream consists of food particles that cannot be recycled."*

chose to do that—managed to retain their popularity with environmentally conscious voters. They obscured the actual costs of recycling by outbidding each other with promises to establish an ever-higher recycling target, expressed as a percentage of the total waste stream that would disappear into new economic production.

The conclusion to be drawn from a comparison of the three alternatives is obvious to anyone who is actually engaged in managing urban wastes: "alternative" disposal methods are not, in fact, viable. A sensible program for disposing of municipal waste would, first of all, minimize moral overtones and emphasize material realities. A program free of moral overtones in any large city would make use of all three methods of disposal.

Such a program would recognize that a very large part of the municipal waste stream consists of food particles that cannot be recycled. This same part of the stream—smelly, infectious, attractive to unpopular animal life—is the least welcome anywhere and can best be rendered harmless by high temperature incineration. . . .

When Your Garbage Leaves Home

New York City provides an interesting example of the practical limitations of recycling waste materials. Its Sanitation Department records that all recyclables diverted from the waste stream constituted about 14 percent of the approximately 11,000 tons of waste handled by it every day in June 1994. The 11,000-ton figure does not include waste handled by private haulers who remove it from all commercial establishments. Some of the unrecyclable remainder of the commercial waste is dumped at the Fresh Kills landfill (for which a substantial fee is charged the private haulers) or, more likely, trucked less expensively by them to other states, most of which accept it with growing reluctance.

On the appointed weekdays in each section of every sanitation district in New York City, black plastic bags, blue plastic bags, and stacks of newspapers and periodicals more or less neatly tied line the sidewalks to be picked up by one of the three designated, but otherwise identical, truck fleets of the city's Sanitation Department. Black bags go into the trucks that collect raw, unrecyclable garbage. Blue bags go into the trucks that collect intermingled recyclable glass, plastic, and metal. Each of the bags is filled by householders. Newspapers, lashed together, go into trucks assigned to pick up nothing but recyclable paper and cardboard.

Those blue bags are surely the bags of virtue, reflecting the stalwart civic effort of householders to comply with Local Law 19, which requires the Sanitation Department to collect no less than 4,250 tons of recyclables each day now that the law has been in effect since 1990. The black-bag garbage trucks outnumber the blue-bag recycling trucks by at least three to one. Simple arithmetic suggests that the legal minimum tonnage of recyclables is not nearly achievable.

"The asking prices for recycled products are as much as 15 percent higher than those of competitive virgin products."

It seems likely that the warm consciousness of virtue that keeps many civic-minded householders faithful to recycling is based on a mistaken notion of what happens to the glass jars and bottles, the plastic flasks and containers, and the tin and aluminum cans that householders collect for reuse.

The householders are likely to imagine that some invisible hand separates and classifies the different types of recyclables, which are commingled in the home, and guides them, almost good as new, back to the manufacturers who filled them before, thus presumably saving civilization great chunks of raw material and fabrication expense.

Lost Value

Alas, the carefully saved glass bottles and jars meet a very different fate after they disappear into the rear end of the blue-bag sanitation truck's enclosed body. As one member of the two-person sanitation-truck team pulls levers, an immense jaw of steel reaches back over the trough into which one or more blue bags have been deposited, cramming them further into the body of the truck. There, a blade, rising from the bottom inside the truck body, presses the newly acquired bags against the rear face of an immense piston, crushing the bags and gradually forcing the piston to retract toward the inside front of the truck body.

In the process, most of the glass bottles, cans, and jars inside the bags are smashed or shattered. Glass shards and glass dust mix with the plastic containers, foodstuffs, and refuse that some less-conscientious householders forgot to wash out of their discards. Inevitably, the reuse value of the carefully saved containers is compressed with them, until the fragments are subject to a new, costly, and only partially effective process for restoring them to marketability. . . .

Industry Leaders' Suggestions

It seems clear to everyone who does not live near the prospective site for a major landfill or a future waste-to-energy plant that one or both of these unwanted neighbors is necessary because recycling alone will not by itself absorb the discards of urban civilization. Some industry leaders urge the privatization of the entire process, including the organic wastes that are not now included under the heading of recyclables. These, advocates claim, could be composted like organic yard waste in the backyard of the city, a process that, perhaps mistakenly, sounds like planned disintegration through rotting. This is a smelly potential health hazard, no more welcome in any neighborhood than landfills, incinerators, or hospitals for the mentally ill.

Other industry leaders suggest that the recycling business needs what they call "a level playing field." By this they mean that products made with recycled material should be as readily acceptable to potential buyers as anything made from previously unused fibers and chemicals. Their specific proposal, already adopted by some governmental institutions, gives a new slant to the meaning of "level." It suggests that all local and state governments, together with the national government, be required to purchase and use a defined percentage of their office supplies and other sundries made from recycled materials. They recommend further that governments be allowed to accept bids, even though the asking prices for recycled products are as much as 15 percent higher than those of competitive virgin products. Such price concessions favoring recycled products are already offered by some local governments. While they demonstrate that recycling is not the cheap and easy matter that would make a substantial market share easy to obtain, this favoritism is simply a tax that prefers one class of producer over all others. . . .

Garbage Doom

Urban Americans have every right to worry over how long it will take, and what sacrifices will have to be made, before an adequately comprehensive set of systems will be available to keep their communities from burying themselves in their own detritus. That seems now to be the inevitable consequence of the confusion between the virtue of recycling and its political attractiveness, and the simple fact that, even with the most efficient collection and reprocessing systems in the world, recycling cannot make the waste stream disappear. To accomplish that, an industrialized society, concentrated in relatively dense communities, needs to strike a balance between recycling and waste-to-energy. It also must find land space for burying the burned and sanitized residues of those two processes.

The modest success in recycling specific materials is interpreted by too many elected officials as a sound reason for pleasing their constituents by refusing to consider waste-to-energy plants and modern landfills as essential parts of a waste-disposal program. If they think deeply about the issue, they may assume that when the day comes on which there will be no place to put the waste that cannot be recycled—

> *"An industrialized society . . . needs to strike a balance between recycling and waste-to-energy."*

surely more than 50 percent of the daily tonnage—they, the legislators, will be free of their earthly cares, to say nothing of their freedom from having to worry about reelection.

But as the pulp mills save old paper from the incinerators, and thus strongly discourage the development of waste-to-energy, the day of garbage doom comes closer. The image of the garbage barge that, like the Flying Dutchman, sailed from port to port because none would accept its cargo, becomes more relevant. Careful students of this unglamorous subject, here and abroad, are already looking at their watches.

Curbside Recycling Is Not Effective

by Jeff Bailey

About the author: *Jeff Bailey is a staff reporter for the* Wall Street Journal *daily newspaper.*

Remember the garbage barge? Plying coastal waters in 1987 without any place to dump its unsightly cargo, it startled the nation into getting serious about recycling household trash.

Tens of millions of Americans now make a daily ritual of sorting their garbage for collection by curbside-recycling programs, which cover one-third of U.S. households. Environmental groups, government and industry alike lend their support. And why not? Residential recycling—up tenfold since 1987—is widely credited with conserving dwindling garbage-dump space, saving money and protecting the environment.

Besides, it makes people feel good. For many, a little trash sorting has become a form of penance to acknowledge that the values of our high-consumption society don't always nurture the soul. "People are worried about the planet," says environmentalist Paul Connett of Canton, New York. "They ask: 'What can we do?' They can do something about trash."

Unnecessary and Costly

There's just one problem. At least by any practical, short-term measure, curbside recycling doesn't pay. It costs residents and local governments hundreds of millions of dollars more than can be recouped by selling the sorted trash. It requires huge new fleets of collection trucks that add to traffic congestion and pollution. And it does so at a time when landfill space turns out to be both plentiful and extremely cheap.

What's more, some critics say, household recycling gives people such an easy environmental fix that they have started paying less attention to such serious, complex problems as air and water pollution. Trash sorting, contends environ-

Jeff Bailey, "Curbside Recycling Comforts the Soul, but Benefits Are Scant," *Wall Street Journal*, January 19, 1995. Reprinted by permission of the *Wall Street Journal*, © 1995 Dow Jones & Company, Inc. All rights reserved worldwide.

mental fund-raiser Roger Craver, has "done more to hurt the environmental movement than anything I can think of."

How consumers came to embrace household recycling after decades of indifference is a bizarre tale of misperceptions and mistaken assumptions that snowballed into a national myth. The movement was helped along by faulty analogies between commercial and industrial recycling—which are often cost-effective and environmentally friendly—and the much dicier proposition of house-to-house collection. And it benefited from the fact that a lot of people firmly believe recycling is the right thing to do, regardless of cost or provable environmental benefits.

Garbage Market Emerges

It might not have happened, though, if not for a barge named Mobro that owed its existence, it turns out, not to a shortage of dump space but to a dramatic change in the trash-disposal market—and a mob-inspired effort to make the most of it.

Through most of history, of course, there was no garbage market at all: People merely heaved their trash outside for pigs and goats to feed on. About 200 years ago, people began burying trash near their homes and then bringing it to town dumps. But the development of the so-called sanitary landfill in the 1970s and 1980s altered the basic economics of garbage disposal.

"At least by any practical, short-term measure, curbside recycling doesn't pay."

The modern landfill featured a clay or plastic liner, plumbing to collect runoff liquids and to control methane and a daily layer of fresh dirt to keep rats and birds from scavenging. Engineering studies were used to help pick dump locations less likely to foul groundwater.

With construction costs of up to $500,000 an acre, a landfill piled 300 feet high turned out to be many times more economical—and no more environmentally troublesome—than one piled to 50 feet. So entrepreneurs built larger dumps. By the mid-1980s, it actually began to pay to ship trash long distances to bigger, cheaper dumps in less-populated regions.

Financing a Voyage

One of the local haulers seeking to profit from the regional price disparities was Salvatore Avellino. A reputed captain in the Lucchese organized-crime family, Mr. Avellino was allegedly mob overseer of all trash hauling on Long Island, New York. (He went to prison in 1994 after pleading guilty to conspiracy charges in the murders of two rebel haulers.)

In 1987, Mr. Avellino met with Lowell Harrelson, a Bay Minette, Alabama, man who envisioned a fleet of barges connecting New York to $5- and $10-a-ton Southern dumps. The boss was interested, recalls Michael J. Cahill, attorney for the Long Island town of Islip, and haulers from other communities in the New York City area joined in to finance the first trip of the Mobro. In March 1987 it shoved off with 3,186 tons of trash on board.

But Mr. Harrelson, an admitted "novice in the waste business," didn't sufficiently nail down an agreement with a dump. Though he initially planned to unload in Louisiana, Mr. Harrelson tried to line up something closer once the barge set sail, and he contacted Larry Meadows, county manager in rural Jones County, North Carolina. "We had room," Mr. Meadows says of the dump. "And we certainly were looking for something to help with the decreasing tax base."

But before Mr. Meadows and other county officials could consult with state regulators, the Mobro steamed into Morehead City, North Carolina, ready to unload. "It was already en route when he talked to us," Mr. Meadows says. "That had us questioning the deal." What was the rush? Was there hazardous waste mixed in? Who were these people?

The questions were never pursued. State officials took over and ordered the Mobro back out to sea. The news media got word. And everywhere the Mobro went—Louisiana, Mexico, the Bahamas—it was rejected. The U.S. Southeast had (and still has) an abundance of dump capacity and was accepting thousands of tons a week of waste arriving by truck from the Northeast. But nobody wanted to take this famous load of trash. After two months at sea, the Mobro returned to New York, and the trash was later burned in a Brooklyn incinerator.

> *"Big trash-handling companies certainly knew there was no landfill crisis but helped spread the word of one anyway."*

There were various reasons the Mobro's mission failed: Some officials and dump owners shared Mr. Meadows's worry that the unexpected barge concealed toxic waste. Others merely came to see the barge as bad news and didn't want the publicity that came with accepting New York's unwanted garbage. The availability of dump space was never an issue.

But that is not how it played in newspapers and on television, where it quickly became an ominous symbol of a nation buried in garbage. "This barge really dramatizes the nationwide crisis we face with garbage disposal," New York environmentalist Walter Hang told [talk-show host] Phil Donahue, in a declaration typical of many broadcast from the Mobro.

Mr. Hang and other environmentalists who had previously met with little success in selling recycling to the public now could offer an alternative to a future full of Mobros: household recycling. "An advertising firm couldn't have designed a better vehicle than a garbage barge," says John Ruston, a recycling official at the Environmental Defense Fund.

Advocacy groups such as the EDF helped convince the public and government officials that door-to-door collection of recyclables was needed. They also linked up with hundreds of local Nimby ("not in my back yard") groups opposing dumps and incinerators in their areas. "Recycle. It's the everyday way to save the world" was the message in a series of EDF television and print ads supported by $125 million in free air time from the Ad Council.

No Dwindling Dump Space

Perhaps because garbage is local and visible, it receives more attention from news outlets than any other environmental topic. And coverage of household recycling was laudatory right from the beginning. But plenty of people could have challenged the premises of the movement. Big trash-handling companies certainly knew there was no landfill crisis but helped spread the word of one anyway, even as they increased their dump and incineration capacity. The perception of a shortage helped them raise dump fees and fatten profits.

Dean L. Buntrock, chairman and chief executive officer of WMX Technologies Inc., had loaded up on dump space in the 1970s and 1980s. He had also started a trade group and lobbying arm, the National Solid Waste Management Association. After the Mobro voyage, the group was widely quoted asserting that dump capacity was shrinking, and some federal and state officials relied on its data.

The public's belief in a garbage crisis helped WMX (formerly Waste Management Inc.) and its competitors pass along huge price increases to municipalities and other customers. And it helped push up profits at WMX, based in Oak Brook, Illinois, to $684.8 million in 1990, a rapid leap that more than doubled the 1987 level of $327.1 million.

Talk of a crisis was misleading, WMX now acknowledges. Though the company observed some temporary local shortages, "we never believed there was a disposal crisis," says Jane Witheridge, a vice president. "Did we go out and do a public-policy education program on that? No." Given the public mood, she adds, it is unlikely the company would have been believed. Instead, WMX was still telling customers as recently as 1993: "This nation is quickly running out of places to dispose of trash."

"Seventy-seven percent [of U.S. consumers] think household recycling is the solution. About half believe curbside programs pay for themselves."

After the Mobro's voyage, the Environmental Protection Agency [EPA] also publicly backed the view that there was a crisis. Warning in September 1988 of a "deluge of garbage," J. Winston Porter, then assistant administrator for solid waste, called for each state and municipality to devise a voluntary recycling plan that would cut disposal needs nationally by 25%. "We're running out of space to bury it," he wrote in a report titled "The Solid Waste Dilemma."

But a look at that report, and other EPA research compiled about the same time, suggests there wasn't so much to worry about. One study, done in connection with new environmental rules for dumps, found that dumps in the U.S. had an average of 21.3 years of remaining capacity. And even this figure was deceptively low because capacity could be multiplied just by increasing the size of existing facilities.

"I've always wondered where that crap about a landfill-capacity crisis came from," says Allen Geswein, an EPA solid-waste official and one of the authors of the study. The EPA, when asked, now agrees that there isn't any capacity shortage. Yet materials the agency continues to distribute warn of a shortage and cite it as one of the reasons for recycling.

State and Local Recycling

Following the voyage of the Mobro and the EPA's call to arms, more than 40 states set their own recycling goals, ranging from 25% to 70% of trash, often with little effort to gauge the cost. Municipalities rallied residents, at times exaggerating the benefits. San Jose, California, rolled out its curbside-recycling program in 1993, warning: "All over the country we're running out of landfill space." Within its own borders, San Jose actually has between 30 and 50 years of dump capacity, according to city environmental officials.

Los Angeles also embarked on an ambitious recycling program, at enormous expense. City officials predicted dump fees would soar and thus make curbside recycling more viable economically. Instead, dump prices plunged, recycling chief Joan Edwards reports.

Since the market hasn't cooperated, some states have enacted taxes and fees to prop up the recycling effort.

"Curbside programs account for only one-seventh of U.S. recycling."

Iowa now imposes a $4.25-a-ton tax on disposal at dumps and gives the money to recycling businesses and municipal programs. Pennsylvania's $2-a-ton disposal tax has yielded $160 million since 1988 to distribute to local recycling programs and businesses. All together, states budgeted more than $250 million to subsidize recycling in 1994, according to *Waste Age* magazine.

The result of all this: a public that needlessly fears a garbage crisis and holds unrealistic expectations about recycling. Polls increasingly show that U.S. consumers rate trash the No. 1 environmental problem, and 77% think household recycling is the solution. About half believe curbside programs pay for themselves. Parents and children most often define a good environmentalist as "someone who recycles and encourages others to recycle."

To a small but growing number of critics, this last impression shows how curbside recycling has become a dangerous placebo. Mr. Craver, the environmental fund-raiser, fears some people have stopped contributing to environmental groups in part because they feel they have fulfilled their responsibility by faithfully sorting their trash. "It's like attending church on Easter," he says.

"Having recycled, people think they've done their part. [But] consumer waste is insignificant compared to other environmental problems."

"It's an upper-class thing," maintains Susan Young, sanitation chief in Minneapolis. "This is all about guilt."

Recycling has nevertheless become the centerpiece of many schools' ecology lessons, turning children into forceful advocates. In a poll by Peter D. Hart, 63% of children said they had lobbied their parents to recycle. No wonder. The EPA's popular Garbage Gremlin comic book for lower elementary grades has this plot: Garbage dump almost full. Girl proposes recycling. Gremlin thwarts recycling. Boy thwarts gremlin. Boy gets girl.

> *"Collecting recyclables will probably mean more trucks on the road because, compared with trash headed for a dump, recyclables can't be compacted as completely en route."*

The EPA's recommended upper-grade curriculum appeals directly to teachers' pocketbooks, warning that the trash crisis "diverts public funds from other important needs such as education." At Jeanne Meadows Elementary School in San Jose, "recycling is the thread that pulls everything together" in environmental lessons, says project specialist Steve Corelis. He teaches about "dwindling landfills," though they aren't dwindling locally, and has students sort paper, aluminum, glass and milk cartons. "We end up trashing the milk cartons" because there are no local buyers, he confides. "But the kids don't know that."

Kathy Berghoff, a Chicago mother of three who concluded as a result of her husband's legal work for a waste company that "there isn't a landfill crisis," tried telling that to fellow parents at Park West Cooperative Nursery School. The school teaches recycling "and people were shocked I would believe such a thing," Ms. Berghoff says. "It was like I was going to burn the American flag." Her daughter Emily, a second-grader, didn't buy the argument either: "I was a villain in my daughter's eyes," Ms. Berghoff says.

To be sure, reuse of old paper, metals, glass and even some plastics makes great sense. It almost always lowers raw-material costs in manufacturing, usually reduces energy consumption and in some cases cuts air and water pollution. Increased recycling thus helps the U.S. paper industry remain globally competitive and reduces reliance on foreign steel. Commercial recycling is a springboard for hundreds of entrepreneurs who find ways to turn industrial discards into marketable products. And, unlike in past years, markets for nearly all recyclable items now exist and prices are strong.

The problem is that collecting from consumers is far less efficient than salvaging commercial and industrial scraps, and—despite all the effort—curbside programs account for only one-seventh of U.S. recycling. Surprisingly, old-fashioned paper drives, drop-off bins and buyback centers still account for more tonnage than curbside and cost far less to operate, according to a study by

Franklin Associates Ltd., a consulting firm whose clients include packaging companies and the EPA. Even with strong resale markets, curbside-collection costs aren't covered.

Such considerations aside, recycling advocates still argue that curbside programs remain a useful step toward a less wasteful society and, even if it takes a long time, will ultimately prove cost-effective. One reason, they say, is that pressure from consumers will push manufacturers to become more efficient and creative in the use of recycled materials.

Proponents also say collection costs will decline as sanitation trucks are re-configured to pick up trash and recyclable items simultaneously. But widespread use of such vehicles, if practical, is years away. Even then, collecting recyclables will probably mean more trucks on the road because, compared with trash headed for a dump, recyclables can't be compacted as completely en route. For now, recycling is raising sanitation costs as cities face cutbacks in other basic services.

San Jose, cutting library and parks spending because of budget ills, is losing $5 million a year on its curbside-recycling program. Minneapolis gives a $7-a-month rebate to every household that sorts its trash, even though the city's costs go up with additional recycling. And New York City . . . faces $100 million a year in added costs under a court order that it comply with its own law mandating that 25% of all trash be recycled. The city currently recycles 15%. "It's time to pull back and be reasonable," Deputy Mayor Peter Powers says.

"In virtually every community, adding a curbside-recycling program increases costs," says Barbara J. Stevens, president of Ecodata Inc., a Westport, Connecticut, consulting firm. "City councilmen are shocked to find this out. But it's like moving from once-a-week garbage collection to twice a week." Adding curbside recycling increases monthly household sanitation bills by about $2, she says. Other studies indicate added household costs of $1.50 to $3 per month or, at the current level of service, $400 million to $800 million a year nationally.

In New York, where traffic and parked cars make trash collection difficult, the city has added two separate weekly routes for different kinds of recyclable items. In Fairfax County, Virginia, which won a National Recycling Coalition award in 1995 for best regional program, mandatory recycling and yard-waste collections— added to twice-weekly trash pickup— mean four stops at most houses every

> *"With less frequent [curbside] collection, [Philadelphia's] participation fell to 35% of homes from 70%."*

week. "That's 17.3 times per month through the neighborhood," says John Elliott, of AAA Disposal Service, a big local hauler. "And they wonder why it costs so much." Household bills run $25 a month, he says, and haulers can't find enough truck drivers.

Los Angeles, which collects trash, recyclable items and yard waste separately, now has a fleet of 800 trucks, says Drew Sones, a sanitation official. If the trash was all collected together, 400 trucks would suffice, he says. The added truck traffic comes as many cities are going to great lengths to reduce vehicle emissions to comply with the Clean Air Act.

Some municipal programs are complex, requiring expensive public-education efforts. Philadelphia, which cut back to recycling collection once every two weeks to save money, is launching a citywide drive to remind residents which week to set out the recyclables. With less frequent collection, participation fell to 35% of homes from 70%.

Philadelphia still claims to be saving money with curbside recycling. "I'm on a mission from God," says recycling chief Alfred Dezzi. "We brought the cost of recycling below the cost of trash." But that calculation doesn't take into account big state subsidies or recycling's fair share of city overhead and other costs. "If we added all those in to recycling," Mr. Dezzi concedes, "it wouldn't stand a chance."

He might be right. Mr. Porter, the former EPA waste chief who set the 25% goal, fears a public backlash as the higher-than-expected costs of recycling become apparent. Now a private consultant to industry and the government, he says his 1988 study identifying a garbage crisis was flawed because it counted dumps rather than dump capacity—and underestimated the prospects for creating additional dump sites. "We now know enough to get reasonable," he says. "States aren't going to reach their goals."

The country, recycling somewhere between 19% and 24% of trash currently, won't push the figure significantly higher even with a lot more spending, he says. And he doubts the effort to greatly expand curbside programs would be worth the money: "For the people who have a desperate need to feel good, you can always have a drop-off bin."

Recycling Is Often Wasteful

by Lawrence Reed

About the author: *Lawrence Reed, an economist, is president of the Mackinac Center for Public Policy, a free market research and educational organization in Midland, Michigan.*

If there's a buzzword in the business of managing America's solid waste problem, surely it is "recycling." At times the term seems to have taken on an almost religious meaning, with the faithful assuming that "disposable" is bad and "recycling" is good by definition.

There's nothing wrong with recycling when it's approached from a perspective of sound economics, good science, and voluntary cooperation. Too often, it's promoted as an end in itself without regard to whether it's worth the time and expense.

Recently, a speaker on this subject told my local Rotary Club that we should all recycle more of the paper we use so America could save its trees. The implication was that we're using too much paper, that trees are endangered, and that our civic duty requires that we do more with less.

No Tree Shortage

As it turns out, most of the trees that are planted in America are planted with the intent of eventually harvesting them to make things like paper. This means that if we all used less paper, there would be fewer trees planted. Maybe some people ought to use less paper anyway (bureaucrats, for instance), but no one should assume that the people who are in the business of growing and harvesting trees are going to continue to do so even if we don't buy their products.

"We're running out of trees" is a fiction older than most of the trees alive today. The truth is that though the total area of forestland in the continental United States is about the same as it was 75 years ago—600 million acres—there are far more trees because of greater tree density per acre. Market-driven

From "Recycling Myths" by Lawrence Reed, *Freeman*, March 1995. Reprinted courtesy of the Foundation for Economic Education.

technological changes, such as the development of wood preservatives, have led to more efficient use of forest resources. Market incentives have given private land owners good reason to replant nearly three million acres of trees every year. So when it comes to paper, recycle to your heart's content, but not because you think we'll run out of trees if you don't.

A recycling mania has been sweeping the country for nearly a decade. More than 6,000 curbside programs

> *"Too often, [recycling is] promoted as an end in itself without regard to whether it's worth the time and expense."*

are operated by local governments, serving at least 70 million Americans. In a recent year, more than 140 recycling laws were passed in 38 states—mandating the activity or requiring taxpayers to pay for it, or both. All this has occurred at the same time that cost-cutting entrepreneurs are busy producing less and less packaging to contain more and more goods.

Without any edicts from politicians, plastic milk jugs today contain 30 percent less plastic than they did just 20 years ago. The weight of aluminum cans declined by 36 percent between 1960 and 1990. Experts like Lynn Scarlett of the Los Angeles–based Reason Foundation point out that America's solid waste problem is a public policy failure, not a market failure.

Because of flat rate charges for municipal garbage pick-up and disposal, government policies in most areas subsidize those who throw away large quantities of refuse at the expense of those who throw away very little. Entrepreneurs know how to construct landfills now that pose absolutely no hazard to the environment, and anyone who has ever flown over almost any state knows there's plenty of land for this purpose, but naysaying regulators have almost closed down this efficient waste management option.

Recycling Often Fails

The fact is that sometimes recycling makes sense and sometimes it doesn't. In the legislative rush to pass recycling mandates, state and local governments should pause to consider the science and the economics of every proposition. Often, bad ideas are worse than none at all and can produce lasting damage if they are enshrined in law. Simply demanding that something be recycled can be disruptive of markets and it does not guarantee that recycling that makes either economic or environmental sense will even occur.

Many people believe that simply segregating plastic containers, glass bottles, newspapers, and metal cans and then placing them in colorful boxes at curbside means that recycling has somehow taken place. Without ever questioning either the cost or the outcome of the process that starts at the curb, they assume that whatever happens must be both economically and environmentally sound.

√ Recycling, however, doesn't really happen unless all that plastic, glass, paper, and metal is turned into new, useful products that are actually in demand in the marketplace. Some of what we put at curbside actually ends up in a landfill or piled to the ceiling in warehouses with no place to go. Recycling programs may make a lot of civic-minded citizens feel good, but the whole rationale is undermined to the extent they are nothing more than expensive, politically motivated, and circuitous methods of old-fashioned garbage disposal.

Quite often, more energy and resources are spent than saved in the process of recycling. Municipal governments, because of the inherent shortcomings of public sector accounting and budget information, routinely underestimate the full costs of their recycling programs.

One area where recycling plainly works is in the disposal of aluminum cans. Since the process requires 10 percent less energy than transforming bauxite into aluminum, it pays for producers to use recycled cans. Hence, a market has developed for these cans, and market incentives encourage entrepreneurs to find efficient ways to collect them.

Containers and Bottles

One area where recycling doesn't make sense is in the disposal of juice containers used principally by school children. Aseptic disposable packages such as those small juice boxes were banned in Maine and are a target of the more extreme environmentalists. But as a 1991 study from the National Center for Policy Analysis (NCPA) in Dallas showed, such knee-jerk, interventionist, pseudo-solutions to nonproblems are rooted in misinformation or incomplete information:

> *"One area where recycling doesn't make sense is in the disposal of juice containers used principally by school children."*

- Filling disposable boxes requires about half as much energy as filling the supposedly preferable alternative, glass bottles.
- For a given beverage volume, transporting empty glass bottles requires 15 times as many trucks as the empty boxes—thus using more fuel and causing more air pollution.
- Because the end product is lightweight, small, and rectangular, the filled boxes can be transported more efficiently than full glass bottles—using 35 percent less energy.

Some states have threatened to ban disposable diapers as a way to encourage the use (and recycling) of cloth diapers. Studies show, however, that when all environmental effects are considered, cloth has no clear advantage over disposables. In California and other western states where there is relatively abundant landfill space and a shortage of water, the case for disposables is actually quite strong. Residents of those states who avoid them and wash cloth diapers with scarce water may actually be doing harm to the environment. The marketplace, once again, is not as dumb as certain do-gooders think it is.

157

Polystyrene Versus Paper

Several cities, including Portland, Oregon, and Newark, New Jersey, have essentially banned polystyrene food packages. That's what McDonald's used to put its burgers in until it was pressured into switching to paperboard containers. The average American thinks these efforts are positive for the environment because they will somehow promote recycling. They also believe that because paper is "biodegradable" and polystyrene is not, the switch will reduce the need for landfills. The truth of the matter is more complicated than that.

Polystyrene, it so happens, is completely recyclable, which isn't always true of the paper used in, say, drinking cups. And those paper cups, by the way, cost the consumer about 2 1/2 times as much as polystyrene.

Studies from NCPA and other respected organizations show that production of the old polystyrene McDonald's hamburger shell actually used 30 percent less energy than paperboard and resulted in 46 percent less air pollution and 42 percent less water pollution. The average 10-gram paper cup consumes 33 grams of wood and uses 28 percent more petroleum in its manufacture than the entire input of a polystyrene cup.

> *"Polystyrene, it so happens, is completely recyclable, which isn't always true of the paper used in, say, drinking cups."*

Furthermore, the paper cup requires 36 times more chemical input (partly because it weighs seven times as much) and takes about 12 times as much steam, 36 times as much electricity and twice as much cooling water to make, compared to its polystyrene counterpart. And, about 580 times as much waste water, 10 to 100 times the residual effluents of pollutants, and three times the air emission pollutants are produced in making the paper cup.

Environmentalists who put their faith in government, with hardly a scrap of evidence that suggests they should, seem oblivious to these realities. To them, mountains of refuse waiting to be recycled into things people don't want at a cost they would never freely pay is not a reason to abolish mandatory recycling schemes. Instead, it gives them a reason to pass new laws that would force-feed the economy with recycled products.

Market economists—by nature, philosophy, and experience—are skeptical of schemes to supplant the free choices of consumers with the dictates of central planners. The recycling mania confirms their suspicions.

Chapter 4

Are Government Regulations Necessary for a Cleaner Environment?

Chapter Preface

When Republicans gained control of Congress in 1994, House of Representatives Speaker Newt Gingrich and other conservatives announced plans to repeal or amend many federal environmental laws. In 1996, the House passed a bill that would have drastically overhauled the 1970 Clean Water Act, easing restrictions on dumping chemicals in lakes and rivers. The Senate, responding to protests, let the bill die without a vote. Nevertheless, critics of the Clean Water Act and similar legislation contend that these regulations are outdated, cumbersome, and a burden on businesses and individuals that must comply with them. According to Arizona governor Fife Symington, "After a given period—say, five years—all regulations that are not demonstrably protecting the health and safety of the American people should be scrapped."

In response to Republican-led reform efforts, environmental activists and organizations rallied to defuse the perception that environmental regulations are out of control. In 1995, environmental expert and author Gregg Easterbrook wrote, "Environmental regulations have not crippled the nation—as the conservative doomsday crowd loves to say. They've been making the nation safer, healthier, and stronger."

Heeding public demand for both reasonable and safe environmental laws, many federal environmental officials argued that adequate environmental protection could be achieved with fewer and more effective regulations. In the words of U.S. Secretary of the Interior Bruce Babbitt in 1996, "We need rigorous national standards. But there is no immutable law that says such standards must be reached through reams of detailed, cookie-cutter instruction codes." Babbit suggests that America set a national environmental goal and "invite businesses and communities to reach that goal in whatever way they choose."

Observers on both sides of the regulatory debate recognize that laws alone will not prevent the fouling of the environment. These individuals maintain that a sense of responsibility for a clean environment is required of all Americans. As Earth First! cofounder Dave Foreman puts it, "Until we can do something about the lack of responsibility, neither free markets nor federal law can accomplish what they should." The authors in this chapter debate the role of each in protecting America's environment.

Legislators Should Not Gut Environmental Regulations

by Philip Shabecoff

About the author: *Philip Shabecoff is the founding editor and publisher of* Green-wire, *a computer-accessed data bank on environmental studies, legislation, and court decisions. Shabecoff served as the* New York Times *environmental correspondent from 1977 to 1991 and is the author of* A Fierce Green Fire: The American Environmental Movement.

If Republicans can get away with calling what is happening on Capitol Hill "environmental reform," then the Nazi blitz of London during World War II could have been called urban renewal. As the usually restrained columnist David Broder put it in the *Washington Post*, "The Republicans, as far as anyone can tell, are preparing to take the country on the greatest leap backward in American history."

Conservatives' Lies

Many of the stories that the conservatives in control of Congress are telling to justify their ferocious assault on the nation's environmental and public health protection laws are fabrications:

- "The constitutional interpretation right now is that if an owl flies and lands on your land, that owl gets all of your land and you are not compensated."—Representative Linda Smith (R-WA).
- "[Toxic-substance regulation] would have cost the wood preserving industry $5.7 trillion per premature death averted. This huge amount would prevent one cancer case every 2.9 million years."—Representative Charles Norwood (R-GA).
- "Under the Safe Drinking Water Act, Columbus, Ohio, must monitor a pesticide that is only used to grow pineapples. I do not know how many pineapples are grown in Columbus."—Representative Robert Walker (D-PA).
- "One of those regulations was a rule that apparently would bar the tooth fairy

From "Unlike George Washington, Republicans Can Tell a Lie" by Philip Shabecoff, *Washington Spectator*, August 15, 1995. Reprinted courtesy of the *Washington Spectator*.

in the United States. It was a requirement that every dentist not give baby teeth back to [the baby's] parents."—Representative David McIntosh (R-IN).

These and many other horror stories about regulatory excesses are being told by those who now hope to rapidly dismantle the system painstakingly built up over the years to protect Americans and their environment.

They share one distinctive trait: they are lies.

The distortions are being deliberately or carelessly purveyed by the so-called conservative Republicans as they methodically slash away at the federal government's ability to control pollution of the air, land and water, to safeguard public health from poisons and disease, to improve worker safety and to preserve our public lands and resources.

There is certainly room for reform in our environmental laws and in the way some are interpreted and enforced. The landmark environmental statutes of the 1970s brought sweep-

> *"Horror stories about regulatory excesses are being told by those who now hope to rapidly dismantle the [environmental protection] system."*

ing changes in the way the country does business. Changes of that magnitude inevitably bring some waste, inefficiency and misplaced priorities. Some money has been misspent and some Americans have been made the victims of bureaucratic ineptitude and arrogance.

But the Republicans—aided, it must be said, by a number of Southern Democrats—have mounted a fierce, sustained, unrelenting war across the entire environmental front, and on public health, too.

Antienvironmental Targets

They are, first of all, seeking to gut the landmark environmental statutes that have been passed since the first Earth Day in 1970, starting with the Clean Water Act, the Safe Drinking Water Act and the Clean Air Act, and then the toxic waste laws, the pesticides laws and, with particular venom, the Endangered Species Act. Others are also targeted.

In case they can't get away with undoing regulations that restrain polluters and other despoilers of land and resources, the Republicans will use the budget to make sure the regulatory agencies do not have the resources to carry out what remains of the laws. As this was written [in August 1995], a House Appropriations Subcommittee had voted to reduce the budget of the already overburdened and understaffed Environmental Protection Agency by 33 percent. EPA Administrator Carol Browner calls this "the clearest evidence to date there is a concerted, systematic effort by Republicans to undermine public health and take away the tools we need to do the job the American people expect us to do."

They also used manipulation of the budget to try to blackmail the President [Bill Clinton] into signing anti-environmental legislation he might have otherwise vetoed. There may yet be an attempt to require opening the Arctic National Wildlife Refuge to oil and gas exploration, a move rejected by Congress on several occasions over recent years. . . .

Costs in the Millions and Billions

Probably the single most effective weapon the Republicans have devised to paralyze federal efforts to protect American citizens is their disingenuously styled "regulatory reform" legislation. This legislation, passed by the House but derailed by a Democratic filibuster in the Senate, would have required that rules drafted by federal agencies—particularly environmental and public health rules—be subjected to intricate and staggeringly expensive cost-benefit analysis before they could be put into effect.

This cynical ploy makes a mockery of the Republicans' complaints that federal environmental protection is excessively bureaucratic and expensive. If enacted, it would add new layers of bureaucracy and millions—some analysts say billions—of dollars to the current cost of regulating. Of course, the chief effect would be to chill any effort to control the polluting activities of business and industry. The legislation would undo major provisions of almost every pollution control law passed in the last 25 years.

"Takings" legislation introduced by the Republicans would require the federal government to pay landowners if they are required to take actions to protect the environment—wetlands or endangered species, for example—that reduces the value of their property. If a developer buys a swamp and plans to drain it to build a shopping mall, and then the government says he can't because it is a protected wetland, the government would have to compensate him for the loss of profit he would theoretically have made from building the mall. This is another bureaucratic nightmare that could drain billions of dollars from the Treasury and allow environmental law to be flouted by property owners, especially big corporations with huge landholdings.

Not content with enfeebling the federal government's power to protect citizens and their habitat, the "Contract With America" [reform legislation attempted in Congress in 1995] Republicans are trying to weaken the power of individual citizens to protect themselves in the courts.

Proposed "tort reform" laws would raise the hurdles that individuals or grassroots groups must clear if they want to sue corporations whose activities threaten their property or survival. These "reforms" would substantially limit damages that could be collected by the injured—children sickened by toxic pollution from a nearby factory, for example—and a

"[Regulatory reform] legislation would undo major provisions of almost every pollution control law passed in the last 25 years."

"loser pays" provision pushed by the Republicans means that anyone suing General Motors or Exxon, with its limitless resources, would have to pay the corporations' legal costs if he or she lost the case.

The Republican right captured Congress in 1994 because, as the writer Joe Davis noted in the *Amicus Journal*, a publication of the Natural Resources Defense Council, "[W]e have a public that is convinced that Congress is little more than an amalgam of thieving rascals and special interests." The irony is that, due to the 1994 election, we now have what Davis calls "a Congress that is living up to that myth. Never in recent history have big-bucks special interests—chemicals, oil, coal, timber, mining, real estate and agri-giants—had a freer hand to loot the nation's treasures."

Federal Lands at Risk

Looking at the scope of their agenda, it is clear that the Republicans are planning to turn back the clock a full century to the days of the robber barons, when a rapacious few were able to ravage public lands and resources to accumulate great wealth, and when industries were freely allowed to engage in practices that sickened and killed people and put their workers at risk.

Republicans on Capitol Hill have already proposed selling off National Parks, particularly those most used by urban dwellers. They want to allow logging, grazing and mining on what are now protected federal lands. They want to allow a foreign company to mine gold at the edge of Yellowstone National Park and risk contaminating park waters. Resource industries and land developers, supported by states' rights and property rights ideologues, are lobbying hard for the transfer of federal lands to the states, where they will become easier pickings.

An Advantage to Industries

Industries are getting a sympathetic hearing in Congress. In fact, theirs are often the only voices heard. Committee hearings on environmental issues are frequently stacked with opponents of environmental protection. Environmentalists and other supporters are not let into the committee hearing room, and even their written submissions are not entered in the record. A bill introduced by Senator Slade Gorton (R-WA) to drastically weaken the Endangered Species Act was actually written by representatives of industries that oppose the current act. Water from federal lands that is now reserved for urban areas and for wildlife needs in the water-scarce West may be re-diverted to serve powerful agribusiness interests.

> *"Committee hearings on environmental issues are frequently stacked with opponents of environmental protection."*

If the Republican Congress is able to follow through on its agenda for public lands and resources, it will return the nation to conditions that existed before the progressive reforms adopted during the administration of President Theodore Roosevelt, which emphasized public control of those resources as an issue of democracy. Since that era, the public domain has been protected for the benefit of all the people, not just the rich, the powerful and the politically influential.

Protecting the health and safety of Americans from the rapacity of industry was set as a national goal at the beginning of the twentieth century. After the publication of Upton Sinclair's *The Jungle*, which exposed the grotesquely unsanitary conditions in the meatpacking industry, we agreed as a nation that Americans should not be exposed to tainted foods. Now the Republicans in Congress have tried to push through legislation that would, as Marian Burros reported in

> *"The anti-environment activities of Congress are certainly contrary to the public will."*

the *New York Times*, limit the federal government's authority to regulate food safety and "reduce the burden on business to prove that food is safe."

An episode that underscores the cruelty of the right-wing ideologues now in power was the attempt by the House Appropriations Committee to kill a new meat inspection system adopted by the Agriculture Department. One of the chief targets of the new system was a strain of E-coli bacteria that kills at least 500 Americans each year, most of them children and the elderly. As they kill, the bacteria cause excruciating pain by dissolving the victims' internal organs. The Republican approach has been that the problem can be handled by the free market—when enough children die agonizing deaths, meat packers will do something about sanitation, okay?

There are many other cases where common decency is falling victim to the anti-government frenzy—for example, efforts to ease the rules that protect children from lead paint.

It should be noted, too, that while the attack on environmental and public health regulation has been especially savage, no federal program that protects consumers, workers, the poor and minorities from abuse and exploitation appears to be safe from the Republican onslaught.

A Reckless Attack

The Republicans who now dominate Congress came to power calling themselves conservatives. But my dictionary, *Webster's Third*, defines a conservative as "one who adheres to traditional time-tested, long-standing methods, procedures or views: a moderate, cautious or discreet person."

With their reckless attack on time-tested, long-standing federal methods and procedures for curbing abuses of economic power, providing equal justice for all citizens, shielding consumers from fraud and abuse, and protecting public health, safety and the environment, the current crop of Republicans who dominate the legislative agenda in Washington have demonstrated quite clearly that they are no conservatives.

Some of the Republicans, including House Speaker Newt Gingrich, have called themselves "revolutionaries." But for good or evil, a revolution creates a new political and social order. These right-wing Republicans are not trying to create a new social order—the phrase is anathema to them. They are attempting to force the country backward to the social order that prevailed before this century, an order that gave unrestrained freedom to private economic power. When they talk about getting government "off the backs of the people," they really mean getting it off the backs of business and industry and wealthy landowners, and allowing them to do whatever they choose to the backs of ordinary citizens. These are not revolutionaries—they are reactionaries seeking to roll back 100 years or more of social progress.

The anti-environment activities of Congress are certainly contrary to the public will. Opinion poll after opinion poll shows that a large majority of Americans continues to support strong environmental protection.

Until fairly recently, the phrase "conservative environmentalist" would not have been considered an oxymoron. Protection of the environment enjoyed bipartisan support until Ronald Reagan became President. Indeed, some of the most effective defenders of the environment remaining in Congress today are old-line Republican conservatives like Senator John Chafee of Rhode Island and Senator James Jeffords of Vermont. But they are a tiny minority, without honor in their own party.

So far, the Republican assault has not succeeded in tearing down the edifice of environmental protection Americans have built up over the years. If we're lucky, they may prove unable to wreak irremediable damage. Some of their excesses may be tempered by public outrage, and President Clinton's veto may prevent some atrocities.

Government Programs and Regulations Can Revitalize Abandoned Urban Brownfields

by Barbara Ruben

About the author: *Barbara Ruben was the editor of the former quarterly magazine* Environmental Action.

On a slate gray day the wind off Lake Erie whips stray Cheetos bags, Burger King coffee cups and dry brown oak leaves past barren blocks of pockmarked and boarded buildings. Hunkered between a padlocked loan shop and the defunct 61st Street Pier seafood carryout, the garish marquee of the long-shuttered Fascination Playland is bereft of most of its yellow and red lights. Scrawled on the doorway of the former adult bookstore and movie house is a somehow fitting epitaph for this post-industrial ghost town: 'There was not much love from God."

A Cleveland Brownfield

But if this scarred block of Cleveland's east side hasn't seen any divine intervention, it is scheduled for help from a worldlier source: the U.S. Environmental Protection Agency [EPA]. The 73-year-old Williston Building, which has housed a range of businesses, from a car dealership in the early days of automobiles to its last X-rated incarnation, is one of the city's 700 abandoned industrial sites known as brownfields.

In 1994, EPA awarded Cleveland a $200,000 grant to assess and clean up some of its contaminated sites. EPA plans to make similar grants to seven other cities; so far, Bridgeport, Connecticut, and Richmond, Virginia, have also been chosen.

From "Fields of Dreams?" by Barbara Ruben, *Environmental Action*, Winter 1995. Reprinted with permission.

First on the list for Cleveland's cleanup is the Williston Building, where officials have discovered soil and groundwater contamination caused by leaking solvents. They say that asbestos will have to be removed from its interior before the site can be redeveloped into office and retail space as part of a larger revitalization effort in the city's midtown corridor.

"Sixteen states have developed brownfields laws since 1989. The programs offer a combination of tax abatements, loans and cleanup held to entice developers."

"Sites like this are the result of the industrial heritage of Cleveland. We want to demonstrate how a community can bring these brownfields back to life by encouraging businesses to locate in the area and at the same time cleaning up contamination," says Virginia Aveni, environmental manager for the Cuyahoga County Planning Commission, one of the first agencies in the country to focus on brownfields issues.

Cleanup Plus Development

Across the country, the EPA and state and local governments hope that by merging environmental cleanup with economic development they can revitalize aging cities by encouraging industry to halt their flight to the greener fields of the suburbs. The General Accounting Office estimates that 130,000 to 425,000 brownfields sites need cleanup nationally at a cost of $650 billion. Brownfields can range from having no contamination to a significant amount, but they are all less polluted than sites considered for Superfund [an EPA waste cleanup program].

Brownfields development proponents are quick to cite the advantages of reusing inner city facilities. "When a contaminated site sits in the middle of a community, even after the immediate danger to public health has been removed, that neighborhood loses jobs, loses its tax base, loses hope. Meanwhile, development goes on outside the city, in fields and forests never before developed, leading to more driving and creating more pollution," EPA Administrator Carol Browner said as she toured Richmond, Virginia, brownfields in October 1995.

Sixteen states have developed brownfields laws since 1989. The programs offer a combination of tax abatements, loans and cleanup held to entice developers. But in the enthusiasm to revive inner cities, some environmentalists and social justice activists worry that regulators could be using new voluntary cleanup programs to thwart Superfund, stymie public participation or shield property owners from liability for contaminants on their land.

"At first blush, brownfields are something we can all agree on, everyone is nodding their heads. But the devil is in the details. What do we mean by flexibility in cleanup? What do we mean by faster processing?" asks Jo Patten at the Center for Neighborhood Technology in Chicago about the various incentives that have been used to hook developers.

Private "Cleanup"

For example, while environmentalists generally laud the Cuyahoga County Planning Commission's initiative on cleaning up brownfields in Cleveland. they fear that a state law passed in 1995 will do more harm than good. Under the Ohio law, cleanup of contaminated property will be controlled exclusively by private companies approved by the state. Although the Ohio EPA is expected to monitor 25 percent of the sites. environmental groups in the state worry fewer than one in ten will be inspected due to inadequate staffing. Because there are almost no avenues for public participation, residents would not be informed when companies conduct private cleanups of seriously contaminated sites. In addition, once a cleanup is approved, the company would be exempt from any liability for their cleanup work. The law also allows companies in many instances to cover over contaminants with cement or asphalt instead of removing them.

"The Voinovich [Ohio's Republican governor] Administration consulted only with corporate lawyers and bankers in the bill's drafting, and the bill reflects that bias from top to bottom," says Richard Sahli, executive director of the Ohio Environmental Council, which represents 170 local grassroots groups. "The Administration has taken an idea that everyone supports, the voluntary cleanup of contaminated property, to camouflage the biggest corporate rip-off in the state's history. "

Chris Trepal, co-director of the Earth Day Coalition, a Cleveland environmental group, says that rather than demonstrating the promise of brownfields cleanups, Ohio "may be a model for the whole country for keeping a brownfield a brownfield forever."

Superfund and Corporate Liability

But that's exactly what many administrators don't want to see. They say the brownfields issue has emerged because developers are afraid to buy old industrial facilities for fear of endless liability and cleanup costs under Superfund.

Superfund, officially known as the Comprehensive Environmental Response, Compensation and Liability Act, can hold anyone who has owned a property since it became polluted liable for cleanup. Banks that lend money for companies to buy the property have also been held responsible for the pollution. Because of this, they have been reluctant to lend money if there

"While some brownfields are very contaminated, others may not be polluted at all."

is a chance a company will default on a loan because it can't pay cleanup costs, thus making the bank the owner of the site. These are some of the issues addressed in state voluntary cleanup laws.

"Just the specter of contamination is more than enough to kill a real estate deal," says Jim Bower, who chairs the U.S. EPA's brownfields task force in the upper Midwest states.

But while some brownfields are very contaminated, others may not be polluted at all. Property already declared Superfund sites are considered too contaminated for brownfield cleanup.

"Developers say, why should I take the chance of having a potential Superfund site on my hands, when I can drive five minutes outside the city

> *"The variety of cleanup projects reflect the array of approaches taken to the brownfields issue."*

and bulldoze a cornfield?" observes Ciaran Mannion, executive director of the Minnesota Environmental Initiative, a statewide coalition of environmental and business groups. . . .

Job and Population Loss

How federal legislation will complement state programs remains to be seen, but in the meantime the variety of cleanup projects reflect the array of approaches taken to the brownfields issue. Many of the programs were pioneered in the aging cities of the Midwest's Rust Belt, where hundreds of thousands of jobs in steel plants, auto factories and shipyards have been lost in the last two decades.

For example, in ten large midwestern metro areas, from Chicago to Detroit, 39 percent of the population lived in counties nearest the cities in 1970. But as urban sprawl and edge cities proliferated, that number dropped to 30 percent in 1990. At the same time, jobs shifted out of these cities, with the percentage of manufacturing jobs dropping from 74 to 60 percent in the cities, while outlying areas took up the slack, rising from providing 26 percent of the jobs in 1970 to 40 percent two decades later. During this time period, the roles of the central city as a job provider and the suburb as a bedroom community have changed dramatically, with the number of people living in the central city, but working in the suburbs rising by 64 percent.

"High density cities evolved because of economic forces 75 or 100 years ago; it was part of economies of scale to have a centralized industrial base. Now in the information age you can open a business on top of a mountain as well as in downtown Detroit. But that doesn't help in deciding what to do with the decaying urban sites," says EPA's Jim Bower.

Minnesota's Successes

Minnesota, which instituted the country's first brownfields program in 1988 with its Voluntary Investigation and Cleanup program, stands in sharp contrast to Ohio. For example, the state has oversight of every stage of the cleanup, and no special standard for industry cleanup has been established, making cleanups generally more stringent than in states that have developed use-specific standards. The Minnesota Pollution Control Agency holds semi-annual meetings with residents in corridors of contamination to explain local cleanup projects.

"The voluntary program is working in Minnesota because the state had a strong Superfund program to begin with. The voluntary program was the carrot, and the state Superfund was the enforcement stick. Environmentalists have been very supportive of the legislation, been looking over our shoulders and we've encouraged that," says Joe Zachmann, a project manager for voluntary cleanup with the Minnesota Pollution Control Agency.

Zachmann cites a successful cleanup in the northern Minnesota town of Staples, where a plant that manufactured rubber products planned to move out of state. The plant manager proposed to buy the facility, but because soil and groundwater were contaminated, he had trouble finding financing. Through the voluntary cleanup program, the manager obtained assistance in formulating a plan to treat and remove the contaminated soil and groundwater and was able to find financing. In addition to cleaning up pollution that was threatening wells off site, the company was able to save the 60 to 80 jobs at the plant.

In another case, near the banks of the Mississippi River in St. Paul, the UNO-CAL Corporation's aboveground oil storage tanks released oil and volatile organic compounds into the soil and groundwater. The bulk storage facility shut down in the late 1980s, and the land has been vacant since then. UNOCAL agreed to clean up the site so that the city of St. Paul can incorporate it into a planned $46 million expansion and improvement of a regional park, which will include new docks, a marina and walkways.

Chicago's Brownfield Landscape

Illinois began the country's second brownfields program under the somewhat arcane name of the Pre-Notice Site Program, which refers to cleanups done voluntarily before state enforcement authorities investigate to write notices of violation of environmental laws. Since 1989, 82 cleanups have been completed and another 200 are underway.

In 1994, the city of Chicago started a demonstration project of its own with assistance from the U.S. EPA. Since 1990, the city had a net loss of 600 manufacturing plants, and 18 percent of its industrial areas lie vacant or inactive. Roughly 2,000 brownfields sites dot Chicago's landscape.

> *"The Minnesota Pollution Control Agency holds semi-annual meetings with residents in corridors of contamination to explain local cleanup projects."*

With $2 million in bond funds, the city has set out to rehabilitate and find buyers for five brownfields. The city hoped for $10 million more in funding from the Department of Housing and Urban Development's Community Block Grant program.

Jim Van der Kloot, special assistant commissioner with Chicago's Department of Environmental Protection, says the program started out with one environmental attorney. But he soon found that the efforts needed to be multidisciplinary, involving the assistance of the city's departments of Planning and Development, Buildings and Law.

"The lesson we've learned is that if you don't link cleanup with reuse you end up with the midnight dumpers coming right back in. We're not looking to create empty lots," he says.

> *"In 1994, the city of Chicago started a demonstration project of its own with assistance from the U.S. EPA."*

And empty property can also serve as a breeding ground for crime, Van der Kloot says. For example, in 1983, a wire manufacturing plant exploded, and the building was torn down. The festering pile of rubble attracted gangs, and crime skyrocketed. The city, which now owns the land, cleared more than a hundred truckloads of debris, including six dead dogs, from the site and is now completing a work plan to remove underground storage tanks and heavy metal contamination.

As the city cleaned up the lot, a business across the street that refurbishes used car parts eyed the progress with interest. The company had hired armed guards to escort its employees to their cars after several armed robberies and carjackings, and it had given up hope for starting a nighttime shift, when they feared crime would become even more prevalent. The company now hopes to buy the lot for possible expansion.

Bridgeport's EPA Grant

States outside the Midwest have come to recognize brownfields issues within their boundaries as well. In the West, Oregon and Colorado have voluntary cleanup programs in place, and California began a pilot study of sites late in 1994. In the Northeast, from New Jersey to Connecticut, states have also enacted legislation.

In August 1995, the U.S. EPA chose the deep sea port city of Bridgeport, Connecticut, as a recipient of a $200,000 brownfields redevelopment demonstration grant. Gritty and poverty-stricken, Bridgeport attempted to declare bankruptcy in 1993. Approximately 50 percent of the manufacturing jobs have been lost since 1985, and per capita income stands at 60 percent of the state average. Nearly half of the population of 141,000 are people of color or immigrants. Most of the city's 2,200 acres of industrially zoned land is contaminated to some degree.

"Bridgeport is the most economically, fiscally and demographically distressed community in Connecticut by almost every available measure of distress," says Kevin Gremse, an economic development planner for the city, in the application for EPA brownfields redevelopment grant.

"Bridgeport is really one big dump site. The challenge is, where do you start?" asks Alma Maya, a business development officer for the Connecticut Development Authority. "All of the sites are in people of color neighborhoods. Zoning in the town is absolutely ridiculous, auto factories tower next to people's homes. And now the businesses that want to come in are garbage-related industries, sludge and trash burners. We don't want to become the garbage capital of the world."

Instead, like the proverbial phoenix, Gremse and community development advocates believe the city can rise above its grime and destitution. The city has applied for status as an "empowerment zone," part of a redevelopment program instituted by the Clinton administration in 1994. Each of nine empowerment zone cities will receive $100 million in social service block grants and employer tax credits for new jobs created.

In the meantime, the EPA grant will be used to assess three corridors of contamination within the city, two industrial and one residential. In one of these areas alone, 2,000 jobs are at risk, but redevelopment of the 2 million square feet of empty industrial space could bring in 8,000 jobs. Gremse says he hopes to be able to tap some of the $25 million for remediation of sites in the state's voluntary cleanup program.

Assessment and Redevelopment Controversies

Laurayne Farrar-James, the chief executive officer of the non-profit Neighborhood Enterprises United in the city's impoverished east side residential area, recalls a massive dump, dubbed Mount Trashmore, that continued growing for years on an abandoned lot in a residential neighborhood. After six years of complaints from residents, the owner finally torched the dump, not exactly the environmental solution activists had hoped for. Today, however, environmental assessments are under way for developing the site into houses for first-time buyers and a health clinic. Similar redevelopment of industrial land that would provide jobs within walking distance of the houses is now on Farrar-James' wish list for brownfields reuse.

Both Maya and Farrar-James are members of a coalition of businesses, banks and community groups called the CLEAN (Community Linkage for Environmental Action Now) Task Force, which will coordinate the brownfields project.

"In one [Bridgeport area], 2,000 jobs are at risk, but redevelopment of the 2 million square feet of empty industrial space could bring in 8,000 jobs."

"Right now I'm feeling optimistic. Once you get people involved in making decisions and reinvested in the government of their city, Mt. Trashmore won't happen again," says Maya.

But Mike Horvath, executive director of the Bridgeport Development Preservation Trust, doesn't share Maya's bright-eyed optimism. He says that few residents in the study areas have been consulted and that he fears that consultants hired to do the assessments will minimize the amount of contamination to expedite development.

"Let's face it, $200,000 is not going to put a dent in these areas. It's going to be used to assess damage, but we've already had enough assessment. We already know the damage. I want to see that money used for cleanup," he says.

Horvath criticizes the now-defunct Carpenter Technologies, a massive steel plant, now a field of broken concrete covering soil soaked with fuel oil and PCBs [polychlorinated biphenyls]. Without any city assessment at all, Donald Trump and gambling tycoon Steve Wynn are already vying over the site to either build an amusement park with the world's tallest roller coaster or a glitzy casino. Horvath says that no matter which plan gets approved, the enterprises won't provide the same high-paying manufacturing jobs that were lost and aren't compatible with a residential area. He also wonders if the pressure to bring in jobs quickly to the area will compromise the measure of cleanup at the site.

> *"We do have a significant concern that any voluntary cleanup programs might be a way of escaping cleanup under Superfund."*

Questioning Brownfields Programs

Horvath points to questions that plague brownfields programs across the country. Some activists fear that developers anxious to extricate themselves from the Superfund quagmire will be allowed to clean up industrial sites to a less stringent standard than residential ones and won't leave the area clean enough. This issue is not one that just affects brownfields programs, but is expected to be debated during Superfund reauthorization as a way of reigning in astronomical costs for cleanup.

"We do have a significant concern that any voluntary cleanup programs might be a way of escaping cleanup under Superfund. The programs might not protect public health but pretend to," says Sierra Club's Blake Early.

Chris Trepal of Cleveland's Earth Day Coalition questions why some of the brownfields laws are creating what she sees as a dangerous double standard for cleanup.

"I spend as much time at work as I do at home. I don't understand why I shouldn't be as safe there," she says.

But determining a cleanup level can be a tricky balancing act between luring businesses back from the suburbs and protecting human health.

"Anyone who approaches cleanup to pristine standards is going to be waiting a long, long time for businesses and jobs to move in. You clean it up so that human and ecosystem health are high priorities, but you have to understand that industrial activity is dirty. There's no such thing as clean industrial activity," says Jim Cummings, executive director of the Calumet project for Industrial Jobs, a coalition of labor, religious and citizen groups studying brownfields issues in the heavily industrialized areas of Hammond and Gary, Indiana, and East Chicago, an area that has lost 100,000 manufacturing jobs since 1983.

The Environmental Justice Issue

Chicago's environmental official Jim Van der Kloot suggests that brownfields redevelopment is a "very constructive way to work with the environmental justice issue since so many of these sites are in minority areas." Still he cautions that too much public participation in actual cleanup plans could turn off potential businesses. "There's a value to bringing jobs to a neighborhood. You don't want to jeopardize that," he says. "We're trying to to do cleanup that is protective of real people in the community. But the reality is we're not going to remove every last molecule of contamination."

But Steve Virgil, who is studying brownfields programs for the Ohio Legal Aid Society, doesn't buy that argument. "Laws are being passed without mentioning the fact that there are inequities in them. They're saying it's okay for pollution to be in the ghetto. It gives the appearance that the environmental agencies care less for inner cities than for the suburbs."

Virgil also says that brownfields redevelopment programs may promise more positive change than they can deliver.

"The fact is that cities began to die in the 1960s, long before Superfund. Businesses began to run from the cities then. It's myopic to think brownfields laws alone are going to bring business back. There is no guarantee that people who live in the neighborhoods will get the jobs," he says.

Cuyahoga County's Virginia Aveni also attests to the fact that it takes more than environmental cleanup to lure businesses back to the city: She has tried to market one inner-city site to 26 potential users, but so far has no takers.

"The real thing to recognize is that a lot of businesses are using environmental problems as a symbolic scapegoat not to talk about why they are moving. They are getting poor city services, inadequate tax breaks, and their employees live in suburbs. There's a perception of crime and more than a little racism involved. When people say they can wave the magic brownfield wand and they're going to have economic development, that's a lie. The problems are deeper than that," says David Barnhizer, a law professor at Cleveland State University who runs the school's Environmental Law Center.

> *"The ideal program would be one that fuses redevelopment with pollution prevention programs."*

Still, Barnhizer and others recognize the potential for brownfields programs, in conjunction with other environmental and economic development projects, to steer cities toward a more sustainable path. They say flexibility must be tem-

175

pered with strong standards and caution that without safe cleanup, economic development will not take root.

Elizabeth Collaton, who analyzes brownfields issues for Congress through the Northeast-Midwest Institute, asserts that "the ideal program would be one that fuses redevelopment with pollution prevention programs, one that takes another step to look at what happens once the site is cleaned up."

Says the Center for Neighborhood Technology's Jo Patton, "There are pretty significant questions remaining to be answered. Will development be done in existing characteristics of the area? It's not just a question of cleanup standards, but how does the community get involved after cleanup? If these are considerations that can involve a broad cross-section of people—not just the banks or developer, but nearby residents and potential workers—then we can navigate around some of these trickier issues and hopefully come up with solutions that will be in everyone's best interests."

An Improved Superfund Program Can Help Clean Up the Environment

by Richard J. Mahoney

About the author: *Richard J. Mahoney is the chairman of the executive committee of the Monsanto Company, a chemical company based in St. Louis, Missouri. He served on the National Superfund Commission from 1993 to 1994.*

Most observers would agree that the Superfund law is among the most poorly crafted and counterproductive statutes of recent years. Because of its perverse and conflicting incentives, parties are inclined to litigate and delay, rather than clean up.

However, the law and its follow-on regulations, which led to expenditures through Fiscal Year 1994 of about $28,000,000,000 (not including corporate legal costs) have not been a total waste. While the price per site cleanup has been exorbitant, at least *something* got done.

Just the Beginning

At 293 Superfund sites, according to Environmental Protection Agency (EPA) assessment, the cleanup process is complete and more than half of the remaining sites are moving along in the process. The EPA is targeting 650 completions by the year 2000. Yet, the approximately 1,300 Superfund National Priority List (NPL) sites potentially are only the beginning. There still are some 19,000 sites that have had a preliminary EPA assessment indicating that they "appear serious" and need a site inspection to determine if they officially should be placed on the Superfund List. Thus, one cannot be complacent about the "progress" of cleaning up the current NPL sites.

Nearly 4,000 emergency removal procedures have been carried out at NPL sites and many more sites not yet officially on the list. Emergency removal, as

From "Revising the Superfund: This Time Let's Get It Right" by Richard J. Mahoney, *USA Today* magazine, January 1996. Copyright 1996 by the Society for the Advancement of Education. Reprinted by permission.

defined in the Superfund statute, is designed to remove and provide remedial actions for "any pollutant contamination which may present an imminent and substantial danger to the public health or welfare." In theory, therefore, at least by this definition and assertion, the "imminent and substantial danger to the public" is largely past. Some would argue, then, that—to paraphrase Sen. George Aiken's (R-VT) advice on the Vietnam War—"It's time for Superfund to declare victory and go home." They cite the origin of the statute, which came in the aftermath of Love Canal [a dioxin-contaminated neighborhood in Niagara Falls, New York] in the 1970s. At the outset, the intent was limited to removing hazardous waste. The expanded purposes of returning the site to "pre-disposal conditions" came later in the enlargement of the legislative debate. Many, though—particularly site neighbors—would dispute the idea that the risk has passed, and others would argue that environmental repair remains largely to be done.

Hazardous waste disposal practices have been changed dramatically. For most companies, it would be inconceivable that the old practices would return. The consequences of improper disposal now are clear to all, and the Resource Conservation and Recovery Act provides future deterrent incentives.

In an ironic way, the Superfund process and its incredible cost for limited cleanup have been a rallying point around which all participants can coalesce. Indeed, the Superfund Commission, in 1993–94, brought the various constituencies together to hammer out compromise legislation. That, however, failed passage in the contentious closing days of the 103rd Congress.

Points of Agreement

The constant debate about Superfund over the years has resulted in some principles for which there is the basis for general agreement—with admittedly a good deal of give and take needed in the details. Among the points of agreement are:

• Cleanup standards should meet the intended end use. An industrial warehouse and a playground need very different remedy approaches, and costs could be reduced dramatically with suitable remedy selection.

• The community should be involved as a full partner in all important site decisions and should have access to resources to enable that participation.

• There should be a so-called *de minimis* standard. Parties that had only peripheral involvement or a very minor part in the Superfund site should have a limited liability. As soon as the over-all law is "repaired," they should be dealt with promptly and released. Major industrial participants want these *de*

> *"In an ironic way, the Superfund process and its incredible cost for limited cleanup have been a rallying point around which all participants can coalesce."*

minimis parties released only as part of comprehensive Superfund reform for fear that, otherwise, the impetus for needed changes might evaporate.

• Joint and several liability should be abolished in favor of proportionate liability—that is, a party should be responsible only for its own contribution to the site. Any unallocatable, so-called "orphan shares" should come from the Superfund pool. While not all groups agree on this philosophically, a sort of grudging acceptance has evolved because this one provision has caused enormous process costs and slows down cleanup, as parties seek to limit their total liability.

> *"Current funding procedures should be re-examined. Large amounts of available Superfund monies currently are not being spent."*

• Properly engineered containment of the site is a legitimate temporary remedy. In many cases, such as preparing it for a future industrial warehouse, containment may be an appropriate, permanent remedy. The fact is that there simply are no currently available, generally accepted, cost-effective procedures for complete restoration (remediation) of most sites. Until cost-effective and neighbor-friendly solutions are developed, containment—when properly done and monitored—wins by default for most sites. However, Superfund money should be set aside for research and development (R&D), seeking economical solutions acceptable to the community where cleanup to standards higher than industrial use is appropriate.

• Despite the multi-year EPA emergency removal program, if there are any sites remaining that have obvious dangers—such as leaking containers, pools of hazardous materials, or removable "hot spots" that might migrate into groundwater or surface water—they should be handled on an emergency basis.

Possible Further Agreement

This is not a long list, but it is, nonetheless, a substantial area of potential agreement. It is possible to make an additional list of areas where some tradeoffs among interested parties might produce further agreement. This would include:

• Limitation of new sites to the Superfund NPL. Many argue that, after 15 years, with all the public awareness, if a site has not made it onto the Superfund NPL, its addition should be challenged strongly. The threshold numerical rating for inclusion on the NPL is highly arbitrary and does not necessarily separate cleanly hazardous from non-hazardous sites.

• After emergency removal is complete, many more sites can be delegated to the states, along with Superfund pool funding, to let local officials decide the best course of action, using guidelines, but not prescriptions, from the EPA.

• Current funding procedures should be re-examined. Large amounts of available Superfund monies currently are not being spent and, in effect, are offsetting discretionary spending for other domestic programs to avoid increases in the Federal budget deficit.

• The existing or reformed Superfund program should come to an end—perhaps in 10 years at the outside.

Two Impediments

Beyond the "agreed principles" and more that might yet find agreement, there are two major issues that appear to defy solution and are the most contentious impediments to complete overhaul of the system:

Elimination of retroactive liability for then-legal disposal acts occurring before the Dec. 31, 1980, effective date of Superfund or before its reauthorization date of Dec. 31, 1986. Potentially responsible parties (PRPs) argue that the statute is unfair since much of the disposal was legal at the time. Proponents of retaining retroactive liability argue that the "polluter pays" principle is inviolate and an important future deterrent.

If retroactive liability were to be eliminated, establishing which materials in many sites were placed there prior to the date liability is established and which came later would open the same "process loss" litigation problems that currently plague this program. A further complication is that, if retroactivity is to be removed, no one has yet determined who will do the cleanup of these pre-1980 or -1986 sites and where the money will come from. Glib statements like "a new agency," "the Corps of Engineers," or "the states" and "existing or new funds" have defied reduction to specificity so far.

The relationship between the insurers and insureds for Superfund liability. So far, courts have held almost equally for both—that is, historic insurance policies did and did not apply to environmental liability. It

> *"Retroactive liability should be retained as in the current law. This issue has so many difficult aspects that it virtually defies resolution."*

seems highly unlikely that Congress could craft an equitable solution that the courts have failed to reach after years of litigation. Indeed, one could argue that this is a contractual matter between insurers and insureds—and not an appropriate subject for Congress.

Points of Resolution

The above has indicated many areas of agreement or potential agreement, as well as two nearly intractable problems. With this as background, I propose that Superfund Reauthorization proceed along the following Ten Points of Resolution:

1. Retroactive liability should be retained as in the current law. This issue has so many difficult aspects that it virtually defies resolution. However, to provide fairness, partial compensatory offsets are made for PRPs in the following recommendations.

2. Insurance issues would be left to settlement by the parties involved. To in-

clude insurance resolution in Superfund reauthorization would lead to certain gridlock. With the containment process described in the following recommendations, future costs and liabilities can be more predictable and settlement between insurers and insureds more feasible, compared to the current open-ended liability situation.

3. Joint and several liability would be replaced by proportionate liability with Superfund paying for "orphan shares."

4. The highest priority is to complete the emergency removal process at all NPL and a select number of major sites awaiting NPL listing. Emergency removal would be limited to leaking or otherwise damageable containers, highly concentrated areas of hazardous materials, and plumes from the site. A time limit should be established for emergency removal program completion (perhaps on the order of three years).

5. No new additions should be made to the NPL during the life of the emergency removal program except for obvious sites of extraordinary hazard.

Categorizing Sites

6. NPL sites and a certain number of priority sites not currently on the NPL (to be capped arbitrarily at about 100–200 new ones), would be divided into two categories:

Sites where properly designed containment is a satisfactory permanent remedy—i.e., sites restricted to future industrial or similar uses. For these, RPRs and the Superfund (if needed for orphan shares) will complete the work. An amount—for example, 10% of actual construction costs of containment—would be put in escrow by the funding parties. This would be a monitoring and maintenance fund. At that point, with containment complete, and the escrow funds in place, PRPs would be relieved of all future liability. This liability relief is a critical part of the tradeoff to PRPs for retaining retroactive liability.

Those sites for which the future use is not known or is unlikely to be industrial. These also would receive containment procedures and a maintenance escrow fee. In addition, an amount equal to the maintenance escrow would be escrowed for future remediation should suitable technology become available and the community choose to use it. If remediation to a higher-than-industrial-quality standard is selected, the state or appropriate local body would be required to match the Superfund share of the remediation escrow. If, after a period of, for instance, 10

> *"There might be clearly cost-effective, full remediation procedures now available for a limited number of sites."*

years, the site still is unused, the amount escrowed for remediation would be returned to the PRPs.

The incentives in this section are aimed at encouraging industrial or other restricted use. In the overwhelming number of cases, it makes sense to do so to avoid the future possibility of Love Canal–like behavior where a site is developed for a school or for residential use. In any case, for illustration purposes, the total surface area of Superfund sites (excluding military and national laboratory sites) can be estimated very roughly at 50,000 acres (about the size of a half-dozen large wheat farms). While this acreage is not trivial in total, the contentious history and potential future problems argue that it best is used industrially or alternatively contained and left unused.

There might be clearly cost-effective, full remediation procedures now available for a limited number of sites. If so, they should be remediated, rather than contained. Based on Superfund experience to date, though, these will be few indeed—otherwise, cleanup already would have happened on a reasonable cost basis.

In sites not yet well under way in construction, but where a noncontainment remedy has been directed, the EPA-proposed remedy should be challenged for cost-effectiveness against the containment alternative. This is necessary since many "remedies" are directed with grossly inadequate support for their choice.

A Superfund Trust

For all sites, an independent Superfund Trust would be established to hold the escrow account and disperse it as needed—as well as to assist in determining future sites use. These funds would be kept separate from general Federal use or local access (except through the Trust). Public policy should dictate whether to have one National Trust for all sites or individual local ones (local administration appears a better choice). Models for this Trust concept exist in current EPA containment sites. PRPs may or may not choose to participate as Trust members.

7. A substantial amount of Superfund monies ($50–100,000,000 per year) should be allocated to peer-reviewed competitive R&D proposals to develop cost-effective, neighbor-friendly permanent remediation. These funds, plus the remediation escrow and potential land value increases, should be adequate incentives for R&D efforts to be undertaken by the private sector.

8. Communities should be empowered and funded for full participation in the Superfund Trust, remedy selection, and the completion process. However, the procedures in points 1–6 above should govern over all.

9. After satisfactory reauthorization of Superfund, so-called *de minimis* participants should be relieved from

> *"Communities should be empowered and funded for full participation in the Superfund Trust."*

all future liability upon payment of a nominal share. The terms "*de minimis*" and "nominal" need definitional debate, but the intent of the definition should be to relieve those who made very small contributions to the site, such as the casual small business participants in municipal sites, etc. Municipal operators would remain subject to PRP procedures. Banks and other "casual, nondisposal" participants would be relieved from liability. Contractors doing containment or remediation would be relieved of future environmental liability upon acceptance of the site by the Trust (except for standard industry contractual liabilities).

10. Minority and/or poor communities would get preferential priority in the resolution processes to ensure that they receive recognition for any past "second-class" treatment by Superfund.

These Ten Points of Resolution represent an outline for Superfund reform. They provide a basis for tradeoffs among the political parties' interests, incentives for directing solutions, and, most of all, a hope that, within the next five to 10 years, the nation can accomplish the original worthy purpose of Superfund—to remove the hazards of decades of waste practices that are unacceptable by today's standards and inappropriate to an enlightened society.

Markets Can Ensure Environmental Protection

by Lynn Scarlett

About the author: *Lynn Scarlett is the vice president for research at the Reason Foundation, a Los Angeles public policy research organization that advocates free-market principles.*

The 25th anniversary of Earth Day came and went in 1995, with little fanfare and no public demand for more environmental laws. The new Republican Congress tried, and mostly failed, to enact reforms designed to lessen the burden of environmental regulation. Behind the scenes and in public forums, various schools of environmental reform debated and discussed. They talked cost-benefit analysis and "takings" compensation, emissions trading and "win-win" environmentalism. They disagreed about many things, including basic principles. But there was general consensus about two ideas: that environmental goals are important, and that the current structure of regulation isn't that great.

Setting Environmental Policy Right

Environmental policy is finally growing up. But to make genuine improvements, rather than merely tinker around the edges, we first need to understand where the demand for environmental regulation comes from, and where it went wrong. And we need a vision of how environmental policy might be set right—of the general principles and concepts that might guide a new environmentalism.

Environmentalism is not, as its critics sometimes portray it, simply a New Age ideology foisted upon an unwilling public. The environmental *movement* has important ideological components, but the demand for cleaner air and water or for wilderness and species preservation is not that different from the demand for any other good. As living standards rise, people want to buy more environmental "goods." Pollution is as old as human activity, but only recently have we been rich enough to worry about it.

From "Evolutionary Ecology: A New Environmental Vision" by Lynn Scarlett. Reprinted with permission, from the May 1996 issue of *Reason* magazine. Copyright 1996 by the Reason Foundation, 3415 S. Sepulveda Blvd., Suite 400, Los Angeles, CA 90034.

Looking across countries, University of Chicago economist Don Coursey finds a clear correlation between increased wealth, measured by per capita GDP [gross domestic product], and increased allegiance to environmental protection. As incomes rise, per capita expenditures on pollution control increase—a phenomenon Coursey observes in most advanced industrialized nations. The amount of land set aside for protection also rises with GDP. Green groups may decry economic growth, but it is growth itself that makes environmental protection possible and popular.

Coursey's work also points up a fact often forgotten in public discussions: "The environment" is not an all-or-nothing good, but a bundle of different goods. In surveys, he asks people to indicate how much they'd be willing to spend to preserve different species. The results are wildly varied. Animals like the bald eagle and grizzly bear consistently rank high, while spiders, beetles, snakes, and snails are barely valued. The varied costs of real-world regulations reflect this distinction: Coursey calculates the amount spent to preserve a single Florida panther at $4.8 million, compared to a mere $1.17 to preserve a single Painted Snake Coil Forest Snail.

Values and Knowledge

Political maneuvering may produce such disparate results, but the law does not actually recognize such distinctions, or the implicit tradeoffs they express. It declares species protection, like many other environmental goods, an absolute. Early environmentalist thinking—influential to this day—did not recognize environmental values as some goods among many but rather proclaimed them preeminent: Earth First! A California regulator describes his state's water policy this way: "If Mother Nature didn't put it in, you had to take it out—everything—that was the goal. This drove us to rigid, grossly exuberant attempts at clean up."

This absolutism suggests one way that environmental policy went wrong. It did not recognize that quality of life resides in pursuit of multiple values. People seek shelter, nourishment, health, security, learning, fairness, companionship, freedom, and personal comfort together with environmental protection. They even seek many, sometimes competing, environmental goals. They don't agree on how to marshal their resources (and time) in

> *"'The environment' is not an all-or-nothing good, but a bundle of different goods."*

pursuit of these many goals. And it is often difficult for outsiders—or even individuals themselves—to know in advance how they would prefer to trade off among different values.

Competing values are not unique to the environmental arena. In fact, people make such tradeoffs every day. They also deal with another conundrum of environmental policy: the "knowledge problem."

On the one hand, environmental problems involve matters of "general" knowledge, scientific knowledge of facts that are constant across time and space. In some cases, the general knowledge is a matter of settled understanding: the boiling point of water, for instance, or the bonding patterns of chemicals. In others, it is a matter of ongoing research and scientific contention. General knowledge includes such still-controversial issues as the health hazards of various substances or the effects of CFCs [chlorofluorocarbons] on the ozone layer. Much environmental debate takes place over issues of general knowledge, and these questions are important. But they aren't the whole story.

> *"[Conflicts] include potentially big nuisances such as toxic air emissions or discharges of waste into water bodies."*

Environmental problems and problem solving also often involve "specific" knowledge—the knowledge of time, place, and experience described by Nobel laureate F.A. Hayek in "The Use of Knowledge in Society." This information varies by circumstance and location and may change over time. Specific knowledge is decentralized—it resides on the factory floor, at a particular Superfund site, or on a specific farm.

The impacts of a landfill in a desert will differ from those near the Florida Everglades. Emitting effluent into a fast-moving stream is different from emitting waste into a pond. Using two coats of paint will have different effects than using just one coat. Resources use and emissions associated with cloth and disposable diapers will depend on how many are used each day, what kinds of disposal systems are available, and where those systems are located. . . .

Using Markets for a Clean Environment

For too long environmental policy has been shaped by people who demanded that environmental values trump all other considerations and who assumed that a regulatory elite possessed all necessary knowledge. Rather than figuring out how to perfect or create institutions that would allow a market for environmental goods to develop and flourish, they have been bent on opposing and destroying markets. They have seen markets not as processes for addressing values and conveying knowledge but as symbols of base commercialism and greed. This moralistic approach is finally fading. We can now begin to examine what sorts of institutions different environmental goods require—to explore a new environmental vision. . . .

Markets work for goods [that] have certain characteristics that make transactions relatively simple. It's possible to clearly specify who owns what, to identify buyers and sellers, and to convey all the necessary information for trades to take place. As a result, the market operates as a discovery process to address the knowledge and value problems—and to encourage improvements over time. . . .

In other cases, however, things aren't so clearly defined. There are frictions:

hard-to-divide goods, parties too numerous or scattered to be identified, vital information that isn't easily shared or easily known, blurry property lines. Institutions must evolve to deal with these hard cases.

One such institution is the common law. The common-law approach asks, "What happens when one person's sphere of activity conflicts with another person's?" The result is a focus on the concepts of liability, nuisance, and trespass; the role of courts in evaluating harms and benefits; and their role in resolving conflicts by clarifying the scope of different intersecting rights.

This blurry realm is not confined to a few difficult air pollution problems (and, in fact, common law may not work well for air pollution). Anywhere people congregate, conflicts emerge over sights, smells, and physical invasions that include everything from factory smoke to ugly houses to one neighbor's leaves falling on another's yard. They also include potentially big nuisances such as toxic air emissions or discharges of waste into water bodies.

The Common-Law Framework and Tradition

The common-law framework offers a means of further clarifying rights and refining just what "enjoyment and use" of one's property means. It is thus both a mechanism for conflict resolution and a means of discovering the scope and limit of rights.

Consider an apartment building with a noisy air-conditioning unit that disturbs a neighbor. Asked for injunctive relief, one tool of common law, the court may emphasize the neighbor's rights, requiring the apartment owner to eliminate the air conditioner noise—unless the neighbor agrees to some other arrangement. Or it may assign the owner the rights, declaring that the neighbor must put up with the noise unless he can make a deal with the owner. In actual conflicts, injunctive relief usually balances the two interests. "The law of nuisance," says Chicago economist Coursey, "actually would tend to use a rule that looked like a combination. . . : the apartment owner may make noise with impunity up to some critical level, and, if the apartment owner makes more than the critical level of noise, the single family may obtain an order of the court directing the apartment owner to reduce the noise down to the critical level."

> *"Unlike statutes, common law takes into account the particular circumstances of specific situations."*

In his famous "Coase theorem," Nobel laureate Ronald Coase developed the theoretical underpinnings of this sort of institution. In a friction-free world, where there are no "transaction costs," he argued, it doesn't matter which side is given the rights, because the two parties can always make a deal. (This calculation covers only the question of whether activities will occur, not issues of fairness, where distribution of rights does matter.) If your air conditioner is making noise you have every right to make, I can pay you to stop; if, on the other hand, you have no right to a noisy air conditioner without my permission, you can pay me to grant that permission. Problems arise in the real world, however, because transactions aren't free and the way rights are defined affects the cost of reaching agreement. So social institutions, such as courts, step in and assign rights to minimize conflict and maximize wealth, at least in theory.

> *"Traditional regulations . . . ignore the location-specific and ever-changing information critical to all production and consumption decisions."*

Common-law tradition embodies a discovery process that clarifies and refines rights boundaries and obligations in those blurry realms where different sets of rights intersect. Common law tends to follow precedent, and precedent can only be disturbed by private parties bringing new cases with slightly different circumstances or new arguments. As the law gets better and better at maximizing the welfare of the parties in a particular kind of case, fewer and fewer such cases will be brought. As a result, the common law tends to settle on fairly efficient rules—those that make the value pie larger. Private parties then bargain "in the shadow" of settled law, dividing a larger pie than they would under rules not tested over time.

Common law, write economists Bruce Yandle and Roger Meiners, "continues to evolve. Changing preferences and improved understanding of pollution problems continuously enter the arena of law." And, unlike statutes, common law takes into account the particular circumstances of specific situations.

Rely on Markets, Not Regulations

The common law can work to mediate disputes between discrete, identifiable parties. But, concede Yandle and Meiners, "It is hard to imagine how common law could address urban auto emission control, ozone layer problems, and global warming, to the extent that the science of those problems becomes more settled." In such cases, it is much too difficult to identify a clear-cut "polluter" and a clearcut "plaintiff." Either most people fall simultaneously into both categories or the cost of dividing the environmental good—clean air, an undisturbed ozone layer, etc.—is much too high (sometimes approaching infinity).

Yet the problems of knowledge and values remain, and so does the demand for environmental goods. The trick for environmental reformers is to develop a vision of evolving institutions that permits different sorts of institutions to address different kinds of issues, and to do so at the appropriate decision-making level. It helps to think of this challenge as a sequence of interrelated questions, a decision tree based on the characteristics of the particular environmental goods involved.

In some cases, what is needed is not political rule making but business institutions. In these cases, environmental goods are divisible, rights are assignable, and we are in the ordinary realm of markets, where entrepreneurs are rewarded for finding ways to address the knowledge and value problems effectively. Here the only issue is allowing time for institutions to evolve on their own.

Markets for some recyclables, for instance, are hampered because buyers and sellers sometimes lack information about available supplies and demand, and uniform quality is not guaranteed. These problems resemble those of many farm commodities in the 1800s. One remedy is to mimic the experience of corn farmers a century ago: Establish a coordinated process for trading in recyclables. The creation of electronic listing of some recyclables with the Chicago Board of Trade is a first step in this direction.

This approach differs markedly from political activists' calls to mandate recycled content in products. Those proposed mandates simply override the specific knowledge of circumstances so critical to efficient resource use. For example, mandating high levels of recycled content in certain paperboard products can require adding extra virgin (nonwaste) fiber to maintain adequate strength of the paperboard. The result is a heavier product that uses more total fiber.

Often, however, environmental goods are indivisible and present challenges to ordinary markets. Faced with these "market failures," the traditional response from the green movement has been to substitute government coercion for individual choice. Yet absolutist regulation that suppresses knowledge and imposes a single value hierarchy is not the only way to achieve such goals as clean air. It is possible to create evolvable institutions that, while they are not as simple or politically neutral as traditional markets, capture much relevant information about knowledge and values.

Tradeable Permit Schemes

Traditional regulations, such as technology prescriptions and resource-use mandates, ignore the location-specific and ever-changing information critical to all production and consumption decisions. Performance standards, by contrast, allow individuals and firms to figure out how best to achieve the stated standards: to lower overall air pollution to a certain level, for instance. This is the central insight of economists who have articulated the case for market-oriented regulations like the tradeable permit [which allow industrial facilities to emit a certain amount of pollutants] scheme set forth in the 1990 Clean Air Act Amendments.

> *"If most relevant knowledge is location-specific and dynamic, decisions about 'how clean is clean' and what remedies to use should take place closest to where the problem occurs."*

Tradeable permit schemes and pollution charges [taxes] provide flexibility to producers (and consumers, in the case of vehicle emission charges) that should, in the long run, result in more efficient responses to air pollution problems. These approaches still require top-down goal-setting, and they are still therefore subject to political pressures. In setting such standards, general scientific knowledge is critical, and often a matter of dispute.

But the problem of indivisibility—especially in the case of air pollution—makes some sort of collective goal-setting inevitable. The number of affected

> *"Bargaining itself may serve as a discovery process, revealing more accurate information about both risks and benefits."*

parties makes common-law approaches or voluntary bargaining cumbersome, given today's technologies. What is attractive about tradeable permit schemes is their potential to prepare the groundwork for creating enforceable "clean air rights" over time. For this to happen, however, legislators need to eliminate all the current language that insists these pollution credits are not rights—language that renders investment in such credits uncertain.

Making Environmental Decisions

Tradeable permits and pollution charges are promising mechanisms. But even if we decide they are the right mechanisms to address a certain environmental problem, we still must ask who the affected parties are—who is breathing the air in question—and where, then, the goal-setting ought to be done. For three decades, we've taken for granted the idea that there should be one single environmental standard for the whole nation. But understanding the roles of knowledge and values in defining and pricing environmental goods suggests that that may not be the case. For some problems, impacts are strictly local and narrowly circumscribed. Other environmental problems may impose regional, or even global, impacts. The locus of impact should help determine where decision-making authority resides.

If most relevant knowledge is location-specific and dynamic, decisions about "how clean is clean" and what remedies to use should take place closest to where the problem occurs. For air-emission problems, that might mean a local air basin. For decisions about siting a hazardous waste facility, that might mean bargaining between landowners adjacent to the site and the site owner.

The rationale for using decentralized bargaining approaches to address environmental problems lies not with any mystical faith that small is always beautiful, nor with the now-faddish notion that all that is good must come from communities. The rationale for these approaches builds, instead, on two premises. One is the importance of decentralized information in understanding and remedying environmental problems. The other is the importance of finding ways for real people affected by real conflicts of social space to undertake their own balancing act among competing values.

Several years ago, when the Mobro garbage barge out of Islip, New York, roamed the high seas in search of a place to unload its unappetizing cargo, nightly newscasters regaled viewers with tales of the NIMBY (not-in-my-backyard) problem. People increasingly don't want landfills—or any other "nuisance" facility—sited in their communities. But people do want to be able to throw out their waste, and the trash must go somewhere.

Political edicts directing communities to site landfills are one possible remedy. But such edicts simply override the concerns and preferences of affected individuals. Bargaining between would-be landfill operators and local communities offers another option—one already used by waste management companies. Sometimes called YIMBY-FAP (yes, in my backyard, for a price), these arrangements involve negotiations in which landfill operators offer a package of protections and benefits, including compensation, to affected landowners—or sometimes entire communities—in exchange for permission to site a landfill. The costs of the landfill are thus borne by all its customers, rather than only the property owners in the surrounding area. (The same principle applies in legal reforms aimed at requiring government "takings" compensation to landowners who bear the cost of such policies as wetlands protection. Society as a whole is buying an environmental good, and all the "purchasers" should bear the cost.)

Perceptions and Fears

These bargaining processes have shed light on several important decision-making conundrums.

First, surveys of New York citizens showed that acceptance of benefit packages depends on how the package is offered. Early direct involvement in the bargaining process is important to participants.

Second, perceptions matter. Just as people may "irrationally" want to buy cars with tail fins, so too they may "irrationally" dislike living next to a landfill, even if it poses no health hazards. In our study, "Too Little, Too Late? Host-Community Benefits and Siting Solid Waste Facilities," economist Rodney Fort and I note that "perception costs might be portrayed as distortions of reality, or as the inability of lay people correctly to assess the problem, but individuals will react according to their perceptions. . . . The [perception] costs are real regardless of whether public perception is viewed as correct or rational by policy makers, scientists, and technical experts."

Technocratically minded environmental reformers fear that public perceptions will yield irrational demands, driving up costs to solve environmental problems—whether those problems involve building landfills or cleaning up Superfund sites. Those fears do not appear to be justified in circumstances where citizens face *both* the risks associated with a facility and enjoy directly the benefits—in the form of lower costs or higher compensation—associated with a particular remedy. Bargaining itself may serve as a discovery process, revealing more accurate information about both risks and benefits.

Unbounded fears may, in fact, be more likely to drive decisions toward "zero risk" in centralized decision processes. There, the costs of decisions are spread over an entire population, while the benefits from pursuing pristine clean-ups are enjoyed by those few near a particular site. The few then have an incentive to invest heavily in lobbying, while the many do not—with obvious results. Experience with many EPA regulations, and the very high cost per year of life saved associated with those regulations, confirms this observation.

> *"Congress needs to get the EPA out of the business of prospectively approving state and local environmental protection programs."*

The contrast between costly Superfund site clean-ups, which have occurred in a top-down, regulatory framework directed by the EPA, and more recent local remediation of abandoned industrial sites through negotiated settlements offers further testament to this point. Processes that create closer links between those who pay for clean-up costs and those who enjoy the benefits of clean-up offer a discipline missing from traditional top-down approaches. The locally negotiated clean-ups have, in general, been achieved at a fraction of the cost for Superfund sites. . . .

Decentralization

Clearly, an environmental vision based on evolving institutions will not please everyone. It acknowledges tradeoffs among values, and it admits both the necessity and the limits of political decision making—positions guaranteed to upset both traditional environmentalists and free market absolutists. It does not promise a perfect world, merely a slowly improving one. And it faces squarely the underlying problem with current environmental regulations: Centralized, top-down rule making is ill-suited to addressing environmental problems in a complex, dynamic world in which most relevant information is location-specific and different people have very different priorities.

Applying such a vision cannot be a matter of waving a single legislative wand. Three decades of statutes have created layer upon layer of regulations. But Congress could start with a few basic reforms. The National Environmental Policy Institute is exploring ways to craft a single statute that would phase in devolution of most environmental decisions to states. The concept is worth pursuing. Devolution to states does not really go far enough, since, ultimately, what is needed is further decentralization to local communities and, where feasible, privatization of environmental decisions. But devolution to the states is a good place to start in any reform agenda.

Similarly, Congress needs to get the EPA out of the business of prospectively approving state and local environmental protection programs. Under the Clean Air Act, for example, Congress sets air-emission standards and states are delegated responsibility for developing State Implementation Plans. Using computer models and other criteria, the EPA assesses those plans to determine whether they comply with federal law. States get full emission-reduction "credits" when the EPA's computer models show a state program achieving over time some estimated pollution reduction. But this means the EPA's assumptions about everything from population growth to commuting patterns, not actual pollution levels, determine the outcome. The process prevents experimentation. It locks states into using technologies or programs that the EPA thinks—but has not necessarily demonstrated—will work. Eliminating the prospective approval process would give states the latitude to design programs they believe will achieve emission reductions, and to evaluate and adjust those programs based on real-world data.

Above all, what is needed is a fundamental shift away from an approach that is primarily regulatory and punitive to one that emphasizes bargaining, improvement in information flows, and incentives for stewardship.

Environmental Policy Should Recognize Common Law and Community Needs

by Bruce Yandle

About the author: *Bruce Yandle is an alumni professor at Clemson University's Center for Policy & Legal Studies in Clemson, South Carolina, and a senior associate for the Political Economy Research Center, a Bozeman, Montana, organization that advocates free-market solutions to environmental problems.*

Since around 1970, the U.S. and most of the industrialized world have been engaged in a massive effort to improve and guard environmental quality. It is a gross understatement to say that the struggles along the way are well documented. Indeed, anyone who has attempted to stay abreast of the topic has built a veritable library of hearings, books, journals, and special reports.

Pursuing Effective Change

What have we learned? How can we improve? Can we identify a better path than the one we have traveled? Some call for a revolution in policy. Others expect to see evolutionary change. One thing is certain. There will be change. The reasons? Our current command-and-control-based policy [of enforcement and punishment] is obsolete. It is time to replace the 1970 centralized model that emerged when information was costly with something that fits a world calling for flexibility, decentralization and improved environmental protection.

I hope for metamorphic change: A new butterfly to replace the old caterpillar. I hope to see policy based on results, not inputs. It is my hope that our measure of success will be environmental improvement, not technologies, suits, and number of enforcement actions. In my comments, I will speak first about some

From "Environmental Policy: Thoughts on a Positive Agenda," a speech by Bruce Yandle, delivered to the Progress and Freedom Foundation, Washington, D.C., March 18, 1996. Reprinted by permission of the author.

broad principles. I then use those principles to consider some flowers that have emerged in the concrete of control. By examining these exceptions to the rule, we may find ideas that form some elements for a revised environmental policy agenda.

There are two very broad options that can be selected when a community of people seeks to regulate collective behavior. I refer to one option as a systems approach. The other, a process approach.

The systems approach involves detailed study of key features of the particular problem being addressed, for example, air pollution. Those directing the approach seek to understand minute features of the problem, to develop detailed rules of behavior, and then to enforce those rules. The focus is on inputs, behavior, technology; it is what we all call command-and-control regulation.

Command-and-control assumes that if inputs are right, outcomes will take care of themselves. Monitoring is not necessary. It is a rigid, rule-filled approach to the problem that works pretty well for static situations and homogeneous polluters, where most important features of the problem do not change and the pollutants being controlled do not interact with or form other pollutants. Unfortunately, there are not many situations like this in today's world. The systems people believe that well-specified pollution problems can be solved so long as the incentives faced by human agents have little bearing on the outcome. The methods used to control automobile emissions provide a pertinent example of the systems approach.

Superiority of the Process Approach

In contrast, the process approach develops constraints and linkages to them that cause individual decision makers to account for their actions. It focuses on broader environmental outcomes, not inputs. Monitoring is crucial. And community participants have an incentive to help monitor.

The process approach is better geared for dynamic, multiple pollution situations, where the decision makers and conditions are heterogeneous and the cost of continuously gaining highly technical information and implementing it is very large. The constraints may be rules of property and liability that give rise to costs and rewards to all who are a part of the process. For example, simple common law rules say polluters—air, water, odor, solid waste—have no right to impose uninvited costs on their neighbors, but that the neighbors and polluters can negotiate solutions.

> *"The process approach develops constraints and linkages to them that cause individual decision makers to account for their actions."*

River basin associations and multi-state compacts, which are enlarged common law approaches, embody rules of property and law that yield incentives to reduce the cost of meeting a community's environmental quality constraint.

River basin managers monitor outcomes. The responsibility of paying for damages disciplines polluters; the ability of lovers of environmental quality to purchase more environmental quality provides some flexibility. Outcomes—the river, not inputs, are what matter in the process approach. Indeed, no one really cares very much about inputs other than those who sell and service them.

Cracks in the Systems Approach

After 25 years of experience, we know that systems approaches worked relatively well for some things in some settings. We also know that taking a systems approach to process problems or applying a process approach to certain systems problems encourages frustration and generates unneeded costs. Sadly, it seems, the systems approach diverts attention from the goal being sought. Environmental outcomes are often relegated to the back seat, while regulators drive toward input compliance.

"The ['responsible care'] program encourages chemical firms to form partnerships with communities, to invite third-party audits, and to show what firms are doing."

By and large, the U.S. has taken a systems approach. Consider a few capsules of highly stylized results: Air quality regulators cannot readily focus on related water pollution problems. Hazardous waste regulators are not allowed to make comparative assessments of priority sites and to vary their allocation of efforts. Property rights are bruised in an effort to protect wetlands, which themselves are not well defined. Command-and-control causes endangered species to become liabilities instead of assets. In short, we have learned that the "one suit fits all approach" works well for a static population of identical actors, but not so well for a diverse and rapidly changing industrial economy.

The high cost of uniform input management has led to some creativity and alteration of rules. Cracks develop in the command-and-control concrete, as individual actors try to custom tailor the regulatory suits that do not fit so well. At some point, after all, people become concerned about the environment and what is happening to it. By looking closely at what goes on in the cracks, we may discover a positive agenda for revised environmental policy.

Evolving Approaches

Let me quickly list some evolving approaches to the goal of environmental protection that I believe help to identify elements of a future agenda.

Facility focus with complete flexibility in achieving goals. The Amoco Yorktown story informs us of a remarkable experiment where EPA [Environmental Protection Agency] and Amoco formed a partnership and did a top-to-bottom assessment of the Yorktown refinery. Putting command-and-control to one side, the two parties for the first time assessed the environment. They found that some things were far better than expected; other things that previously received little or no regulatory attention offered low-cost opportunities for environmental improvement. By focusing on goals and allowing flexibility, everyone won—the community, EPA and Amoco.

Third-party audits and open doors. The world chemical industry has embarked on a program called "responsible care." The program encourages chemical firms to form partnerships with communities, to invite third-party audits, and to show what firms are doing, how they are controlling pollution, and to illustrate how more can be accomplished if flexibility is allowed. To reduce the understandable fear of using third-party audits, the State of South Carolina is considering legislation that would prevent the use of such findings from incriminating firms and individuals where violations are voluntarily discovered and corrected.

"Future environmental policy should place a premium on measuring, monitoring, and reporting on environmental quality."

River basin associations. North Carolina's Tar-Pamlico River Basin Association is North America's only operating association that brings together point and nonpoint sources of pollution in a combined trading effort to reduce nitrogen and phosphorous loadings in a river. I should point out that this approach is commonplace elsewhere. Property rights and contracts provide the vehicle. Command-and-control simply could not do the job in North Carolina. EPA wiped away the systems approach, focused on the process and allowed complete flexibility in achieving a water quality goal. This could not have been accomplished without the vital support of the Environmental Defense Fund. Again, everyone won—the community, the polluters, the regulators, and the river.

ISO 14000 and the State of Pennsylvania. Global markets are pushing environmental goals with forces that sometimes surpass those of the regulators. The International Standards Organization, a nongovernmental organization, assists and audits firms that seek to be ISO certified, a contractual requirement in many cases for selling goods in world markets. The State of Pennsylvania now accepts ISO 14000 certification as a substitute for evidence that firms located there meet Pennsylvania standards. The market has replaced the regulator.

Superfund and the Dutch system. The Dutch system for dealing with abandoned hazardous waste sites has been adopted generally across all of Europe, which has far more abandoned sites than the U.S. The triage system allows for some sites to be contained, not mitigated, some to be returned to full use because of low risk, and some to be mitigated, often at public expense. The mitigated sites must be cleaned to the level of customary use for the land in question. The result: There is no celebration of litigation. Sites are being cleaned. Property rights tend to be protected and costs contained.

Chapter 4

A New Environmental Policy

What does this say about an agenda? Let me suggest the following:

Goal orientation. Future environmental policy should place a premium on measuring, monitoring, and reporting on environmental quality. Progress toward specific goals, as set by communities, should be the measure of success, not the number of suits, enforcement actions, and installation of technology.

Flexibility. Performance goals with complete flexibility for attaining them should be the general foundation for all environmental policy, with command-and-control occupying the default position. Innovation should be rewarded, not penalized. Valuable knowledge must be conserved.

Biological envelopes. The larger environmental envelope that surrounds a community of environmental users should form the zone of control. River-basin, water-shed, and air-shed associations, as well as multi-state compacts, should be encouraged and given flexibility in accomplishing goals. Again, the monitoring function is crucial.

Community common sense. Decision making for environmental protection should be located where outcomes and costs matter the most—at the level of the environmental user. People in communities can be trusted to protect themselves from harm. Those facing the problems have the greatest incentive to find the least-cost way of dealing with the problems. Local communities should rise to the top of the regulatory hierarchy.

Common law. Steps should be taken to salvage common law protection of private environmental rights. Statutory shields against common law remedies should be eliminated, provided the community has participated in determining environmental goals and solutions.

Property rights. Property rights should be respected. When private parties are asked to provide public benefits by altering the use of privately held rights, they should be paid.

As we consider elements for a new environmental policy, we do so recognizing that we live in a world that faces many other compelling demands. We hear about health care, safety, retirement security, education, and emerging communities elsewhere that grapple with even more primitive wants and needs. Global competition is mentioned endlessly, and it is real.

The basic blueprints for the nation's environmental policy are now 25 years old. Not many things that old have survived into today's dynamic world. We no longer have a smokestack economy. But we still have countless smokestack regulations that stand in the way of effective environmental improvement. In prehistoric times, we are told sharks and dinosaurs lived in the same periods. The dinosaur, full of bones, and not very flexible, did not adjust and adapt. The shark, which does not have a bone in its body, only cartilage, made it to modern times. Our new environmental policy should be shark, not a dinosaur.

The Superfund Program Should Be Privatized

by James V. DeLong

About the author: *James V. DeLong is a lawyer and an adjunct scholar at the Competitive Enterprise Institute, a Washington, D.C., research and advocacy group that supports environmental policies that give the private sector responsibility for protecting the environment.*

Superfund is not a program devoted to the protection of public health. It is an expensive mechanism for reclaiming a limited amount of land for general use. The number of parcels of real estate covered by the law or otherwise needing remediation runs into the hundreds of thousands (though the level of contamination of the vast majority is probably minimal), yet federal policy is to clean up the 1,238 sites on the National Priorities List [NPL] to operating-room standards and ignore the others.

Mistaken Policies

The effort to justify that policy results in exaggeration of the risks to public health posed by Superfund sites. Those risks are trivial and could be contained at low cost. Furthermore, the effort to "make the polluter pay" has enmeshed over 32,000 people in a regime of injustice, waste, inefficiency, and bloated transactions costs and is discouraging the redevelopment of properties.

The policy of concentrating on NPL sites ignores the arbitrary nature of the process by which sites are listed. There is no convincing evidence that those sites are significantly more threatening than are many non-NPL sites. The focus on the NPL also ignores the growing burden of private litigation, which is becoming an increasing drain on national economic resources and represents a significant reallocation of property rights.

The [Superfund] law should be repealed and site remediation privatized so that decisions are made by market processes, not bureaucratic ones. Existing federal

From "Privatizing Superfund: How to Clean Up Hazardous Waste" by James V. DeLong, *Cato Policy Analysis*, no. 247, December 18, 1995. Reprinted by permission of the Cato Institute, Washington, D.C.

sites and abandoned sites should be auctioned off to private parties for either a positive or a negative price. The buyers should be obligated only to contain the contamination and prevent harm to public health. Whether a site is cleaned up for use or left idle should be determined by the market for the property.

The Failure of Superfund

Superfund—the Comprehensive Environmental Response, Compensation, and Liability Act (CERCLA)—is often described as "broken." That description is not quite accurate, since it implies that the program was once in good repair. In fact, Superfund has never worked. The law, based on misunderstanding and distortion, was zipped through a lame-duck Congress in 1980 in a spirit of vengeance against "the polluters." It has been amended and operated on the same principle and stands as a sad reminder that revenge mixed with hypochondria is a poor basis for public policy. Watching the program evolve is like watching the characters in a Greek tragedy move to a doom compelled by their hubris. Perhaps a better metaphor is an English farce, in which nonsense is normal and expected.

"The [Superfund] law should be repealed and site remediation privatized so that decisions are made by market processes, not bureaucratic ones."

At this point, the wreckage is too complete to be fixed by tinkering. Because Superfund is a bipartisan problem—the vote in favor of stringent amendments in 1986 was 88 to 8 in the Senate and 386 to 27 in the House—perhaps both parties can recognize that the best course is to repeal it, take steps to provide rough justice to those who have been caught in its traps, and rethink the problem.

Superfund is actually five different programs with five different goals. It is:

- an emergency response program to protect public health against urgent hazards;
- a public health program to protect neighbors of waste disposal sites and users of drinking water against possible long-term harm associated with the escape of hazardous substances;
- a program to complement the Resource Conservation and Recovery Act (RCRA), which governs the generation and disposal of hazardous wastes, by imposing severe consequences for failure to control such wastes;
- a program to reclaim polluted land, returning it to productive use and enhancing the property values of its neighbors; and
- an expression of the belief that contaminated land is aesthetically offensive and that the quality of public life will be improved by cleanup (that belief can also be cast in stronger, religious terms—some people seem to regard pollution as a sin that must be prevented or atoned for, regardless of costs or benefits).

Many of Superfund's problems are due to miscommunication and confusion generated by the intermingling of the different goals. The law was originally sold as a broad public health measure (in pursuit of the first three goals above), and the Environmental Protection Agency's [EPA] public rhetoric and formal criteria for decisionmaking are still phrased in terms of public health protection. Yet in the course of its evolution, Superfund has become a land development and aesthetic enhancement program. Its connection to the protection of public health is exceedingly tenuous.

How to Achieve Cleanup Goals

The beginning of good policy is to recognize that each of the five goals requires its own approach. The first objective of Superfund—emergency response—can be pursued effectively by a government agency (although not necessarily at the federal level) concentrating on protection of public health. The second—long-term containment—is best handled by private landowners acting under the lash of legal responsibility for the escape of hazardous substances. The third—enforcing RCRA—may be important in the future, but it has nothing to do with the current problems of Superfund, which involve cleaning up releases that predate the passage of RCRA.

The fourth and fifth goals, which concern land reclamation and the development of property for productive or aesthetic purposes, cannot be pursued effectively by a government agency. Those efforts should be ruled by market processes, not bureaucratic ones, and should be governed by three principles:

• For government-owned and orphan sites, the government should establish a regime of private decisionmaking by auctioning off contaminated sites (for either a positive or negative price) on the sole condition that the buyer prevent the spread of contaminants. For privately owned sites, the law should require only that hazardous substances be contained.

• For both kinds of sites, cleanup should occur when economic forces dictate it as a step toward returning the site to industrial, commercial, residential, or recreational use, and decisions about the type of use and the timing of cleanup should be left to the owner.

• Ideally, specification of the levels of cleanup would be based on rules governing liability for harm to others. However, the current liability system contains many imperfections, and for the time being those specifications will have to be the product of government decisions. They should be based on realistic risk assessment methods, not the worst-case approach that dominates current decisionmaking, and should vary according to the use to which the owner decides to put the site. . . .

> *"Many of Superfund's problems are due to miscommunication and confusion generated by the intermingling of the different goals."*

Perhaps Millions of Sites

Before the passage of Superfund, the EPA's ballpark estimate was that between 30,000 and 50,000 sites contained hazardous waste and that 1,200 to 2,000 might present significant problems. That estimate is impossible to square with definitions contained in the law. Superfund's defined scope, applied literally, sweeps in hundreds of thousands, and perhaps millions, of sites. The implications of that were not considered at the time and have received little consideration since. The breadth of Superfund's formal coverage and uncertainty about the EPA's intentions hang over all reform proposals like a potential avalanche.

The all-encompassing nature of Superfund's definitions was tempered by the establishment of the National Priorities List. The EPA was required to develop a National Contingency Plan for discovering and assessing sites where hazardous substances might be found. The plan contains criteria for determining priorities for cleanup based on possible harm to human health or the environment, and the EPA is to use those to compile the NPL. The full weight of the program is applied only to the sites placed on the NPL. The federal super "fund" can be used to clean up hazardous wastes only on NPL sites, and only those sites are subjected to government-forced cleanup actions, potential responsible-party investigation, the preparation of formal risk assessments, and in general the full panoply of Superfund. . . .

Costs of Superfund Sites

Total Superfund spending on NPL sites, including cleanup and transaction costs and the tax bill, runs about $6 billion per year. The estimated cost of an average NPL cleanup is about $29 million, but the true cost varies greatly with the type of site. A mining waste site might cost $170 million, a manufacturing site only $13 million. Remediating some of the big federal facilities will be an even more expensive task.

"Superfund's defined scope, applied literally, sweeps in hundreds of thousands, and perhaps millions, of sites."

The cost estimates exclude the transaction costs of determining liabilities when multiple parties are involved. If only four or five PRPs [Potentially Responsible Parties] exist, transaction costs might turn a $29 million cleanup into a $30.5 million job. The transaction costs for 50 PRPs might raise the total from $29 million to $41 million.

Polluters are also liable for "natural resource damages," which means they pay for general damage to the environment regardless of any economic harm. "Natural resource damage" is an esoteric topic with a specialized literature of its own, but its flavor is captured by a recommendation for reform by Ridgway M. Hall Jr. in 1995 that states, "Legislation is needed to limit natural resource damage liability to cases where there is actual damage to natural resources." Only under Superfund would liability for phantom damages come to be the natural order of things and the idea that damages should actually exist before they must be paid for come to be regarded as a proposal for reform.

The nation's total potential cleanup bill cannot be calculated, given the uncertainty surrounding the number of contaminated sites. Two thoughtful analysts [Milton Russell and Kimberly L. Davis] put the range at between $44.4 billion and $135 billion. The low bound assumes 1,350 sites at an average cost of $32.9 million; the high estimate is for 3,000 sites at a cost of $46 million each. Such estimates could be expanded. If 10,000 sites need cleanup at an average cost of $30 million each, the price tag is $300 billion. If 1 million sites require an

> *"[Superfund's] potential future costs are in the hundreds of billions, and maybe in the trillions, of dollars."*

average investment of, say, $1 million, then the total price is $1 trillion. Neither of those figures would represent an unreasonable guess, and even $5 trillion is not an upper bound under the EPA's present cleanup policies. . . .

Escalating Costs and Grievances

Superfund is perceived, accurately, as unjust. It is also perceived, accurately, as expensive and ineffective, pouring out money without creating value. Its potential future costs are in the hundreds of billions, and maybe in the trillions, of dollars. Its requirements are inscrutable, creating substantial uncertainty for the people within its ambit and subjecting them to heavy penalties at the whim of an arbitrary bureaucracy. It transfers mountains of money to litigation lawyers and environmental consultants for work of little or negative social utility. It siphons resources into a limited number of sites on the NPL while ignoring broader cleanup problems, and it contains no system for establishing priorities. It has created a huge problem of "brownfields" [abandoned urban industrial areas] because hundreds of thousands of parcels of land are blighted for development while new industries are built on virgin ground. Incentives are perverted, as contractors have little reason to seek efficiency or pursue innovation. Finally, despite years of heavy criticism, Superfund never gets fixed.

Those issues reinforce each other in a steadily intensifying spiral of grievance. A minor PRP who gave trash to the local municipal collection service feels irked if asked to contribute a few dollars toward cleaning up the dump. Up the ante by making him or her pay part of the cost for all the unknown contributors, and for the whole dump, and the sense of grievance grows. Add other factors, such as cleanup standards that have no relationship to real risk and that increase costs dramatically, and irritation soon turns to a raging sense of injustice. Put enforcement in the hands of hard-nosed federal attorneys, and then let Congress dither over the problems for years without correcting them, and the public anger grows accordingly.

That is an extensive bill of particulars for a single program. As one industry lawyer said to the author, "Imagine. They accomplished all this in just 15 years. Usually it takes decades for a government program to become this fouled up.". . .

The Privatization Option

The only way to [improve cleanup policies] is to privatize Superfund. The virtues of privatization are the virtues of the free market. Markets allocate resources to their most productive uses, enlist the talents and energies of millions of people, establish values in situations of uncertainty, and provide efficient administration of complicated systems.

Privatization can best be accomplished by auctioning off the sites. Auctions are a mechanism for privatizing decisions, and they are, increasingly, used for decisions that have traditionally been made through bureaucratic processes. . . .

The auction mechanism could be used initially for sites owned by the government, either because they were contaminated by a federal agency or because they have been abandoned and the government has taken them over. Two other substantive reforms, however, would have to be made in Superfund, or the mechanism would be of little value.

• The government would have to abandon the idea that all sites must be cleaned up regardless of cost of remediation or ultimate value of the site. The buyer would agree to prevent human exposure but would not be required to clean up the site.

• The government would establish standards for cleanup appropriate for different types of uses, such as manufacturing, transportation terminal, residence, park, school, playground, and nature preserve. Those standards would be based on realistic risk assessments, not on worst-case phobias. An owner wanting to develop the property would have to meet the standard for the desired use. (As a matter of theory, that function could be performed by the private liability system, which would make the owner liable for any harm caused by

> *"The only way to [improve cleanup policies] is to privatize Superfund."*

contamination. However, the liability system for "toxic torts" is in considerable disarray at present, and Superfund reform cannot be suspended pending liability reform. The adoption of cleanup standards based on realistic risk assessment is a reasonable compromise solution.)

At the auction *the price could be positive or negative.* That is, the buyer of the property might pay money to the government in exchange for the land, or it might take the land only on the condition that the government pay money to the buyer. . . .

Privatization by auction, combined with abandonment of the policy of valueless cleanup, addresses most of the current problems with Superfund. It creates a mechanism for allocating cleanup resources to their most productive uses. They will be devoted to those sites that can be brought back into productive use most cost-effectively. "Worst-first" prioritization disappears automatically. The impossible problems created by using a bureaucratic process to allocate resources among competing sites according to some elaborate checklist are eliminated. That is a key benefit of the scheme. The government is not just privatizing the responsibility for conducting a cleanup. It is privatizing the decision about whether cleanup should be undertaken at all and, if it should, to what level of use. . . .

Use Market Forces to Correct Superfund Mistakes

One of the standard maxims of the followers of W. Edwards Deming, the great quality control expert whose teachings helped move Japanese industry to preeminence, is, "Fix the problem, not the blame." The obsession with fixing blame for contamination has been the curse of Superfund and has frustrated not only the nation's efforts to fix the problem but all efforts to even define the issues.

Once the problems are sorted out and the basic division between emergency response, containment and cleanup, RCRA enforcement, and real estate development established, the answers become much clearer. The worst possible approach is the present one, in which a few sites are selected haphazardly for intensive remediation while questions of value and payoff go totally ignored. Fifteen years of congressional posturing and agency bureaucracy have brought the program to its present condition, and there is no reason to believe that more of the same physic will improve matters. The only viable way to bring order out of the current chaos is to enlist the forces of the market to make the decisions about which of the many thousands of sites should be remediated and to what level.

Bibliography

Books

Frank Ackerman	*Why Do We Recycle? Markets, Values, and Public Policy.* Washington, DC: Island Press, 1996.
Judd H. Alexander	*In Defense of Garbage.* Westport, CT: Praeger, 1993.
Joseph L. Bast, Peter J. Hill, and Richard C. Rue	*Eco-Sanity: A Common Sense Guide to Environmentalism.* Lanham, MD: Madison Books, 1996.
Colin Crawford	*Uproar at Dancing Rabbit Creek: Battling over Race, Class, and the Environment.* Menlo Park, CA: Addison-Wesley, 1996.
Michael Gerrard	*Whose Backyard, Whose Risk: Fear and Fairness in Toxic and Nuclear Waste Siting.* Cambridge, MA: MIT Press, 1994.
Lois Marie Gibbs and Citizen's Clearinghouse for Hazardous Waste	*Dying from Dioxin.* Boston: South End Press, 1995.
John Lemons and Donald A. Brown, eds.	*Sustainable Development: Science, Ethics, and Public Policy.* Boston: Kluwer Academic Publishers, 1995.
Arjun Makhijani et al.	*Nuclear Wastelands: A Global Guide to Nuclear Weapons Production and Its Health and Environmental Effects.* Cambridge, MA: MIT Press, 1995.
Katherine N. Probst et al.	*Footing the Bill for Superfund Cleanups: Who Pays and How?* Washington, DC: Brookings Institution: Resources for the Future, 1995.
Lewis G. Regenstein	*Cleaning Up America the Poisoned.* Washington, DC: Acropolis Books, 1993.
Michael Sanera and Jane S. Shaw	*Facts, Not Fear: A Parent's Guide to Teaching Children About the Environment.* Washington, DC: Regnery, 1996.
Andrew Szasz	*Ecopopulism: Toxic Waste and the Movement for Environmental Justice.* Minneapolis: University of Minnesota Press, 1994.
U.S. House of Representatives, Committee on Small Business	*The Effects of Superfund Liability on Small Businesses.* Washington, DC: Government Printing Office, 1996.
John Wargo	*Our Children's Toxic Legacy: How Science and Law Fail to Protect Us from Pesticides.* New Haven, CT: Yale University Press, 1996.

| Laura Westra and Peter S. Wenz, eds. | *Faces of Environmental Racism.* Lanham, MD: Rowman and Littlefield, 1995. |

Periodicals

Beth Baker	"Curbside Recycling Revisionists," *Environmental Action*, Summer 1995.
Stuart Batterman and Yu-Li Huang	"Determining the Disproportionate Impacts from Pollution Sources," *Poverty & Race*, July/August 1996.
Gregg Easterbrook	"Ignore All Doomsayers on EPA Laws," *Los Angeles Times*, December 1, 1996. Available from Reprints, *Los Angeles Times*, Times Mirror Square, Los Angeles, CA 90053.
Brandy E. Fisher	"Dissolving Medical Waste," *Environmental Health Perspectives*, July 1996. Available from PO Box 12233, Research Triangle Park, NC 27709.
Michael Fumento	"Dioxin on Trial," *Regulation*, no. 4, 1994. Available from Cato Institute, 1000 Massachusetts Ave. NW, Washington, DC 20001.
Nancy Glaser et al.	"Recycling Pays!" *Yes!* Fall 1996. Available from PO Box 10818, Bainbridge Island, WA 98110.
Michael Gough and Steven Milloy	"EPA's Cancer Risk Guidelines: Guidance to Nowhere," *Cato Policy Analysis*, no. 263, November 12, 1996. Available from Cato Institute, 1000 Massachusetts Ave. NW, Washington, DC 20001.
Chris Hendrickson, Lester Lave, and Francis McMichael	"Time to Dump Recycling?" *Issues in Science and Technology*, Spring 1995.
Issues in Science and Technology	"Don't Dump Recycling," Letters to the Editor, Summer 1995.
Roger Meiners and Bruce Yandle	"Get the Government Out of Environmental Control," *USA Today*, May 1996.
Alva Morrison	"The Nuclear Triangle: Has the Southwest Been Selected as America's Nuclear Waste Dump?" *E Magazine*, February 1996.
Salim Muwakkil	"Moving Mountains," *In These Times*, February 19, 1996.
Neal Peirce	"Brownfields: Issue for the 90s," *Liberal Opinion Week*, September 16, 1996.
David Pescovitz, ed.	"The Future of Garbage," *Wired*, January 1997. Available from PO Box 191826, San Francisco, CA 94119-9866.
David Peterson	"Let Them Burn Garbage," *Z Magazine*, April 1996.
Pat Phibbs	"Birth Defects, Other Disorders Linked to Superfund Site Exposure, ATSDR Says," *Environmental Science & Technology*, vol. 30, no. 10, 1996. Available from 1155 16th St. NW, Washington, DC 20036.
James Ridgeway	"Glow Fish," *Village Voice*, November 5, 1996. Available from 36 Cooper Sq., New York, NY 10003.
Robert Steuteville	"Keys to Curbside Efficiency and Performance,"*BioCycle*, July 1996. Available from JG Press, 419 State Ave., Emmaus, PA 18049.

Bibliography

Robert Steuteville   "The State of Garbage in America," *BioCycle*, April 1996.

Elizabeth Striano   "Lowering Collection Costs, Improving Rates in Curbside Recycling Programs," *Waste Age's Recycling Times*, October 1, 1996. Available from 4301Connecticut Ave. NW, Suite 300, Washington, DC 20008.

Judy Stringer and   "Companies Embark on New Outreach," *Chemical Week*,
Kerri Walsh   July 3–10, 1996. Available from 888 7th Ave., New York, NY 10106.

Mike Weibacher   "Toxic Shock: The Environment-Cancer Connection," *E Magazine*, June 1995.

John E. Young   "The Sudden New Strength of Recycling," *World Watch*, July/August 1995. Available from 1776 Massachusetts Ave. NW, Washington, DC 20036.

Organizations to Contact

The editors have compiled the following list of organizations concerned with the issues debated in this book. The descriptions are derived from materials provided by the organizations. All have publications or information available for interested readers. The list was compiled on the date of publication of the present volume; names, addresses, phone and fax numbers, and e-mail and Internet addresses may change. Be aware that many organizations take several weeks or longer to respond to inquiries, so allow as much time as possible.

American Council on Science and Health (ACSH)
1995 Broadway, 2nd Fl.
New York, NY 10023-5860
(212) 362-7044
fax: (212) 362-4919
Internet: http://www.acsh.org

ACSH is an association of scientists and doctors concerned with public health. It seeks to educate the public about what it believes is the exaggerated danger from exposure to chemicals. ACSH's publications include the semiannual *Media Updates* and *News from ACSH* as well as the quarterly magazine *Priorities.*

American Crop Protection Association (ACPA)
1156 15th St. NW, Suite 400
Washington, DC 20005
(202) 296-1585
fax: (202) 463-0474
Internet: http://www.acpa.org

ACPA is an association of firms that produce agricultural chemicals such as herbicides, pesticides, defoliants, and soil disinfectants. It contains legislative and regulatory departments and maintains committees on environmental management, public health, and toxicology. The association promotes the use of chemicals in farm production. It publishes the periodic *Bulletin* and the quarterly *Growing Possibilities.*

American Public Information Center on the Environment (APIE)
124 High St.
South Glastonbury, CT 06073
(800) 320-2743
e-mail: apie800@aol.com
Internet: http://www.americanpie.org

APIE is an environmental organization that serves people and communities through several programs, including a toll-free telephone information line that responds to callers' environmental questions and concerns. APIE also publishes the quarterly *American PIE.*

Canadian Wildlife Federation (CWF)
2740 Queensview
Ottawa, ON K2B 1A2
CANADA
(613) 721-2286
fax: (613) 721-2902

The Canadian Wildlife Federation is Canada's largest wildlife conservation organization. Through summits, educational materials, and research, the organization works to conserve wildlife and ensure the wise use of Canada's resources. CWF publishes booklets and pamphlets on a variety of topics, including recycling and toxic chemicals, as well as the periodical *Canadian Wildlife.*

Cato Institute
1000 Massachusetts Ave. NW
Washington, DC 20001-5403
(202) 842-0200
fax: (202) 842-3490

The institute is a libertarian public policy research foundation dedicated to promoting the principle of limited government and to achieving greater public involvement in questions of governmental policy. It publishes the triannual *Cato Journal,* the bimonthly newsletter *Cato Policy Report,* and the quarterly magazine *Regulation,* which include articles on limiting environmental regulations.

Center for Waste Reduction Technologies (CWRT)
345 E. 47th St.
New York, NY 10017
(212) 705-7407
fax: (212) 705-3297

CWRT comprises corporations, government agencies, academicians, and other individuals who are interested in promoting public awareness of waste reduction technologies. The center identifies areas for research, conducts educational programs, and facilitates the exchange of information. It publishes the periodic newsletter *WasteNotes* and numerous brochures, including *Waste Reduction Priorities in Manufacturing: A DOE/CWRT Workshop.*

Chemical Manufacturers Association (CMA)
1300 Wilson Blvd.
Arlington, VA 22209
(703) 741-5000
fax: (703) 741-6000

CMA is a national association of chemical companies. It conducts technical research and monitors legislation and regulations regarding environmental safety and health. The association also provides health and safety information about chemicals to the public. In addition to numerous booklets, its publications include the magazine *ChemEcology* and the newsletter *CMA News,* each published ten times a year.

Coalition for Responsible Waste Incineration (CRWI)
1133 Connecticut Ave. NW, Suite 1023
Washington, DC 20036
(202) 775-9839
fax: (202) 833-8491

The coalition promotes responsible incineration of industrial waste as part of an overall waste management strategy. It publishes the CRWI Information Kit, which supplies technical, safety, health, and environmental information concerning waste incineration.

Council on Packaging in the Environment (COPE)
1255 23rd St., NW
Washington, DC 20037-1174
(202) 331-0099
fax: (202) 833-3636

COPE works to increase awareness of solid waste management problems and to promote a balanced combination of source reduction, recycling, waste-to-energy recovery, and landfilling. The council publishes the monthly *COPE Update* and the factsheet series Backgrounders.

Environmental Defense Fund (EDF)
257 Park Ave. South
New York, NY 10010
(212) 505-2100
fax: (212) 505-0892
Internet: http://www.edf.org

The fund is a public interest organization of lawyers, scientists, and economists dedicated to the protection and improvement of environmental quality and public health. It publishes the bimonthly *EDF Letter* and the report "Plastics Recycling: How Slow Can It Grow."

Environmental Research Foundation (ERF)
PO Box 5036
Annapolis, MD 21403-7036
(410) 263-1584
fax: (410) 263-8944
e-mail: erf@rachel.clark.net

ERF strives to help people fight environmental injustices in their own communities. It specializes in information about hazardous waste and waste disposal and seeks to educate the public on their adverse health effects. The foundation publishes *Rachel's Environment and Health Weekly* newsletter and various fact sheets and reports, including "An Odor Like a Skunk Dipped in Creosote and Burned: EPA's Regulation of Commercial Hazardous Waste Incinerators."

Friends of the Earth
1025 Vermont Ave. NW, Suite 300
Washington, DC 20005
(202) 783-7400

Friends of the Earth is dedicated to protecting the planet from environmental disaster and to preserving biological diversity. The organization encourages toxic waste cleanup and promotes the use of tax dollars to protect the environment. Its publications include the bimonthly newsletter *Friends of the Earth* and the books *Crude Awakening, the Oil Mess in America: Wasting Energy, Jobs, and the Environment* and *Earth Budget: Making Our Tax Dollars Work for the Environment.*

The Heritage Foundation
214 Massachusetts Ave. NE
Washington, DC 20002
(202) 546-4400
fax: (202) 546-0904

The Heritage Foundation is a conservative think tank that supports free enterprise and limited government in environmental matters. Its publications, such as the quarterly magazine *Policy Review* and the occasional papers *Heritage Talking Points,* include studies on environmental regulations and government policies.

National Recycling Coalition (NRC)
1101 30th St. NW, Suite 305
Washington, DC 20007
(202) 625-6406
fax: (202) 625-6409

NRC advocates the recovery, reuse, and conservation of materials and energy. It seeks to encourage recycling efforts through changes in national policies on energy, waste management, taxes, and transportation. The coalition publishes numerous reports and articles, as well as the bimonthly newsletter *NRC Connection.*

National Solid Wastes Management Association (NSWMA)
4301 Connecticut Ave. NW, Suite 300
Washington, DC 20008
(202) 244-4700
fax: (202) 966-4818

NSWMA is a trade association representing private sector companies involved in garbage collection, recycling, and the disposal of hazardous and medical wastes. It lobbies for laws that are environmentally sound but that still allow communities to dispose of their waste. It publishes the monthly magazine *Waste Age: The Authoritative Voice of Waste Systems and Technology,* the biweekly newsletter *Recycling Times,* and the fact sheets *Waste Products Profiles.* The association also publishes several reports, including "The Cost to Recycle at a Materials Recovery Plant."

Natural Resources Defense Council (NRDC)
40 W. 20th St.
New York, NY 10011
(212) 727-2700
fax: (212) 727-1773
Internet: http://www.nrdc.org

The council is an environmental group of lawyers and scientists who conduct litigation and research on toxic waste and other environmental hazards. NRDC publishes pamphlets, brochures, reports, books, and the quarterly *Amicus Journal.*

Political Economy Research Center (PERC)
502 S. 19th Ave., Suite 211
Bozeman, MT 59715
(406) 587-9591
Internet: http://www.perc.org

PERC is a research and education foundation that focuses primarily on environmental and natural resource issues. It emphasizes the advantages of free markets and the importance of private property rights regarding environmental protection. PERC's publications include the quarterly newsletter *PERC Reports* and papers in the PERC Policy Series.

Index

Agency for Toxic Disease Registry, 80
Agent Orange, 99
alachlor, 46
alar apple scare, 65, 68
Alexander, Judd, 58, 64
Alter, Harvey, 58, 140
American Medical Association, 98
American Public Works Association, 58
American Water Works Association, 48
America the Poisoned (Regenstein), 97
Amicus Journal, 164
Anderson, Douglas L., 105
Annual of Environmental Quality in Offshore of China (1989), 39
Aquapore Moisture Systems, 122
Archives of Environmental Contamination and Toxicology, 85
Arctic National Wildlife Refuge, 162-63
Arizona Daily Star, 88
Atgeld Gardens (Chicago), 79
atrazine, 46, 66
Avellino, Salvatore, 148

Bagwell, Keith, 88
Bailey, Philip, 123, 124
Baltic Sea, pollution of, 40-41
Barcelona Convention, 42
Barnhizer, David, 175
Bast, Joseph L., 96
Bean v. Southwestern Waste Management Corp., 103
Bhopal, India, 18, 21
biologic pathogens
  in sewage sludge, 86-87
  testing for, 111
  in wastewater, 110
Bird, Dwight, 24
Black Sea, 37-38
Bleifuss, Joel, 84
Boerner, Christopher, 101
Bohai Sea, 39
Bolch, Ben, 98
Bower, Jim, 170
Bridgeport, Conn.

brownfield cleanup in, 171-74
Broder, David, 161
Brown, George, 21
Browner, Carol, 162, 168
brownfields, 167
  in Bridgeport, Conn., 172-74
  in Chicago, 171-72
  cost of cleanup of, 168
Brownstein, Ronald, 97
Bullard, Robert D., 102
Buntrock, Dean L., 150
Burger family, 132-33
Burros, Marian, 165

Cancer Alley, 72, 80, 82
Carson, Rachel, 92
Charles River Associates, 119
chemical AIDS, 73
Chemical Manufacturers Association, 24
Chicago
  brownfield cleanup in, 171-72
China
  pollution of Yellow Sea by, 39
chlorine
  importance of, 116-17
  pollution in Baltic Sea, 40
  restrictions on, 41
  use in paper industry creates dioxin in wastes, 75
Christiansen, Kendall, 140
Citizens' Fund, 23
CLEAN (Community Linkage for Environmental Action Now), 173
Clean Air Act
  is target of conservative legislators, 162
  tradeable permit schemes under, 189-90
cleanup
  of brownfields, 171-76
    GAO estimates of cost, 168
  of nuclear weapons wastes, cost of, 26
  should be handled at local level, 191-92
  under Superfund
    can be improved, 177
    con, 200-201

Franklin, Marge, 62
Franklin Associates, 139

garbage
  co-collection with recyclables, 127
  crisis, is a myth, 50
  per-capita generation of
    is decreasing, 57-58
    recycling has reduced, 62-63
Garino, Robert, 124
General Accounting Office (GAO) study,
  103
General Chemical, 19
Geswein, Allen, 151
Gibbs, Lois, 74, 77, 97
Gibertson, Mike, 117
Giuliani, Rudolph, 139
Gore, Al, 18, 20, 22
Granado, Lorraine, 19
greenfields, 28
Gremse, Kevin, 172
groundwater
  contamination by nuclear weapons waste,
    27
  pollution by sewage sludge, 114
    is not addressed by rule 503, 86
Gulf Coast Tenants Association, 82

Hammer, Steve, 123
Hanford Site, 28, 29, 30, 31
Hang, Walter, 149
Hayek, F.A., 186
hazardous waste, 33
Hazardous Wastes in America (Epstein), 97
Health Advisory Levels, 67
heavy metals
  in sewage sludge, 86, 112
  in Yellow Sea, 38-40
Hebert, Joe, 68
herbicides
  contamination of tap water by, 45-46
  monitoring and standards are inadequate,
    48-49
  risks of, 47
high-density polyethylene (HDPE), 136,
  137
Hill, Peter J., 96
Horvath, Mike, 173, 174
Houk, Vernon N., 98

incineration
  is expensive compared to recycling, 125
  is part of sound waste-disposal system,
    141
  public opposition to, 142

vs. recycling, 140
should be halted, 76
utility of, 143
In Defense of Garbage (Alexander), 58, 64
International Joint Commission, 117
International Standards Organization, 197
Invisible Houston (Bullard), 103

Jacobson study, 118
Johnson, Dirk, 66
Jungle, The (Sinclair), 165

Kaufman, Hugh, 88
Kimbrough, Renate D., 99
Kisspotlight system, 136

Lake of Santa Gida, 42
Lambert, Thomas, 101
landfills
  are expensive compared to recycling, 125
  are part of sound waste-disposal system,
    141
  are safe, 53-54
  crisis concerning, is not nationwide, 59
  vs. dumps, 58
  public opposition to, 142
  space is not a problem, 55, 147, 156
Land Practices Peer Review Committee, 89
LeBlanc, Gerald A., 92
Leonetti, Carol, 130
Lifetime Health Advisory (LHA)
  for cyanazine, 45
Litvan, Laura M., 122
Logan, Terry, 89
Love Canal, 74, 97, 178
  Paigen report on residents of, 100
  studies have not shown dangers from
    dioxins, 98
Lyons, Harold, 98

Magnesium Corp. of America (MagCorp),
  17, 24
Mahoney, Richard J., 177
market forces
  can correct Superfund mistakes, 205
  vs. mandates, for recyclables, 189
  should be relied on for environmental
    protection, 188-89
Maximum Containment Level, 46
  EPA's calculation of, 66
Maya, Alma, 173
Mediterranean Action Plan, 42
Mediterranean Sea, 42
Meiners, Roger, 188
Merco Joint Venture Co., 88

postconsumer plastic, 136
  technologies for, 136-37
  public opinion on, 151, 152
  saves energy, 125
Reed, Lawrence, 155
Regenstein, Lewis, 97, 99
Repa, Ed, 62
Resource Conservation and Recovery Act,
  33, 80, 141
  deters hazardous waste disposal practices,
  178
Richard, John, 97
river basin associations, 197
Roberts, Bill, 21, 22
Rockefeller, Abby, 91
Ronneby Declaration, 43
Roosevelt, Theodore, 164
Rothbard, David, 116
Rothstein, Linda, 26
Ruben, Barbara, 167
Rubin, Alan, 89
Rucker, Craig, 116
Rue, Richard C., 96
Ruston, John F., 125, 149

Safe Drinking Water Act, 162
salmonella, 111
Sandhill Plastics Inc., 137
Savannah River Site, 29, 31
Scarlett, Lynn, 184
Schulz, Max, 65
seas
  essential steps to protect, 43
  waste threatens, 36-37
Seattle
  recycling program in, 126, 128
  economic benefits of, 129
Selcraig, Bruce, 17
sewage sludge
  biologic pathogens in, 86-87
  chemicals in, 85-86
  endangers human health, 84
  grades of, 87
  heavy metals in, 112
  manipulation of public's perception of, 90
  presents negligible risk to consumer, 115
  quality standards for home use of, 113
  restrictions on disposal of, 108-109
Shabecoff, Philip, 161
Shaw, Susan, 41
Shedenhelm, Richard, 56
Sikorski, Gerry, 21
Silent Spring (Carson), 92
Sinclair, Upton, 165
sludge. *See* sewage sludge

Sludge, 88, 89, 90
smelter operations, 18
"The Solid Waste Dilemma" (Porter), 150
Solid Waste Disposal Act, 86
*Standards for the Use or Disposal of
  Sewage Sludge* (EPA), 89, 109
  augments existing regulations, 114-15
  does not address groundwater
  contamination, 86
Starr, Roger, 139
Stauber, John, 77, 89
Steck, Sara, 134-35
Steuteville, Robert, 136
Superfund, 81, 168, 169
  categorization of sites under, 181-82
  costs are excessive, 202-203
  and Dutch system, 197
  has never worked, 200-201
  liability under, 179, 180-81
  locally handled cleanups cost less, 191-92
  reform of, 178-79
  should be privatized, 199, 204-205

Tap Water Blues (Environmental Working
  Group), 48
Taylor, Dorceta E., 79
Third Citizens Conference on Dioxin and
  Other Synthetic Hormone Disrupters, 74-
  78
Thomas panel, 98, 100
Tierney, John, 50
Times Beach, Mo., 97, 98
Tokar, Brian, 72
"Too Little, Too Late? Host-Community
  Benefits and Siting Solid Waste
  Facilities" (Fort and Scarlett), 191
Total Recycling, 136
Toxic Releases Inventory (EPA), 18
  opposition to, 21
  unequal treatment of industry under, 23
  weaknessess in, 20
*Toxic Sludge Is Good for You: Lies, Damn
  Lies, and the Public Relations Industry*
  (Stauber), 77
Toxic Substances Control Act, 93
toxic wastes
  minority communities are
  disproportionately victimized by, 183
  release of, 20
  see also specific chemicals
tradeable permit schemes, 189-90
transuranic waste, 32
Trepal, Chris, 169
tributyltin, 94
TV Nation, 88

Index